Lonely Avenue

Lonely Avenue

The Unlikely Life and Times of Doc Pomus

ALEX HALBERSTADT

DA CAPO PRESS
A Member of the Perseus Books Group

Editorial management and production by Word Craft Publishing Services
Design by Asterisk Typographics, Inc.

Cataloging-in-Publication data for this book is available from the Library of Congress.

First Da Capo Press edition 2007
ISBN-10: 0-306-81300-9
ISBN-13: 978-0-306-81300-9
Published by Da Capo Press
A member of the Perseus Books Group
http://www.dacapopress.com

Da Capo Press books are available at special discounts for bulk purchases in the
U.S. by corporations, institutions, and other organizations. For more information,
please contact the Special Markets Department at the Perseus Books Group, 11
Cambridge Center, Cambridge, MA 02142, or call (800) 255-1514 or (617) 252-
5298, or e-mail special.markets@perseusbooks.com.

1 2 3 4 5 6 7 8 9

To my mother and my father

Contents

Introductory Note

WHAT I LOVED MOST about Doc—well, I loved everything, really—was his sense of constant engagement. Not just creative engagement either, though that was certainly part of it. When I first met him, in the late 1970s, I had much the same experience that so many others did when they first met Doc, whether as a young man discovering his métier or at the very end of his life. Within moments, it seemed, we were fast friends, within minutes we were off to the races, caught up in a dialogue which for me will go on in my mind's ear for as long as I live.

I certainly can't claim any credit. If it had been left up to me, I might have just sat there for hours, for days maybe, a timid acolyte in the presence of the legendary songwriter. But Doc didn't permit that. He quizzed me, he grilled me, he voiced his enthusiasms, he sought out mine—he conveyed this incredible life force, this pure energy and love for people and ideas that I've rarely encountered in so undiminished, so *undisguised* a form. "Peter, you got a minute?" he would say on the phone and then just launch into whatever was on his mind at that particular moment: music, politics, philosophy, friends, it didn't matter. The dialogue just bubbled along irrepressibly, taking its own natural course but always brought down to earth, and into perspective, by Doc's inevitable conclusion: "What can I tell you? Just the same old nonsense." Which, of course, it was and it wasn't—but it was.

The thing about Doc was that he unfailingly put himself on the line. Not just in his songs but in every aspect of his life. I think that was what I learned most from Doc, the notion that you *must* put yourself on the line, whether for friends or politics or art or merely in expressing your opinions honestly. He used to talk about how when he was a kid, after he was stricken by polio, he had dreams of becoming the first heavyweight champion of the world on crutches, what his father called "a man among men." It was a perfectly understandable fantasy for a lost, lonely child, but that, in effect, is what he did become: if he was not the heavyweight champion in boxing, he became a champion of another sort. He maintained his perspective. He maintained his humanity. He maintained his sense of compassion, his omnivorous interest in everything and everyone (tell Doc a story, and you'd always get two in return), his commitment to helping you or me or anyone else who needed it—without forfeiting his right to grumble about it before, during, or after. What was astonishing about Doc was that he denied no element of his humanness. He didn't bullshit himself, and he didn't bullshit anyone else, which I think as much as anything was what sustained his creativity.

In the last ten years of his life Doc wrote some of his very greatest songs, songs that matched, and in some cases surpassed, the quality of his biggest hits. With them—with songs like "From the Heart," "Blinded by Love," "There Must Be a Better World Somewhere," "Prisoner of Life," "The Real Me"—he achieved the kind of profound simplicity that he had been striving for all his life. He knew it, and was proud of it—but he also knew that it wasn't what went before that mattered; it wasn't honors or validation (though he liked those, too) that yielded satisfaction. No matter what you have achieved, no matter what recognition may come your way, he would say over and over again—and mean it—it was what came next that counted; it was the next challenge, creative, personal, political, the arena was irrelevant. Life was living up to the challenge.

He kept writing almost up to his last breath. He kept on reaching out a helping hand to others, too. Toward the end he could honestly say, "I'm doing the same stuff I always did. I'm acting the same way I always acted. The only difference is that now I talk about it. At one time I wouldn't express my opinions except to maybe my closest friends, because it wasn't cool to be that animated. Now I don't hold anything back. I don't know, maybe it's just so I'll get noticed, but I really don't want to live to see a day where the space that I take up in this world is like some musty closet, some little broom closet somewhere. I want to be able to talk out—even if I'm wrong."

Doc did talk out, and he filled an enormous space. To Doc, as *Lonely Avenue: The Unlikely Life and Times of Doc Pomus* perceptively points out, there was no separation between life and art; he was one of those rare creative spirits who continued to grow, both through his work and through his humanity.

PETER GURALNICK

The fencer's weapon is picked up and put down again.
The boxer's is part of him. All he has to do is clench his fist.

— MARCUS AURELIUS

George's, 1943

Greenwich Village

DOWN THE STREET from Sheridan Square, straddling the dogleg corner of Barrow Street and Seventh Avenue, George's was a dark, low-ceilinged room wrapped in a haze of cigarette smoke and loud conversation. Like most neighborhood taverns it specialized in veal *bolognese*, cheap Chianti in the straw-wrapped bottles, ten-cent schooners of beer, forty-cent tumblers of whisky, and hotter jazz than you'd find just about anywhere uptown. It was Saturday night. The tables were crowded with the usual mix of painters, writers, musicians, low-rent dilettantes, GIs returning from the European front, and a couple of upperclassmen from Columbia and City College. The cobblestoned corner of lower Manhattan really did feel like a village, albeit a village of exiled sectarians. The men wore their hair long and sported beards; the women favored herringbone trousers and no make-up and dangled cigarettes from their serious faces. Everyone talked about music and politics and sex. Jimmy Baldwin, a regular, was saying something to Trent, a hard-looking union organizer in dungarees; all night he drifted in and out with a sailor named Johnny Williams.

On the bandstand, a tall black man sat in a chair with his legs crossed and played a blues on a muted trumpet. He had large hands and tired eyes and wore a corduroy blazer with patches on the elbows and proper loafers, looking more like a football coach than a jazz musician. Nearly everyone in the room knew Frankie Newton's improvisations from Billie Holiday's "Strange Fruit." That night he played soft and slow.

A teenager with wavy black hair and a brand new satin shirt listened at the edge of the stage. He was broad and heavy, big for his age, but looked out of place at George's, surrounded by the studied casual bonhomie of the Villagers. His legs were strapped into shiny steel and leather braces; a pair of crutches rested in his lap. Despite his carefully cultivated stubble he didn't look old enough to drink. He'd cased the room long enough to know that, if he stationed himself to the left of the narrow high bandstand with a glass of beer in his hand, the crowd would hide him from Dominick and Jerry, the club's owners. His pint glass had been empty for an hour, but he tried to look inconspicuous. It didn't work for long. Between songs, Dominick limped over to the table and in his most heartwarming broken English, said: "Why doncha spenda some money or getta the fuck outta here."

The teenager looked up; his heart was pounding. He had no money but he didn't move. "I'm a blues singer," Jerome Felder blurted out, "and I'm here to do a song." At the other tables, the people turned to look at them. Dominick was unfazed. "If you're really a singer lemme hear you sing," he said, motioning to the musicians. Jerome froze. Slowly he fitted his crutches' padded tops under his arms and lifted himself up. He made his way to the bandstand and haltingly climbed the three tall steps to the stage. Jerome stood on his crutches in front of the room and squinted into the spotlight. The talk died down. "What key?" Frankie Newton asked. "Blues in any key, any tempo," the teenager replied, and the trumpeter began to play a slow undulating blues in B-flat.

Jerome swallowed a breath of air and belted out the first line to the only song he knew, Big Joe Turner's "Piney Brown." Like Turner, the Rabelaisian Kansas City bluesman, he shouted the syllables, eyes shut tight from the adrenaline and fear. He'd never thought about what the lyrics meant. Now, all he could do was try not to forget them. When he finally opened his eyes he was surprised to see about half the people in the room clapping.

On the subway home to Brooklyn, Jerome knew that at long last his authentic life had begun. It happened in the two minutes it had taken him to finish the song. Ever since he could remember, he'd convinced himself that he'd become the first great boxer on crutches, or the first baseball player, or, later, the first saxophone virtuoso. Now he was a blues singer, though he'd never heard of one who was crippled or white or a Jew. He knew he needed another song. As the train car careened over the Williamsburg Bridge, he put together the words to "BB Blues." He named his first composition after Brighton Beach, where the previous summer his family had rented a cabin and where he met the gorgeous, dark-eyed Vivian Popick. She'd let him hang around, but he didn't dare confess his feelings. Unwittingly, she broke his heart, and blues singers always wrote about their broken hearts. That night, as he sat up in bed and listened to Joe Turner records on his parents' Sylvania console, Jerome decided he needed a new name. A blues singer's name. Something foreign and hip like a name out of the Halliburton adventure books he'd read as a kid.

The following night Jerome was back at George's, ready to sing an even finer "Piney Brown" in B-flat. He was waiting to be introduced when Dominick stopped at his table. "Whadda they call you, anyway?" he asked. "My name is Doc Pomus," Jerome replied loud enough for everyone in the room to hear, "and I'm here to sing the blues."

A Teenager in Love

Brooklyn, 1939

> If his destiny is strange, it is also sublime. Haven't I known it myself, haven't I spent ten months in that extranatural existence? And to that question posed by Ecclesiastes, 3,000 years ago—Who can fathom the depths of the abyss?—only two men of all men have the right to answer:
>
> Captain Nemo and I

JEROME CLOSED *Twenty Thousand Leagues Under the Sea* and tossed it on the nightstand. He looked around, remembering again where he was. The clock said it was one thirty in the morning. The room was quiet. A cold breeze bothered the curtains. Jerome took a hold of his legs and pushed. They were inert; it reminded him of pushing against a sleeping dog. He heaved his legs over the edge of the bed and sat up.

Jerome took a deep breath, bent down until he could touch the backs of his ankles, and straightened his legs. He made sure the steel and leather braces strapped around his thighs and calves were extended and locked them in place. He scooped up the crutches propped against the nightstand, fitted them under his arms, leaned forward slowly until they were perpendicular to the floor, winced, and raised himself up.

A table stood next to the window in the kitchen. When he reached it, Jerome lowered his elbows onto it, leaned his crutches carefully against the edge, and hauled himself onto the table. His cheek pressed against its cool surface. He slithered on his stomach and pulled himself forward by holding onto the windowsill. The metal latches of the braces scraped against the wood. Jerome stuck his head through the curtains and inhaled the cold October air. He pulled a Chesterfield from his shirt pocket and lit it. Pulling on it until he felt it saturate his lungs, he blew a huge draft of smoke into the night. Jerome flicked the ashes out the window onto the canopy downstairs, where his cigarette cinders left black smoldering holes in the cloth.

It was his favorite time of night. McKibbin Street was quiet. The stickball games had broken up; the stoop orators had gone inside. The old Jewish women in housecoats who spent afternoons watching the street from their windowsills had drawn their curtains. Only a few windows were lit. The night was teeming with street sounds: the whine of automobile engines, the creak of the pushcart men rolling their carts home after a long day on Moore Street, a lonely rumba wafting down the street from somebody's radio. Jerome flipped on the set and wiggled the dial until he picked up the remote from the Elks Rendezvous in Harlem: Chris Columbus's band was playing "I Can't Get Started," a whole section of muted trumpets woozily carrying the melody. Jerome exhaled another lungful of smoke, rested his head on his arm, closed his eyes, and listened. In those early morning hours he felt like he belonged to the world most acutely, protected by the darkness and solitude of night. At those moments he had access to the entire storehouse of adult knowledge. But he was still fourteen, and tomorrow was a school day. In five hours he'd be dressed and ready to go, his wet hair combed across his head, squinting into the morning sun from the passenger seat of his mother's black Plymouth.

THE CORNER OF McKibbin Street and Manhattan Avenue wasn't Henry Miller's Brooklyn. The overcrowded pocket of Williamsburg was a ghetto populated by European Jews who shared the block tensely with a smattering of blacks and Catholics. The families who lived here didn't believe in Leviticus's vengeful god. Their modern god had delivered them from *shtetls*, from kiosks and hovels on Europe's *Judenstrasse*, to the land of baseball and Tom Mix. That secular miracle had left them with a belief in books, the near-magical power of a steady job, and a distrust of pleasure. As in any of the city's immigrant settlements, the common goal was to leave. In the meantime, the Jews of McKibbin Street toiled for Brooklyn College tuition, a Frigidaire, a new Buick coupe. Though they lived across the river from Manhattan, the City might as well have stood on the other side of the Rockies. Even the St. George Hotel in nearby Brooklyn Heights—with its heated saltwater pool and roof-deck tea service—seemed like something out of a Fitzgerald novel.

The Felders moved to 75 Manhattan Avenue, the only building in the neighborhood that had an elevator, when Jerome was ten. The rent was higher, but his mother, Millie, had insisted. Polio had left her older son with two useless legs, a weak back, and a bum shoulder; he couldn't very well climb the stairs. They lived on the second floor above Goldy's Bridal Shop. When the elevator broke every couple of months, Jerome sat on the bottom step with his back to the stairwell, grabbed hold of the higher step, and pulled himself up onto it. In this way he slowly worked his way butt-first to the top of the two staircases, where Millie, and later his brother, Raoul, waited to hand him his crutches.

Early on, Jerome devised a way of purging his memory. He had the ability to forget something humiliating or painful almost before it was over. This proved useful because he was constantly falling. He fell down staircases, tripped over curbs and doorways, slipped in the ice and snow. Most winter days he came home and found the knees of his trousers caked with sleet and grime. It was the only way he knew he'd fallen. Sometimes he felt that, in this way, he'd forgotten most of his childhood.

His memories began the summer he turned seven, when his parents sent him away to camp in the midst of New York's polio epidemic. His memory, in snatches, went back further, but Jerome, as he understood himself, was born in those lonely, deadening months. The camp was located far from the city's contagion in Connecticut's pristine countryside. On one of his first mornings there, Jerome woke up and couldn't feel his legs. His parents raced up to Connecticut in an ambulance, but for hours weren't permitted to enter the quarantined grounds. By the time they brought Jerome back to Brooklyn, he was hysterical. At the hospital he remembered the faces of other stricken kids and those of their gray, distraught parents, and Millie in the bathroom, running the faucets to mute the sound of her crying. His parents conferred with the doctors out of his earshot. The only way he knew what was happening was by watching his mother's face. Judging by her tear-rimmed eyes, he could tell it was something awful.

The only bright memory was his brief stay in Warm Springs, Georgia, in the late fall of 1932. There, he was able to take some solace in his newly acquired disability—he caught a few glimpses of Franklin Delano Roosevelt, the nation's most famous polio patient, soaking in the mineral water pools. Though he spent only a few weeks at Warm Springs, Jerome would hear about the place for years to come. Millie claimed that when she visited Jerome there, FDR's Scottish terrier Fala bit her savagely on the ankle. She talked about it as though the dog's long-gone teeth marks anointed her as a woman of historical influence. Not long after her visit to Georgia, Millie heard Roosevelt speak in Miami's Bayfront Park. Mid-speech, a bricklayer from New Jersey named Giuseppe Zangara shot at the president with a .32 handgun he'd bought at a local pawnshop. Zangara missed Roosevelt but hit the mayor of Chicago. After that, FDR became an honorary Felder.

After the idyllic weeks in Warm Springs, Morris and Millie brought Jerome upstate to the New York State Rehabilitation Home in Haverstraw, a glum town just north of New York in the Hudson Valley. It was a holding pen for other juvenile paralytics, and for sheer misery, a place rivaled only by the orphanages of Dickens. For years Jerome replayed the scene of a half-dozen twelve- and thirteen-year-olds crowded around his bed, slamming their fists into his arm just to find out how easily he'd cry. He remembered the grin of the ringleader, a jug-eared kid named Bud

Warner. After the second or third beating, Jerome resolved that he'd never let Warner and the others see him whimper. He saved his terror for Dr. Ott, a human ferret in a white lab coat. Dr. Ott made the rounds of the beds every morning. The hack surgery of the day was a foot stabilizing operation that fixed the extremity in one position, a procedure that later rendered the "cured" unable to walk even with the help of crutches. It was Dr. Ott's remedy of choice. On his rounds he perched at the foot of a bed, threw the sheet up from over a pair of paralyzed legs, and examined them with exquisite disinterest. Turning to the nurse, he declared "operate" or "don't operate" with the indifference of a Caesar. In the hours prior to Dr. Ott's rounds, Jerome lay terrified in his dawn-lit room. When Millie visited, he made her promise that she wouldn't let them cut him open, and she kept her word.

When he returned from Haverstraw, Jerome realized he hadn't been home in more than two years. He'd once been a gregarious, hyperactive kid with curly hair, freckles, a loud voice and an intense, leering smile. He preferred to run rather than walk, sing rather than speak. Now he spent his pallid afternoons in bed, rattled by the sounds that used to delight him: the cries of the kids playing stoopball outside, the wail of the fire engines racing down Manhattan Avenue, the morning rumble of coal sliding down the metal chute, the house shifting and creaking in the night. At first Morris and Millie decided to keep him out of school; this meant occasional visits with tutors and a few semiannual exams. Sometimes the exams never arrived—Jerome figured his parents felt too sorry for him to press the issue. He spent most of his afternoons in a daydream. He fantasized that he ran the hundred-meter sprint at the Olympics, KO'd Primo Carnera, belted endless home runs off Lefty Grove and watched the ball sail over the snowy stone garlands above the outfield seats in Yankee Stadium. In those fantasies he still had his crutches, but it didn't matter. Somehow it all made sense.

And he discovered books. He gorged on Jules Verne and James Fenimore Cooper and Alexandre Dumas and anything else

he could check out at the public library. The stories spirited him
away for entire days, into reveries where he wrestled giant mollusks
underwater, a dagger clenched in his teeth, or dispatched col-
umns of Cardinal de Richelieu's guards with a few well-timed par-
ries of a shining, bloodstained rapier. None of it was real, of course,
but he preferred it to waking every morning in a numb, motionless body. He told himself that he'd have preferred anything.

MILLIE AND MORRIS FELDER were locked in a war of attri-
tion that made its presence known only occasionally in sudden,
violent flashes. They reminded Jerome of two aging gladiators
who circled each other, weary and battle-scarred, neither able to
land the decisive blow. When he returned home from Haverstraw,
he discovered that he had a baby brother, Raoul Lionel, whose
name had a suave British ring that must have appealed to Millie.
Raoul became Jerome's occasionally reluctant roommate, yet his
arrival did little to seal the rift between their parents. Their quick,
noisy skirmishes—triggered most often by disagreements about
money—punctured the ritual silence that Morris enforced at the
dinner table. "Tell your father I'm not speaking to him," Millie
would tell Jerome while Morris sat stiffly at her side, his jaw
clenched in anger.

    Moritz Felder arrived at Ellis Island in 1906. He was ten.
Along with his parents, siblings, and hundreds of other Viennese
Jews, he'd boarded the ocean liner Rhynland in Antwerp. He was
the oldest of eight children born in near poverty; in a defiant exertion of will, he put himself through veterinary school. When the
Depression made his career choice untenable—no one could remember a Jew in Williamsburg who'd owned a dog or a cat—
Morris enrolled in law school. It had been his idea to name his
first son Jerome Solon, after the Athenian sage, in tribute to the
litigious deities. After graduating, he put out a shingle at a small
office on Court Street and handled the kind of clients that often
paid him in barter. It was well known in the Felder household
that Morris's law practice was a failure.

Morris defied this circumstance, too, and doled out a heavy share of his earnings to his extended family. Morris's generosity only stirred up resentment between him and the kin he supported—a circle that included brothers, sisters, nephews, nieces, a father-in-law, and of course his wife.

There were other, greater odds to be defied. Morris was short, walked with a stoop that was a remnant of a congenital spinal curvature, and owned a face that was neither handsome nor affable. Yet he dreamed of being a statesman. He presided tyrannically over the neighborhood's insurgent Democratic club and agitated on a whole front of local issues. When the Brooklyn Dodgers sent a third-string catcher, the rare professional ball player who was also a Jew, down to the minor leagues, Morris collected fifteen thousand signatures on a petition from other Williamsburg Jews to bring him back to the majors. It was one of his few victories. He ran for every kind of office—assemblyman, state senator, judge—as often as he could. The constant campaigns, the bound stacks of leaflets, and the cold-weather autumn speeches made up Jerome's earliest memories, none more indelible than the golden afternoon when Fiorello LaGuardia stopped by the apartment. Other than Morris's one prize—an appointment as assistant counsel to the city's Transit Commission—he always lost. The losing campaigns made him angrier at the world, more isolated and domineering, and even more determined to rail against the injustices he saw everywhere around him. It was never long before another envelope from the White House—form responses to Morris's letters to the president—arrived in the mailbox, the return address printed in elegant blue type.

Morris's defeats became the thorn that inflamed the Felders' marital agonies. After all, Millie hadn't married Morris for his looks but for his fine mind, his education, and the worldly ambition they shared in equal measure. Millie wasn't pretty but was striking nonetheless thanks to her steely diction, superior posture, and immaculately tailored outfits of spartan elegance. She ran the household with the propriety and rigid etiquette of Britain's lower bourgeoisie. She kept an ordered house, worked energetically for the Williamsburg Helping Hands Association, raised money for polio charities, and found time to pitch in for various other good causes.

Millie Goldstein was born on Mile End Road in London's East End ghetto and arrived at Ellis Island at fifteen. Too poor to attend college, she went to work as a seamstress. Yet she behaved like an aristocrat who'd found herself stranded among the lower middle class due to a series of absurd, tragic-comic contrivances. The most grievous of these was Morris's failure to keep up his side of their bargain. It was a lapse that Millie wouldn't forgive. Jerome couldn't remember his mother ever treating his father as an equal. It made matters worse that Millie's energy, as well as her abilities to charm and persuade, easily outstripped Morris's. She rose quickly in her jobs and impressed coworkers as hardworking, resourceful and honest. But she couldn't abide anyone she found complacent or lazy, anyone who didn't reciprocate her fierce work ethic. Away from the apartment, everyone called Millie "The General."

Millie and Morris usually erupted at dinner. When the shouting died down, Morris retreated to the bedroom until morning while Millie washed the dishes, thrashing them as though exacting vengeance on the plates and spoons. Their standoff was aggravated by the presence in the apartment of Millie's father, Harris Goldstein, a handsome London window dresser who'd retired before anyone could remember, and who had been a leader in the British Zionist movement in his youth. Harris inhabited a severe world of private judgments and regrets. His taciturn, profane moods vacillated between spells of domineering gregariousness and virulent displays of bile. Harris slept on the living room sofa and lived entirely on the income of his son-in-law, something he managed with panache. In the mornings he emerged in a three-piece worsted suit, a homburg, and a carnation boutonnière, as though headed to a Montmartre salon instead of a kosher deli on Broadway. He shared his daughter's desultory opinion of Morris and treated him with unvarnished scorn. Harris sometimes vanished for days or even weeks. His only wife, a plain, sweet woman, had died young, and Harris maintained a long-standing reputation as a Lothario. At eighty he romanced a woman of fifty, known to the rest of the family only as the aunt of syndicated cartoonist Al Capp.

Jerome steered clear of his grandfather. He rarely invited friends up to the apartment, afraid they'd run into Harris in one of his vituperative spells. But in his calmer moments, his grandfather was the only member of the household who treated Jerome like a grown-up. Perhaps out of a general distaste for children, or mere obliviousness to his grandson's age, he talked and listened to him as an equal. Some Saturday afternoons they walked together to the vaudeville matinees at the Folly Theater on Debevoise Street, where they marveled at the risqué Polynesian dancers, the Hawaiian steel-guitar troupes, the waltzing cats and roller-skating dogs, and Jerome's favorite, ventriloquist Edgar Bergen. At night they'd watch Westerns at the Alba, near the corner of Flushing and Graham: *The Big Trail*, with a baby-faced John Wayne, Tex Ritter in *Song of the Gringo*, or anything with Tom Mix. Afterward, tired and famished, they headed to a Bickford's across the street for ice cream sundaes.

DOC HATED looking at photos of himself taken in the two or three years after he came home with polio. He'd insisted on being photographed without crutches, standing against a post or a wall with a forced smile and a look of feigned nonchalance. Underneath the smile Doc always saw the intense effort it had taken to hold himself upright while somebody focused the camera. A different photo from that period ran in the *Brooklyn Times Union* on July 5, 1933, just days after his eighth birthday. It was taken at Manhattan Beach, a Jewish enclave by the ocean where every summer the Felders rented a bungalow at 241 Sea Crest Street. In the picture his parents, aunts, uncles, and cousins, along with plenty of neighborhood kids—maybe thirty in all—stood around

Jerome, who looked both embarrassed and giddy. Uncle Don, the popular WOR deejay, beamed his seventy-dollar smile beside him. Jerome had written the radio station asking for a puppy, and Uncle Don surprised him at the bungalow with a black Maltese terrier named Crummie. Morris dutifully clipped the photo for his scrapbooks, where he kept a meticulous record of the family's cameos in the local papers and magazines.

Before polio, Jerome had loved the beach. He'd bury himself in the sand, dig for crabs, and scoop up jellyfish, splashing in the brown-green rollers. On weekends, big bands performed at the Brighton Beach Baths, and Jerome never missed a show. An orchestra led by "King of Jazz" Paul Whiteman—featuring for a time the hard-drinking cornetist Bix Beiderbecke—was a mainstay at the band shell. One night when he was three, Jerome jerked free of Millie's grasp and ran onto the stage. The orchestra was in mid-song; Jerome danced and sang along. The audience guffawed, and Whiteman gamely positioned the kid at the microphone. Afterward, the bandleader occasionally brought him onstage for a couple of verses, mostly to get a laugh from the grown-ups. Somebody who caught his act at the Baths even got Jerome a one-time spot on the *Horn and Hardart Children's Hour* on the radio; all he could remember about it was being petrified.

Jerome had forgotten about his beachside debut by the time he discovered Romain Rolland's *Jean-Christophe* at the library. In his imagination, the thinly disguised biography of Beethoven instantly displaced his favorite adventure books. The deaf genius who constructed entire symphonies in his mind enthralled him. For months, Jerome organized his nights around Beethoven broadcasts on the radio. After everyone was asleep, he'd pull a conductor's baton from under his bed and, framed by the billowing curtains, vigorously wave his arms in time to the *Eroica*. The orchestra responded to his slightest move. He slashed the baton to the left, egging on the brass, then lunged to the right, inciting the cellos and violas. It put him in a delicious trance that lasted until the deejay's somber, English-accented voice announced the end of the movement. Jerome laid down the baton and wiped his fore-head. He was sure he was going to be a conductor. He wasn't sure how he'd manage to stand upright on the podium, but he decided he had the rest of his life to figure it out.

Jerome spent whole days glued to the radio. Wiggling the dial allowed him to explore forbidden corners of the adult world with-out leaving his bedroom. He made constant discoveries. Mendels-sohn and Brahms eventually gave way to Jeanette McDonald and Nelson Eddy, Bing Crosby and Charlie Barnett. But nothing pre-pared him for the Negro stations. The first time he heard Fletcher Henderson's orchestra, he sat with his face inches away from the fabric-covered speaker, his eyes wide open and mouth slack.

It was the dusk of hot jazz. The music of the Negro bands in-habited a universe wholly distinct from the shellacked big band swing and vaudeville fare of the Hit Parade. It sounded alter-nately sultry, weary, despairing and, at its most frenetic, like a cacophonous but perfectly syncopated explosion. Jerome found a new musical obsession just about every week: the Basie Band's broadcasts from the Famous Door on Fifty-second Street with Lester Young in the reed section, Coleman Hawkins's remote from Kelly's Stable, Billie Holiday singing with Teddy Wilson, Muggsy Spanier's Ragtimers, the Mills Blue Rhythm Band. Years later, musicologists would categorize these into blues and jazz and swing, but in the mid-thirties black music, in its esthetics and worldview, formed a unified idiom of breathtaking richness and va-riety. Beethoven had been a man of his time, and Jerome decided that he, too, had to be true to his era. He'd take up the sax. A series of piano lessons with a puritanical, metronome-tapping teacher named Dockson had gone dismally. When he banged out scales on the baby grand, which happened to be the only half-decent piece of furniture in the Felders' apartment, Jerome's mind drifted. But after just a couple of brief sax lessons he'd al-ready managed to pick out several tunes he'd heard on the radio. He despised practicing, but loved playing. Jerome decided the alto was his calling.

The first gig didn't go quite the way he'd imagined. That debut took place on a small square of lawn outside a physical therapy facility in Far Rockaway. The boxlike building was perched on the edge of the boardwalk. Jerome spent two summers there, aged eleven and twelve, pretending to learn the rudiments of mechanical drafting, but mostly staring out the windows at the able-bodied beach-goers with the other incarcerated paralytics. It was the saddest group of teenagers he'd ever seen. Jerome was staying there only until the summer's end; most of the others lived there year-round. For a few hours a day, the patients were allowed to graze in the small, fenced-in area outside. They spent the rest of their afternoons crowded around the windows, gaping at luscious tan girls, shirtless muscular boys, buxom women strolling hand-in-hand with their beaus, toddlers running manic circles in the sand.

His solace was an impromptu band of adolescent cripples that performed on the boardwalk once a week. Jerome blew the alto, backed by a drum kit, bass, and piano. He read sheet music haltingly, and decided to memorize the melodies instead. This freed him to watch the bathing-suited beauties who gathered around him and stared with the ruthless pity of teenaged girls. He knew that he didn't have much talent for the instrument, and that the marching-band repertoire was repetitive and square, but Jerome never tired of playing with a group. The mental link between the musicians felt conspiratorial, like a planned prison break. After a while, he conned a softhearted young nurse into letting him slip outside for nighttime furloughs. Jerome propelled himself down the boardwalk on his crutches as quickly as he could and took mental snapshots of freedom: the endless blue-black sky, the murmuring surf, the smell of cooking food and cigarettes, the hoarse whispers of high-school lovers huddling under the boardwalk's wooden planks. After that second summer in Far Rockaway, Jerome swore he'd never let himself be incarcerated again.

In 1939, the year Jerome turned fourteen, Morris and Millie decided it was time for him to attend a regular school, and they enrolled him in the ninth grade at Bushwick High School in September. Neither his brief stint in middle school nor the summers in Far Rockaway prepared him for the social devastation of high school. The teenaged scholars of Bushwick High were proud of the neighborhood's delinquent underbelly. Like any self-respecting, lower middle-class adolescents, they spat on sidewalks, feigned sullenness that verged on coma, and stood ready to fight at the slightest provocation. They bragged about rye whiskey and sex and petty crime. At fourteen, Jerome hadn't even kissed a girl, much less copped a feel in the back of a parked car. He'd never tasted liquor or smoked reefer and hadn't stolen a thing, though all that would change quickly. In those first weeks at Bushwick High, Jerome felt like a Jesuit missionary among a tribe of sub-Saharan cannibals. The first couple of girls that he liked stared right through him. His crutches and braces pretty much guaranteed that the only attention he got from girls were startled, pitying glances followed by the even worse aversion of the eyes.

According to a test Jerome took as a child, he had one of the highest IQs in the borough, but he hated classes. The dictation and note taking slowed his mind to a crawl. He'd already read more books than most of the others, but in the classroom he was bored, staring out the window at the plane trees or drifting off into fantasy. The only class he enjoyed was music. Mr. Souffert, a local bandleader, made the forty-five minutes worthwhile, even exciting. It was the first time Jerome held his own in school. He played alto in the band and with Souffert's help learned to sight-read, compose four-part harmonies, even write out arrangements and lead sheets. For the first and only time he looked forward to coming to class. With a saxophone around his neck, the others respected him. Classmates asked for help; girls spoke to him. But Jerome's confidence evaporated as soon as he stepped into the bustling hallway. Everyone parted to let him pass, while a few stared or even sniggered. It didn't surprise him anymore to hear a staccato shout of "cripple!" or "gimp!" behind him, usually disguised as a cough. By the time Jerome wheeled around to face his attackers, they'd be gone.

He spent most of his nights and weekends with cousins Max and Bernard, the children of Millie's sister Yetta. Max was the quietest—a taciturn, dreamy kid on his way to becoming a gifted writer. He was handsome and had an enviable early aptitude with girls. A mercurial cruelty that emerged in strange, sudden strokes sometimes disturbed the opaque surface of his personality. It was as though he became a different person. You had to watch your back around Max. Bernard was more straightforward, a manic talker who doodled on every available surface, his hands permanently stained with ink. He consumed stacks of newspapers and magazines and delivered angry ad hoc lectures on politics and current events. His tirades often turned into tantrums. They got them in plenty of trouble, but Jerome took a vicarious pleasure in these eruptions. He found Bernard's vitriol instructive.

At school, he was learning to cover up his intense discomfort with a pushy bluster, and the bravado temporarily eclipsed his fear. Soon, he could last an entire afternoon without feeling the clammy, sickening pressure in his stomach. By his junior year, Jerome had learned to smoke, drink and curse, and he had cultivated an acid wit that kept the social predators in the school cafeteria at bay. When someone sniggered now, Jerome made a point of handing it back to them threefold, pelting his attacker with hilarious abuse until everyone around them was laughing, a reaction that discouraged, or at least deferred, reprisals. Jerome wasn't about to turn into the bland, smiling fat boy the social workers at the rehab centers had worked so hard to create. He refused to play the jolly cripple who smiled away insults. He'd make them fear him instead.

MARY BARGET was voluptuous and tall. She was a Latin-Greek girl of sixteen who carried herself with the confidence of a twenty-five-year-old woman. She played piano in Mr. Souffert's class and took to Jerome right away. They recognized in each other a seriousness about music that the other kids didn't share. As far as Jerome was concerned, Mary's ample cleavage didn't hurt, either.

It was Mary who told him about a local dive bar called the Lincoln Cabaret. She said she knew one of the bartenders. If they formed a band, they could play there—and get paid.

They rounded up two boys from music class for their first gig. Jerome remembered only that the drummer was named Johnny somebody. The first night, they played to a few neighborhood barflies and a mostly empty room. No one paid any attention to the fact that the band was blatantly underage; after their set, the bartender peeled some small bills off a roll and handed each of them a pint of beer. They couldn't believe their luck. The Lincoln Cabaret never got much busier, but on the weekends it some-times turned ugly. Jerome and Mary had to keep an eye on the clientele to make sure a beer glass or a knocked-out drunk didn't come careening in their direction.

Millie and Morris were lenient with their son's music. Playing the saxophone was no career for a paralyzed Jewish kid from Williamsburg, but they couldn't see much harm in it, either. Of course they'd never set foot in a dive like the Lincoln Cabaret, and Jerome didn't dare tell them about the gigs. When they asked, he said he was doing homework at Max and Bernard's. Fortunately, Mary managed to line up some gigs at a kosher deli on Broadway, and on a Sunday, Jerome's parents, with Harris in tow, showed up to watch him blow his way through "Alexander's Ragtime Band." Afterward, the band got permission to practice at the Felders'.

JEROME WAS FIFTEEN when he discovered "Piney Brown Blues" in the bins at Lineker's record shop. He didn't know much about the blues, only that he thought he liked it. "Piney Brown" changed that. Jerome played the 78-rpm disk until the label that read Decca, and underneath it "Big Joe Turner & His Fly Cats," was dark with fingerprints and spindle marks. From the moment he first lowered the needle into the groove, the record floored him like nothing he'd heard. The singer shouted the lyrics with such stupendous, effortless force that Jerome imagined him to be

eleven feet tall, six hundred pounds, and powered by a steam engine. When he saw a photo of Turner in a magazine, he discovered he wasn't far off. The man was as big as a warehouse. His
petite, balding head rested upon a mountainous body like a
maraschino cherry on a sundae. Turner's blues was a tribute to his
friend Walter "Little Piney" Brown, the proprietor of Kansas
City's Sunset Club, where Turner tended bar and sang. The
recording was an epochal event in jazz history, a masterpiece and
stepping-stone to both rhythm and blues and rock and roll.
Jerome didn't know any of that in 1941; he scarcely would've
cared if he did. All he wanted to know about was that foghorn of a
voice. That, he thought, is how a man should sound. It made
every other male singer sound like a petulant mumbler. Jerome
wanted to make the same massive sound himself. He just wasn't
sure how.

The notion of being a singer didn't coil itself around his mind
until Jerome was walking home from school one winter afternoon.
His mind, as usual, was fixed on trying not to slip on the icy
macadam. He'd already crossed several blocks with small, tentative steps when he leaned against the side of a building to catch
his breath. On the sidewalk, teenagers lobbed snowballs at each
other across the street. They soaked their ammunition in melted
snow and left it to freeze to make it more lethal. The iceballs were
hard enough to shatter a window. Jerome had propped himself
against the brick wall with his right hand when a block of ice hit
him squarely on the knuckles. He fell to the pavement, clutching
his fingers.

The doctor at the hospital told him that the iceball fractured
several bones. Even after the cast came off, Jerome never re-
gained much feeling in his fingers. The bones hadn't healed cor-
rectly, and there was nerve damage. He tried fingering the valves
on his saxophone, but it was no use. Fantasies of playing sax with
the Basie orchestra had to be retired. Besides, his band was
through. At the Lincoln Cabaret, somebody pulled a knife on
Mary Barget, and the bartender told her not to come back.

AFTER HE'D RETURNED from the rehab home in Haverstraw, Jerome learned to yell at a frightening volume. On those desolate afternoons when Morris was away at the office, Millie remained his only friend and companion. For most of the day she was busy with housework at the opposite end of the apartment. To get her attention, he learned to bellow her name from his bed loud enough for her to hear. After weeks of this, his voice had grown ragged but strong. He never considered it useful until he sat listening to "Piney Brown" and flexing his bandaged fingers. "Yes I dreamed last night I was standing on Eighteenth and Vine . . . ," he'd holler, then yell, along with the record. He added heft to his voice until he could bellow with his entire upper body, bellow so loudly that Millie came running into the room and the neighbors began knocking. His voice didn't sound as effortless and rich as Turner's, but at least it was loud.

He hadn't any intention of getting up onstage the night he first came to George's. His friend Cy Elvert, a saxophone player known in the neighborhood for his left-wing politics, brought him to the Village to take in Frankie Newton's band and try to mingle with the bohemians. Jerome could pinpoint the exact moment when everything changed. It wasn't the lie he told Dominick, nor that terrible hush just before he began to sing in front of Newton's incredulous bandmates, not even the sensation of his voice pressurizing the air in the smoke-filled room. It was the audience's response—not just the lukewarm applause, but the routine acceptance of him as someone who belonged on that bandstand, as a *legitimate performer*, that flipped the switch in his mind. After leaving the club, the cigarette smoke still stinging his nostrils, Jerome knew that everything was now radically, irrevocably different. In the space of a couple of minutes, he'd suddenly become a singer, *was* a singer, and now his aspirations and fears and fantasies rearranged themselves around the new reality. He felt like Romulus or Remus, reared by wolves, realizing that all along they'd belonged to a different species, whose members were willing, however grudgingly, to take them in as their own. The paralyzing sense of not belonging began to lift. Jerome suddenly knew that he wouldn't have to compete with the able-bodied sons of Brooklyn's Jewish matrons, wouldn't have to chase their nine-to-five aspirations, their suburban futures of glad-handing in-laws and bassinets and retirement accounts. He was a blues singer. He'd live in the gorgeous, sepia, underground world of the artist, accountable to no one.

Back home, Jerome and Max worked on a stage name. Jerome had once heard a local blues singer named Doctor somebody on the radio and liked the sound of it. Maybe it was a cockeyed offering to his parents—see, your son's become a doctor after all. And Pomus? Did they choose it because it sounded black, like "Thomas?" Or, with its weird spelling, like the name of some fire-breathing fakir he'd gleaned from *Arabian Nights*? Doc never managed to remember. It sounded foreign and dangerous and hip—that was enough.

Doc swooned when he thought about the life laid out before him. He imagined a singer as a kind of spiritualist or priest. The song was a vessel through which he'd make manifest his very soul—the audience would sense and acknowledge it, and at least until the last chorus died down, the two would be joined. It was a fierce and naïve belief that would take him prisoner. For the moment, it merely filled him with purpose. He was an artist all right, but his essence wasn't trapped between the covers of a book, or fixed on canvas, but for a few minutes it hovered in the air for anyone present to partake. Who but a singer—most of all a blues singer—could make that claim?

The weeks that followed brought Doc's new life into sharp relief. Nightly, when he took the stage with Frankie Newton's group—which included brothers Sam and Jimmy Allen on guitar and piano, and Dave Smith on bass—the veteran players hung behind him with an amused curiosity. Every night the applause in the room got stronger. After a couple of weeks, Doc added Billy Eckstine's lascivious "Jelly Jelly" to his repertoire of "BB Blues" and "Piney Brown Blues." He also remembered that he knew the words to "Sunny Side of the Street." It wasn't in his regular blues line, but it lent his act variety. Now he could confidently perform four songs.

The frosting on the cake was the steady flow of musicians who unexpectedly showed up and sat in. Between songs, the great trombone player Vic Dickerson would stride onto the bandstand; without saying a word, he'd take his horn out of its case and begin blowing. Other times Pete Brown, the rotund, hoarse, perpetually stoned altoist who knew Newton from John Kirby's band, improvised behind Doc with a dirty, growling tone, and Doc never forgot the night—was he dreaming?—that Lester Young climbed the three steps to the stage. Doc shouted a couple of verses, and then, from behind his shoulder, Prez came in with a solo, phrasing in that mellow, aching way Doc had so admired on the radio. He hardly knew what to make of it. A couple of weeks ago, he'd been Jerome Felder, lackluster senior from Bushwick High, and now Lester Young was taking a solo behind *him*.

Between sets, the band members made a beeline out the side door into the alley to share a joint. After a few times choking on the sweet smoke, Doc acquired a taste for grass. On the street a joint was fifty cents, an ounce, twenty dollars. An ounce of the really good stuff, Panama Red or Acapulco Gold, cost an extra five, but it bought enough to roll eighty or eighty-five decent-sized joints. He was getting a taste for whiskey, too, and stayed high until after the last set, when the musicians sat together and gorged on huge sandwiches of veal and peppers on Italian bread—discounted to thirty cents for the house band—and heaping plates of spaghetti marinara. On the subway home, it sometimes took him half an hour to remember where he lived.

JEROME, as one raunchy blues put it, was walking on soft-boiled eggs. He was transfigured. At dinner, his head buzzed with the songs and stage moves that he'd debut during the night's show. His fingers drummed a rhythm in his lap. But he kept his alter ego hidden from Millie and Morris. What would they think of him complicating a life in one slum with the music of another, even worse ghetto? Had they paid all those doctors and social workers and tutors to see their son become a performer of Negro burlesques? Jerome knew that in his parents' eyes he remained a paralyzed high-school graduate with a middling transcript and few prospects.

After graduation, worrying about his future turned into a pre-occupation for his parents. Even the ceremony took a surreal turn. Jerome, in his gown and mortarboard, gaped as his father bounded up onto the stage. Morris had signed on as a commence-ment speaker to surprise his son, but watching his father stooped over the lectern, trying to placate the bored students with con-spicuously telegraphed jokes, only embarrassed him. At home, Millie and Morris fretted out loud about his lack of direction. He knew they didn't expect much of him. They feared he'd end up like those cripples selling pencils they passed daily on the city's street corners. Jerome empathized with their fears because at times he shared them. What could a Jewish, paralyzed, high-school graduate with middling grades and neither property nor inheritance reasonably expect to become? An accountant or an engineer? Hardly. Jerome showed no talent for the quantitative or the analytical, spent money like a sieve, and didn't have much of a work ethic. What did that leave? Would he become an insurance agent? A Fuller Brush salesman? A bookie? At night Millie turned in bed and worried while Morris kept his gloomy convictions to himself. When Millie had been pregnant with Jerome, Morris was convinced his son would be a man among men, the one who'd complete his own prodigal ambitions. Instead, he despaired at seeing in his son a reflection of his own physical disability and fail-ures, and kept his disillusionment to himself.

Always the pragmatic one, Millie decided to act and signed up Jerome for a career-training seminar. The location was an old theater in downtown Brooklyn. Jerome gamely agreed to go, but when he sat down among the hopeful actuaries and loan offi-cers, his hands began to tremble. A vision unfolded in his head: Jerome suddenly witnessed a future so bleak and terrifying that he hustled out of the building as quickly as his crutches allowed. He would've run if he could. As he stood shivering on the sidewalk, doubled over from the effort and a distinct feeling of nausea, he promised himself that he'd never contemplate an office job again.

The General wasn't deterred. Millie invited motivational speakers, disguised as dinner guests, to the apartment. Shortly before dessert, Millie cued the visitor to start grilling her son about his career plans. He or she then trumpeted on about the degrading lot awaiting Jerome among the ranks of the uneducated, the unemployed and the idle. The most prominent of these furies was Ruth Waters, a stern, heavyset judge at Brooklyn's domestic relations court. "You're losing time," she hollered at a shell-shocked Jerome, brusque as a traffic cop. Even a factory job, she told him, was more productive than the life of the home-bound parasite—of living, she went on to say, with his parents and keeping his nose buried in records and books. "Mind you own fucking business!" Jerome told her curtly, leaving the judge open-mouthed over a plate of warm cherry strudel, and slammed the door. Millie's vocational-themed dinner parties came to an abrupt end.

For all of Doc's renegade nighttime adventures, Jerome's daytime routine hardly changed. He still rode the subway, sometimes with Raoul in tow, to Ninety-second Street and Park Avenue on Manhattan's Upper East Side to visit Konrad Hoehler, the elderly German who kept Jerome's leg braces in good repair. The work was minute and technical and had become a specialty among German immigrants. As the old man hunched over the braces with his menagerie of tiny tools, Jerome and Raoul cast wary glances at the bust of Hitler on the desk.

His double life made Jerome acutely aware of how little his parents really knew him, and each other. Surrounded by Morris, Millie, and Harris at the dinner table, he marveled at how seldom they must have wondered about each other—about what the others fretted and fantasized, what they feared and craved. Was it the same with most families? Had Morris and Millie been like this when they met? It didn't matter—now Jerome had another life away from home, his genuine life, and it would take him places no one at the dinner table had ever imagined.

DOC WASN'T SURE when the guys at George's began to take him seriously. He wasn't sure he took himself seriously yet, but after about a month of singing with Frankie Newton, he somehow convinced Dominick to let him bring in his own band. The group he cobbled together was made up of Hal Stein, a sixteen-year-old saxophone-playing wonder from West New York, New Jersey, and Hal's two underaged neighbors—bass player Billy Cronk, who'd later play with the Dorsey Brothers and the Louis Armstrong Orchestra, and Ed Shaughnessy, whom Doc would one day watch on TV drumming behind Johnny Carson. Minutes before their first gig, Doc walked out onto Seventh Avenue to admire the brand-new sign affixed to the side of the awning, just underneath George's red neon:

Doc Pomus and His Blues Men, Featuring Hal Stein!

NO COVER OR MINIMUM.

Having his own band freed him to take risks. During his stay at George's, Doc learned that women liked singers, even singers on crutches. They sat in the front row and telegraphed their pleasure; by the end of the set, it was a cinch to drop by their table and strike up a conversation. Onstage, he was learning to work a crowd. Though his range of motion was limited, Doc realized that he could make up for it by controlling the timing, the song sequence, and the dynamics of his voice—knowing when to drop it to a near hush and when to dig down into his gut and blow. He knew he wasn't a magical stage performer—the kind that held the crowd in thrall from the moment he walked onto the stage to the moment he left it—but Doc was discovering he could be good. Maybe even better. Plus he was making forty dollars a week—not a star's wage, but not a bad payday for a working musician who fronted his own band.

Once he'd worked up a local following, Doc branched out to the Pied Piper, later renamed Café Bohemia, around the corner on Barrow Street. The Piper was a nostalgia club that specialized in Dixieland and old-time hot jazz. He worked the Sunday afternoon jam sessions supervised by the Baron Timme Rosenkrantz, the Danish jazz fan and sometime recordist, and later by Foots Thomas, the sax player from Cab Calloway's orchestra. On one of those Sundays, Leonard Feather—the British jazz critic—asked Doc to record two of his songs. A few days later, Doc showed up at a studio with Hal Stein. After a handshake or two, he was leaning over a microphone and hollering the lyrics to "Blues without Booze" and "Blues in the Red," both written by Feather, who was banging away at the piano. Doc was reading the words from a piece of notebook paper Feather had handed him just minutes earlier.

Doc couldn't figure out why he wasn't more scared. Maybe he was too green, or too dumb. Still a teenager, he huddled in the small studio with the stellar altoist Tab Smith, Chuck Wayne on guitar, and several guys from Duke Ellington's orchestra. If he fretted that he was still the fraud that had wandered penniless into George's on that summer evening, the session put his fears to rest. The recording was released on Bess Berman's Apollo label, soon to become the home of gospel star Mahalia Jackson; the flipside was "Blues Around the Clock" by Willie Bryant, soon to be the famed Apollo Theater emcee. When the record was pressed, Doc came home with a boxful—it was the first tangible evidence of his new career. Doc even found a glowing review in a small magazine called *Music Dial*. Ray Parker, who moonlighted as a pianist, was the author and editor. Doc had trouble putting it together in his mind—he'd made a record that a critic had heard and thought extraordinary enough to commit his praise to paper. It was right there in the pages of the magazine—he was no longer a fake.

DOC FIGURED that lucky breaks came in droves. Every week he played the numbers at the local gambling front, and not long after his first record hit the shelves, his lucky number hit, too. To Doc, money was just a means of floating from one week to the next. But here was a windfall—he never managed to remember the exact amount—and after pocketing the winnings, Doc picked out a tan two-door Chevrolet and paid for it in cash. He shelled out extra for hand-operated Bendix hydraulic brakes, the kind used on tractor-trailers. With the rest of the money, he bought himself a sharp Harris tweed suit and two-tone wingtips. When he drove the gleaming new coupe around the neighborhood, Doc felt like a heavy from a Dashiell Hammet novel.

Like many of the things he'd wanted and somehow managed to get, the Chevy ended up haunting him. He never got the hang of the brakes—they were absurdly powerful and caused the car to lock up and skid at the slightest touch, and one time in five they simply failed. One early morning, driving home from a club in the far reaches of blackest Brooklyn, Doc dozed off behind the wheel. It was still dark outside; besides, he could fall asleep in the strangest places. The Chevy must have coasted into a parked car or a lamppost, because when Doc woke up he was inside an ambulance, and his pockets had been picked. He wasn't hurt badly, but the accident gave rise to a myth—for years, Doc told women that, when he came to in his car, he saw a man picking his pocket and punched him so hard he broke his own hand. The hand that he'd hold up was the one fractured by the snowball.

After the crack-up, Morris became obsessed with his son's driving. First, he got into the habit of hiding Doc's car keys. If that wasn't precaution enough, he began to move the Chevy in secret. Doc would hustle out of the apartment on his way to a gig, done up in a suit and tie and doused with a handful of cologne, only to find the car gone. Raoul had to walk for blocks to flag down a taxi, since cabs rarely passed 75 Manhattan Avenue, and then try to persuade the driver to make a detour to the corner where his agitated brother stood waiting. To the end of his life, Doc was plagued by a recurring nightmare: Morris had hidden the keys to his car, and he was searching for it frantically, stumbling from block to block on his crutches.

AWAY FROM THE CLUBS and the pot smoke, Doc had to admit
to himself that he didn't know how long any of it would last. He
still lived with his parents, who were beginning to suspect the
truth about where he spent his nights, and he figured he needed
an insurance policy. In September 1943, he enrolled at Brooklyn
College and, partly in tribute to Morris, declared a major in political science. Campus life turned out more agreeable than he'd
imagined. He remained bored with classes but thoroughly enjoyed
the social life. So much had changed that summer. No longer the
shy paralytic he'd been at Bushwick High, he was now a working
jazz musician, a veritable Errol Flynn among the bookish undergrads with their horn-rimmed glasses and sensible shoes who still
debated Trotsky and Stalin in the cafeteria. When Doc discovered
a well-attended student jazz club on campus, he installed himself
as president in a quick, bloodless coup. Who was going to oppose
him? Was there another poly-sci major that fronted his own jazz
band and shared the stage with Lester Young? And in Rector
Bailey, a renowned guitar teacher and nightclub sideman affiliated
with the college, Doc found a hip, sympathetic mentor.

Ever since he'd walked on crutches, girls had been disarmed by
his appearance. They treated him as a sexless cipher, pitied him, or
simply ignored him. But at the jazz club, Doc met a girl who was
different. She was dark-haired, pretty, and most remarkably—
since the jazz club didn't attract many girls—devoted to jazz and
the blues nearly as much as Doc. He could tell she was impressed
by his well-larded stories of singing alongside Frankie Newton, so
he casually invited her to hear him at the Pied Piper. Barbara
Silver—for that was her name—told him she'd love to.

Not long after Barbara took the subway to the Village to watch
Doc perform, someone discovered them necking in Doc's Chevy.
The two of them stopped only when they heard a knock on the
window. When Doc opened the car door, he stood face to face
with the indignant president of Brooklyn College. The man assured
them they'd both be expelled, but nothing came of the threat but
a good story. Doc was too pleased with himself to worry—Barbara

was the first girl who ever looked up to him, who understood and validated his music. He needed badly to share his double life with someone who could savor its importance.

Doc waited for Barbara after classes and drove her home to the Bronx. Every time he dropped her off, she asked him upstairs. Barbara told Doc that her parents couldn't wait to meet him; she just knew they'd love him as much as she did. Doc always refused. He was convinced that Barbara's parents expected her to bring home a varsity athlete or a bespectacled pre-law major, and kept imagining their expressions when he'd come shuffling in on his crutches. Doc couldn't get the image out of his mind. After he kissed Barbara goodbye, he'd wait in the car with the engine idling until she reached the front door and, with an awkward wave, nose the Chevy back into traffic.

RECTOR BAILEY, too, had been to the Pied Piper to hear Doc and the new incarnation of His Blues Men. The bass player, Leo Guarnieri, had convinced Doc to hire an army buddy, a drummer named Milt Jackson who later became a member of the urbane Modern Jazz Quartet. Jackson was laying down a lush carpet of vibraphone around Doc's hoarsely shouted blues. The combination couldn't have sounded weirder if he'd been playing a harpsichord. Still, Bailey was impressed enough to ask Doc to work a date with his group, the Herman Chittison Trio. Bailey made good money playing clubs in Brooklyn and New Jersey to nearly all-black, ghetto crowds. Forget the Greenwich Village hipsters, he told Doc. The outer-borough clubs would show him a whole other level of appreciation. The idea intrigued Doc. He knew that his singing never quite jibed with the *haute* jazz ideal of the white aficionados, who worshipped the cerebral, improvised music performed uptown, especially bebop's jagged, avant-garde runs. Doc considered Charlie Parker a genius, but when he closed his eyes and pictured himself onstage, it was the blues he heard, shouted in the virile, open-throated Kansas City style of Turner and Little Jimmy Rushing and Jay McShann. So he told Bailey, sure, he'd sit in.

Doc showed up at that first gig at the Verona Café, a dark, shabby room on Fulton Street, a bustling thoroughfare in poor, dangerous Bedford Stuyvesant. It was a casual, throwaway week-night show. Chittison played piano in the florid style of Art Tatum; along with the rhythm section, Bailey laid in a driving, muscular groove. Even before he stepped up to the microphone, Doc no-ticed the alert, hard-drinking audience eyeing him. In Bed Stuy, you'd sometimes spot a white face or two in the back of a room, but never onstage. Doc soon learned that on most nights the joints were 100 percent sepia—loud black entertainment for a good-time black clientele. Nothing in common, he thought, with the polite, "integrated" rooms on Fifty-second Street, where the tables were jammed with recent Princeton grads in Charvet ties nursing their Scotch and milks and nodding to each other with heavy-lidded eyes in a kind of Confucian approbation.

The blacks watched Doc with rapt curiosity. Who was this ro-tund ofay poseur with his crutches and braces? Doc could tell they didn't know whether to expect imitation or homage or all-out comedy. No audience had ever watched him so intensely, so inter-ested in what he'd do. It hadn't occurred to him then that they'd never seen a white man on this stage—on any stage—singing their music. Doc stepped onto the bandstand, grabbed the mike like it was a sputtering torch and shouted the first note, coming down hard on top of the beat. The room blew up. It was all Doc could do to keep his voice above the hollering and wailing around him; when he was done, they received him as though he'd just punched Max Schmeling into a coma. Rector Bailey was grinning a "told-you-so" grin. He'd been right. Doc's idiom hadn't found its audience until now. They'd loved him all the more because he was white and *owned* the music, without fuss or extraneous rev-erence or apology. Men in work shirts were lining up to buy him drinks; a young woman busting out of her crepe-de-Chine blouse who'd been doing a double-twist right in front of the band-stand was beckoning him over to her table. Easy, Doc thought. This was home.

From Doc's journal, January 12, 1982:

I always believed in magic and flying and that one morning I would wake up and all the bad things were bad dreams and Daddy would be alive and heroic and Mama would understand and be proud of me only because she understood me and my kid brother was a kid again and I would sing to him and he would have that 10-year-old-I-worship-you look in his eyes. And I would get out of the wheelchair and walk and not with braces and crutches. And I would walk down all streets and no one would stare at me and young girls in see-through dresses would smile at me, dazzled by my appearance and glow, and men would listen to my words carefully and I could wander around all night without fear in my soul and I could sit by a lonely stoop at 1:00 am with friends and have a convertible top open at 2:00 am and walk or park in Prospect Park or Central Park. I would always sing and everybody would always love to hear me sing and my children were little children in my arms and the woman or women in my life would stay young forever and love me in a young way forever.

Young Blood

Audiences feel a weak flutter rise in their stomachs whenever blues-singer Doc Pomus comes to the bandstand to perform. It takes him a long time to climb up to the stage, and the crutches make a funny noise. "For that reason," says the 28-year-old entertainer, "agents—they're mostly ex-tap dancers—won't take a chance on me. But when I start singing everybody gets lost in the music. Being crippled just takes a little longer. I got it licked in my head, where it counts. I like the blues because they tell a sad story. They're 'bottom music.' I like to sing for Negro audiences because they're tough, you can't fool them with show tricks. Imagine though! People come to see *me* to forget their troubles."

—*Picture Life Magazine*, September 1954

LIKE ALMOST EVERYONE who'd grown up in its lower middle-class warrens, Doc never felt much allegiance to Brooklyn. It was a place where you ate and slept while you dreamed about the Elysian pastures on the other side of the East River: the townhouses on Sutton Place, the grand ballrooms in the Central Park hotels, the boutiques and haberdasheries on Madison Avenue, the big time nightlife on Fifty-second Street and up in Harlem. Yet nearly two years after he ambled onto a Greenwich Village stage, Doc was back in Brooklyn, having completed a Brooklynite's dream journey in reverse. To Doc it felt like progress. In the space of a few months he made the sprawling borough his playground, claiming all the work and applause and marijuana and late-night pulled pork sandwiches he wanted. Every week he tore up another joint, wailing in the blackest of urban blues styles to another incredulous room. The work wasn't lucrative, and it sure wasn't prestigious—John Hammond wasn't casing the watering holes along Fulton Street for the next giant of jazz. It didn't matter. The reception he got at the black joints awakened a loyalty in Doc. Ever since he was a kid he knew instinctively that being a fat Jewish paralytic made him something others reviled and feared: a thing, a nigger. Now he belonged. Doc was a surefire hotshot on the outer-borough circuit, the teenage white wonder that every Negro blues fan in Brooklyn was dying to hear and see for himself.

Most of Brooklyn's sepia clubs lay scattered around Bedford Stuyvesant and the equally dangerous ghetto neighborhood of Brownsville, but rhythm and blues could be heard nightly as far away as Coney Island. Doc made the rounds at the Verona Café, the Cosmo, McGovern's Tavern, Paul's Café, Farmer John's, the Full Reed (on the corner of Fulton and Reed), Soldier Meyer's, and the Brooklyn Baby Grand. A typical night's lineup included a shake dancer—a stripper who embellished her act with lewd, quasi-jazz-ballet steps—a couple of urban blues singers, a band, and an emcee who had the audience rolling with some rude blue comedy. The raunchier joints had drag queens on the bill. The last set ended at three or four in the morning, but the musicians jammed and partied until dawn.

Doc's biggest gig was at the Elks Club at 1068 Fulton Street. There, he worked in front of a crowd of several hundred as part of a revue that added tap dancers to the mix. The audience threw coins and wadded up bills onto the stage, and on nights when he was good, Doc came away with as much as sixty dollars. The dancers' routines included acrobatic flourishes that allowed them to bend over and pick up the money, while the emcee cleared the singers' loot off the stage and took a cut for the service. The setup made Doc nervous; he was convinced the emcee was ripping him off.

Brooklyn's toughest joint was the Cobra Club, a honky-tonk surrounded by garbage-strewn alleys that stood at the bottom of a dead-end intersection in the heart of Brownsville. Known for its explosive free-for-alls, the Cobra served as a hangout for hookers, pimps, petty thieves, and characters banned from every other barroom in the city. The only man who kept the lid from popping off was the short, squat bouncer Bert "The Chocolate Kid" Lytell. In 1948, *Ring Magazine* listed Lytell as the nation's number one middleweight. Other middleweights refused to get in the ring with him, forcing him to take on light heavyweights. But on occasion even Lytell couldn't keep the Cobra from boiling over. One night, Doc watched from the stage as a soused woman at the bar took off a shoe and smashed the stiletto heel, tomahawk-style, against the head of her even drunker beau. The victim slid off his stool and sprawled on the floor with a wide, stupefied grin on his bloodied face.

Doc usually played the Cobra with the ever-stoned Pete Brown. The paranoid sax player must've weighed close to three hundred pounds and carried a revolver in the waistband of his pants. Whenever anybody got too close, he pulled it out. During one gig, a mid-song volley of gunshots sent everyone scrambling for the exits. Moments later a light-skinned, trembling Negro clutching a Colt .45 ordered everyone who was left to march out the back door and into a dead-end alley. After Doc, Pete, and the rest had filed into the filthy, narrow passageway, the gunman emptied an entire clip into the crowd and ran away. Doc heard the bullets ricochet off the brick walls. Amazingly, no one was hit. But when Pete Brown's drummer, Lionel Trotman, noticed his shirt was covered with blood—a remnant of somebody's nosebleed—he swooned and collapsed on the pavement.

The night scrambled Doc's nerves. The following week, in the back room of another club, he dropped his crutches and lunged to the floor when he heard gunshots. Someone was only throwing beer bottles against the wall in the alley outside. Soon Doc learned to pick out the exits before every gig, to watch for thrown bottles and stools, to stay calm whenever he heard the telltale screams and mayhem caused by a drawn gun. Hardly a weekend passed without a fistfight breaking out, someone pulling a knife, or some hard-luck barfly being carried out on a gurney. Enough whiskey and pot quieted Doc's jitters. The gigs petered out just after dawn. Afterward, Doc stood on the garbage-strewn curb outside the club shivering in the pale light breaking over the warehouses while he tried to remember where he'd parked the car, directions to the nearest breakfast counter, or the most likely corner to flag down a cabdriver brave or dumb enough to have strayed into the Brooklyn slums.

THEY USED TO CALL OTIS BLACKWELL "The Preacher." He had a gospel singer's quiver in his voice, but his delivery was a measure more mischievous. He paced back and forth onstage and jabbed a finger at the audience like a brush arbor reverend driving home some truth about original sin. Otis carried fragments of lyrics and songs scribbled on scraps of paper in his pockets and delivered a song in an offbeat, proto–rock and roll style. As a kid he loved country records and old Westerns, especially ones starring singing cowboy Tex Ritter, whose plummy, deep baritone made Otis grin. Something about those songs percolated into his style—when he sang, he sounded like a Harlem cowboy. In the afternoons, Otis pressed pants at a neighborhood tailor shop. Gigging, as Doc was finding out, rarely covered the bills.

They met at one of Otis's shows at Paul's Café, on DeKalb and Sumner. There were maybe thirty blues joints in Brooklyn, and over the years they figured they must've played them all. Otis introduced Doc to his first manager. Willie Saunders was a tall, smooth-talking reporter for the *New Amsterdam News*, light-complected and suave. He drove a Cadillac sedan and was trailed by a bevy of gorgeous women. Saunders's management amounted to booking Otis and Doc into some local dives for "cocktail sips"— weeknight gigs where a customer off the street could get a free show for the price of two or three cocktails. The owners paid Saunders a finder's fee and plied him and his women with free liquor while Doc and Otis serenaded the empty barrooms. For this they received sums so measly that sometimes they couldn't even cover their tabs. But Saunders strung them along with talk of big-time Manhattan bookings that waited just around the corner. Not that they believed him. Frankly, Saunders's cast-offs in the female department usually made up for his bullshit.

Doc loved being onstage. Recording, on the other hand, was usually a racket and a waste of time. Still, every few months he cut a side or two for some paltry amount and never gave it much thought. None of the records managed national sales or airplay. The labels that approached him recorded local black rhythm and blues and gospel singers for a working-class black audience. The technical standards were shoddy; the business practices mercenary. No one mentioned royalties. Aside from Apollo, Doc recorded for Coral, Derby, After Hours, even a Danish label called Baronette. He sang on a Rex Stewart session for two Jewish brothers from Chicago named Leonard and Phil Chess. And he cut a marijuana-innu-endo tune titled "My Good Pott" for Savoy, the Newark, New Jersey, label headed by Herman Lubinsky, a man known by a broad margin as the cheapest, hardest, most loathsome character in race records, a business already blessed with a surplus of gang-sters, exploiters and goons. Sometimes the labels stiffed Doc even on the tiny advances. At least twice he pulled out a borrowed gun and threatened to kill Lubinsky along with his A&R man Teddy Reig. He also pulled a revolver on Derby's Larry Newton. Doc re-minded him about that stickup years later, when Newton became president of Ray Charles's label, ABC.

If the records didn't sell, the labels weren't entirely to blame. Most often, Doc wrote songs the night before the session, scrib-bling the words in his notebook while in bed or at an all-night diner. They were dirty, conventional blues with titles like "Send for the Doctor" and "My New Chick." What was the point of composing Shakespearean sonnets? Doc didn't expect the sides to travel far beyond the jukeboxes at the local honky-tonks.

In the end, it was his least promising session that made him famous around New York. Doc's radio spot for Alley's Clothing Store, a shop on the corner of Bedford and Fulton that catered to Brooklyn's sharpest black hipsters, was a surprise smash. New

York's top rhythm and blues jocks—Willie & Ray, Symphony Sid, and Dr. Jive—broadcast Doc jive-talking about Alley's fantastic pants in heavy rotation: "You got all those great things in the bug stitches!" The infectious jingle was way more fun and knowing than the competition:

> Alley, Alley, Alley,
> You're so good to me,
> You got those three ring bottoms . . .

After it surfaced on the radio, musicians greeted Doc with shouts of "Alley Alley"; the jingle brought in bookings and sessions. In 1948, Apollo's Bess Berman even asked him to cut a full-length version on record.

Doc changed the words to make it dirtier—naturally, more commercial—and laid down "Alley Alley Blues" at Beltone, a run-down little studio located in the Wolcott Hotel on Thirty-first Street. He brought a trio to back him. Guitarist Ralph Williams was a versatile instrumentalist and singer who'd been with the Orioles, the well-known vocal group. Reggie Ashby, who spent so much time at the Felders' apartment that Raoul swore he forgot Ashby was black, manned the piano. The bass player was John Levy, a sideman from the Pied Piper. Jerry Jerome, the producer, wafted in about an hour before the session and, after contributing some bright chit chat and several hearty claps on the back, disappeared before the first note was played. The engineer gave the signal, the red light went on, and Doc growled out the familiar melody with the new, improved sexual lyrics:

> In the alley, alley, alley,
> She was so good to me . . .

Williams provided the comedy, coming in on the break with a girly falsetto squeal:

> Doc, Doc . . . please don't stop
> It's getting so good to me
> Let's go around the clock!

They cut three other sides: "Clementine," "Fruitty Woman Blues," and "Nagging Wife Blues." They clowned around and re-arranged instrumental parts on the fly, but the whole session lasted only three or four hours. Apollo, like most of the other small companies that made race records, allowed only one take per side.

After the session, they piled into Doc's battered Chevrolet and drove to Fulton Street, where they wolfed down plates of brisket, pulled pork, coleslaw, and collard greens at Smitty's Chauncey Rotisserie. Sated, they headed to the corner of Verona Place to their gig at the Verona Café. They arrived weary but game, wailed until three in the morning, then brought in the dawn with what-ever women were left. The band staggered out of the Verona squinting into the daylight, said their goodbyes, and walked home past the day-people headed to their offices, the unshaven kiosk men unshuttering their newsstands, and the aroma of bacon and eggs and loud up-tempo swing that wafted out the wide-open doors of the coffee shops.

DOC COULDN'T SEE MUCH POINT to sticking with college after the Brooklyn gigs began in earnest. He'd dropped out briefly a couple of times before but had come back out of guilt toward his parents. Still, he couldn't work as a honky-tonk bluesman and at-tend classes at the same time. Besides, his interest in political sci-ence had run dry. Because he no longer saw her on campus and at the downtown club dates, Doc fell out of touch with Barbara Silver. He didn't have the nerve to invite her to the clubs where he now performed—he'd be afraid for her safety. But that wasn't the main thing. Their courtship had come to an abrupt end when Doc's cousin Max confessed to him that one night he'd seduced Barbara up on his rooftop. Max made a show of contrition and re-gret, and Doc pretended to let it go, but he could barely breathe when Max told him. He and Barbara hadn't done much more than neck in his car, and Doc took the revelation as yet another sign that reciprocal love wasn't meant for him. Oh, he'd been with women before, the kind you usually met at the clubs—burlesque performers, barmaids, other men's women, drunks—women with whom sex was a momentary respite for loneliness. The woman he dreamed about—beautiful, warm, decent, smart—would have to wait.

He thought about Barbara all through the forties. Occasionally he worked up the nerve to phone her parents and ask about her, but she never called back. One humid August night Barbara Silver walked into the club on Fulton Street where Doc was singing. Inside, it felt like a hundred degrees. Doc's shirt was sticking to his back. Between sets, Barbara introduced Doc to the smiling boy she'd come in with. She said they'd just gotten married. Doc congratulated them and smiled back. When he stepped onto the stage and began to sing—"Well they call me Doc, I can make you feel so good"—he swayed at the microphone and tumbled to the floor. Later he told himself that he fainted from the intense heat. But every time he thought about Barbara, he felt a twinge in the pit of his stomach.

NO MATTER HOW JADED, broke or beaten-down he might've felt, Doc never quit being a fan. Watching a great gig always fired him up. And there was no one in all of New York Doc loved to hear as much as Little Jimmy Scott. To all appearances, Jimmy was a tiny, wizened, effeminate black teenager who peered at the audience from behind thick glasses and looked part Indian, a claim he endorsed. He passed for fourteen or fifteen when he was nearly twice that age. A rare genetic deficiency called Kallman's Syndrome had left him with a prepubescent body and a choirboy's high voice that he used to stupendous effect. Jimmy lingered behind the beat longer than any singer alive. When he sang it sounded as though he'd miss the beat altogether, but his delivery was exquisitely controlled. His wide vibrato and tart, crying timbre lent his ballads a sorrowful quality that Doc found almost spooky. That combination of timing, pitch, and intonation had a dreamlike feeling—Doc had seen the sob in Jimmy's voice crack the most cynical junkie or pimp and fill their eyes with tears. When Jimmy had first settled in New York, he got a rocky reception. At the rougher joints someone in the audience usually shouted "faggot" when he appeared on the bandstand. Jimmy was used to it. By the time he reached the bridge, the audience was listening to him in rapt and slightly disbelieving silence.

Jimmy met Doc in 1945 in Harlem, at the uptown Baby Grand on 125th and Eighth Avenue, just down the street from the Apollo Theater. During the show, a spot of light that danced across the ceiling distracted Jimmy. When the house lights came on, he saw that it had been bouncing off a pair of shiny steel leg braces worn by a squat white guy in the front row. When Doc reverently introduced himself, Jimmy was struck by the man's utter absence of self-pity. He offered to take Jimmy to the best joints and eateries, and he whisked him up and down Manhattan, from Harlem down to the Lower East Side and back, nimbly working his crutches up and down the stairs to the subway. Jimmy could barely keep up. Later, Doc introduced his new friend and idol to the Brooklyn circuit. They were soon playing on the same bill, mostly gigs emceed by a disc jockey named Tommy Smalls, better known as Dr. Jive. On the off-days, Doc and Jimmy made the rounds of the local clubs. The regulars bought them drinks, and when they performed an occasional freebie, the owners sent them all the beer and food they could stomach.

On nights when they felt especially exultant, they cabbed it to Harlem, where the after-hours joints stayed open all night in cheerful disregard of the city's cabaret laws. Clubs like Monroe's Uptown House on 134th Street, along with Dickie Wells' and Covan's Morocco Club, which stood across the street from each other on 133rd, had the hottest jazz, the sexiest shake dancers, and a drag queen that would perform impersonations or some especially low-down comedy. On the rare but dependable occasions when the police raided the joints, everybody poured out the back door and hopped the fences. Doc never chanced upon a raid and was thankfully spared that necessity. Harlem was also where they'd run into Billie Holiday, another admirer of Jimmy's singing. Billie lounged at their table for hours, nuzzled a lapdog in her Persian lamb collar, and traded gossip in her languid, cigarette-flavored voice.

Jimmy shared an apartment with a proper, religious sister and her husband in an old Quonset hut barracks in Canarsie. Out of respect, Jimmy and Doc didn't get stoned around Jimmy's family, not a small accommodation since they were stoned most of the time. One night Jimmy introduced Doc to his brother's step-daughter, Aida. She was small like Jimmy, but darker skinned and even more exotic looking; she claimed she was "half-Egyptian and half-Arabian." Aida was a singer, too. Painfully shy in public, she still managed to win the amateur night contest at the Apollo Theater. Whenever she showed up at Doc's gigs, he asked her to sit in. Aida sang in a small, pure, perfectly musical soprano, and her phrasing was eccentric and hip. Musicians who heard her asked Aida to sit in with them, too, but she felt too self-conscious. Instead, she fell for Doc. In time, he understood that she loved him fiercely and poetically, but Doc reciprocated her affection only to a point. The prevailing style of the hipster with his chick was to be cool with your feelings; a man wasn't supposed to care for a girl as much as she did for him. Somewhere, too, Doc must have acknowledged to himself that Aida wasn't the kind of girl he could bring home to Millie. But Aida was unreserved with her feelings. She made love to Doc imaginatively, holding nothing back, with an abandon he'd never experienced in his after-hours trysts. Those nights became a scene he'd return to in later years, trying to untangle the strands of nostalgia and regret.

EVERY THIRD WEEK OR SO, Doc, Jimmy, and Aida piled into the tan Chevy and took the Canal Street Tunnel to South Bedford Street in the heart of Newark's black belt. Cookie's Caravan—home to some of Doc's favorite gigs—belonged to Bill Cook, who broadcast the hippest hour of music on Jersey radio. He was a short, stout, light-skinned black man with a pug nose covered in freckles. Cook was a fan of Doc's records and gave them heavy airtime on his show; when he emceed, he talked Doc up to the skies. Doc's confidence leaped whenever Cookie introduced him.

Cookie's Caravan was the best kind of joint—cavernous, with a loud sound system that covered the entire room. The stage was shaped like a boxing ring and stood high off the ground in the middle of the room, with steps at two sides. The crowd was the rowdiest Doc had ever seen. Whenever a singer really delivered, women reached into their handbags and men emptied their wallets and threw their Friday-night earnings in the air. Doc never forgot the sound of quarters bouncing off the wooden stage and the sight of greenbacks cascading through the smoke-filled light. Once in a while a young woman was so moved by a song or a singer that she swooned and passed out. Sometimes, she got another blow when she came to: her man would be so shaken by her reaction that he'd hit her upside the head and send her back to dreamland.

New York performers were the exception at Cookie's. In many ways, Newark's black music scene rivaled the one across the Hudson. The city had cheap rent, good drugs, and a blazing nightlife that lasted into the late morning. Cookie warmed up his audiences with the requisite shake dancers, followed by a young, pretty crooner who sashayed through a couple of ballads, then a local bluesman like Sammy Cotton or the unforgettably named Mr. Google Eyes. The headliner was most often a nationally known performer like Roy Hamilton, the stately balladeer whom Cook managed, Little Jimmy Scott, or one of the club's two resident geniuses.

Big Maybelle was vast and ungainly and ebony black. Her voice was equally outsized, dark-toned and unrestrained from the highest treble to the lowest bass. She could sing a complicated modern jazz ballad or a low-down blues, and everything in between, rendering them with her telltale strangled cry. Onstage she cultivated the persona of the victim, belting out tales of heartbreak in which she was done in by a mean, two-timing woman.

Only rarely did she change the story and let a man do her in. Maybelle used the microphone only for effect; she didn't need it. She sang while striding back and forth onstage like a leopard. Sometimes she rolled down the steps and promenaded among the tables. The object of her interest was always a young woman whom she knew or wanted to get to know better. Big Maybelle moved in close, looked deep into her quarry's eyes, and sang to her until the woman lost her wits.

To many blues cognoscenti, Doc foremost among them, the greatest singer in the nation, save Joe Turner and B.B. King, was Andrew Tibbs. His records failed to capture his genius. Drawing upon authentic feeling in a cramped studio, surrounded by musicians who were anxious to split and an engineer who was likely indifferent to black music, was something he couldn't muster. But onstage at Cookie's Caravan Tibbs held an almost supernatural sway over the audience. People flocked to see him from up and down the East Coast. Tibbs was small and thin and had an innocent, angelic face marred by a knife scar that bisected his cheek, making him look like a choirboy gone bad. That good-evil countenance, plus a voice that had a note of pure mayhem in the middle, drove women and some men, too, into Pentecostal hysterics.

When Doc and Tibbs sang on the same bill, they closed their set with a "Battle of the Blues." They stood at opposite ends of the room; each had a strong voice, and neither one relied on a microphone. Doc and Tibbs traded two choruses they improvised on the spot. Usually they sang to, or about, some dish they'd spotted among the tables. The outcome was usually hilarious and sometimes dangerous. If the woman was alone, Tibbs or Doc might have lucked out when she claimed one of them after hours. Just as often, a disgruntled boyfriend or husband—who for some reason always turned out to be tough, ugly, and impossible to sweet-talk—waited for them at closing time with a beating on his mind. In those cases Doc and Tibbs backed off, humbly apologized, or simply snuck out the back door. As Tibbs had a habit of saying, "Caresses, without a doubt, are never worth a clout."

Doc saved his fondest accolades for Jimmy. Whenever Jimmy shuffled up to the mike in owlish spectacles and a too-loose suit looking like a myopic scarecrow and bent those endless notes for what always sounded like a heartbeat too long, Doc couldn't help but get torn up. Before, between, and after the two sets—at Cookie's they began at 9:30 and 1:30—the performers and half the audience slipped out to the barbeque pit around the corner. There'd be a line around the block. Stoned and grinning, Doc and Jimmy could polish off two or three helpings of ribs covered in hot sauce. They'd shit fire for days, but the flavor was so rich that the agony was worth it.

Doc didn't realize how much he cared for Aida until she left town. A few years later, Jimmy left town, too. Worn down by a usurious contract with Savoy and a failed marriage, he eventually found his way back to Cleveland, where he'd grown up and still had a large family. In the years that followed, Doc rarely went two weeks without listening to one of Jimmy's records. He'd slip it on the turntable, light a Chesterfield, and listen to "A Cottage for Sale" or "Someone to Watch Over Me." When no one was around, Doc sometimes sang along. As the red Savoy label turned on the spindle, Doc wondered what had happened to Little Jimmy Scott. He never suspected their friendship had only begun.

WHEN DOC stopped by his parents' apartment to say hello and scrounge a free meal, he sometimes brought his bass player. Leonard Gaskin dressed like a diplomat, had a mellow, dignified manner, and hardly ever went a day without a gig. He woke up in the afternoons, played two or three sets in Brooklyn or in Harlem or on Fifty-second Street, spent the wee hours inhaling cigarettes and absinthe in the cold-water flats of slumming European nobility and sundry jazz hipsters, headed over to the CBS building to play a square morning radio program, then ate a huge breakfast and fell asleep. To Doc's amazement, over the course of one particular dinner *chez* Felder, his father managed to convince Gaskin—a classically trained musician and one of the most sought-after session bassists in the city—to enroll in a correspondence course in air-conditioning and refrigeration. Morris agreed to pay for it, and did. Gaskin never cracked a single book, and they had a laugh about it later, but to Doc the whole thing demonstrated just how flimsy their livelihoods sometimes felt. Deep down, both he and Gaskin suspected that one day their jam sessions and gigs and record dates would dry up and leave them broke and forgotten. Sure, it was a gas, but it didn't add up to a career. For Doc, sometimes it didn't add up to rent.

By 1948, Doc was bedding down in run-down transient hotels, not strictly the cheapest kind, but close. In the coming years, his most dependable address was a rented room at the Broadway Central, a carpeted palace on lower Broadway that housed semi-failed theatrical types, retired divorcees and loners, scrimping coeds, and the borderline insane. When he wasn't asleep Doc hung out in the lobby, always in close proximity to a cup of coffee and a sandwich, but mostly because it was the least lonely place he could find. There was a kind of fraternity among the lobby regulars. The loudest character was named Siegel. He came to the hotel with his dog to borrow money from his brother, who owned a candy store, then played violin for hours in the lobby. One night, in 1954, Siegel confided to Doc that the man he shared his apartment with, a dishwasher named Harold Weinberg, had told him that he'd murdered Maxwell Bodenheim, the well-known Greenwich Village writer, and Bodenheim's wife. Doc convinced him to call the cops. The following day, the police announced they'd solved the notorious Bodenheim murder.

The man in the room adjacent to Doc's spent every night talking to himself. He lived on an allowance from a family that wanted nothing to do with him. Obsessed with conspiracies, he mailed hundreds of letters to the mayor and governor but never got a response. Once, when he'd talked Doc into writing a congressman on his behalf, he finally received an answer. Doc wrote all his letters after that. The man paid him according to the elected office of the recipient: Doc charged him a dollar for a letter to a congressman, five dollars for one to the mayor, and ten dollars to write the governor.

Doc's room had a record player and a radio, a closet with a few shirts and suits of dubious freshness, and a shelf of books. It was a place to sleep and sometimes bring a girl, but for several weeks a year it became a prison. Anything could trigger the episodes: a rough gig at the joints, another of Willie Saunders's broken promises, too many nights drowned in coffee and bourbon and marijuana, or simply a long stretch of going broke. Doc spent those harrowing days in bed with the blanket pulled up to his ears. Even though the sun had set and he was weak from hunger, Doc sometimes couldn't force himself to put on clothes and take the elevator to the lobby. On those days the levies that held back childhood terrors, the fears of squatting penniless and sick under some staircase, gave way. The terror that convulsed him made Doc's teeth chatter. It straddled his chest for hours; his lungs felt as though they couldn't draw enough air.

The panic chipped away at his persistence. In those moments he enjoyed a cruel clarity about his life. He was in his mid-twenties now; for the better part of a decade he'd squeaked by as a broke, glamorous white Negro. He'd sung in seedy clubs, made penny-ante records, smoked reefer. But he couldn't ignore the fact that all of it had reached a painful circularity. Without a manager or a big-time record deal he'd remain a novelty, notorious among a tiny circle of blues buffs and a colorful slice of Brooklyn's underclass. Doc knew, too, that it had been this way all along, that it had never been different. It never occurred to him that he was the only white man in the entire United States who hollered the blues at nightclubs for a living, and who recorded them on shellac disks. Would it have mattered if he'd known?

After weathering one of these spells, Doc would pack a change of clothes into a bag and take the BMT train across the Williamsburg Bridge to 75 Manhattan Avenue. It was a chance to dry out, to take solace in a few home-cooked meals and some undisturbed sleep, and maybe to pick up a twenty on the sly from

Millie. At home, his parents fought the same calcified war. While Morris's law practice lay as fallow as ever, Millie's fortunes had taken a leap. She'd been made director of the Menorah Home for the Aged, a large nursing home at 876 Bushwick Avenue. It was a position of real influence. If Millie or Morris harbored a hope of reconciling, her promotion cemented their divide. Doc and Raoul heard the rumors about Millie's affair with a neighborhood doctor named Izzie May, but the relationship had ended more than a decade earlier. Millie was in her early fifties now and, as a product of a certain age, wouldn't consider divorce.

Ever since Doc had been a child, Millie was given to short-lived but fierce episodes of brooding. She'd take long walks in the rain or go missing for a day or two and return as though nothing out of the ordinary had happened. One day she phoned Doc and asked him to meet her at a hotel in Coney Island. She said she was staying there alone. It was an odd request, but Doc agreed. They spent an afternoon sipping iced tea in a café off the hotel lobby. Neither one could tell the other about the things that made them miserable. They'd reached the impasse that occurs between mothers and adult sons and bantered about the weather and the prices, separated by the agreed-upon omissions. Doc could hardly tell his mother about losing Aida and singing for pimps and prostitutes at Snooky's on Forty-fifth Street. And what could Millie say to her son about her hopeless marriage?

With his rumpled suit and unshaven face, Doc looked old for his age; Millie appeared younger than her years. Passersby must've assumed they were lovers shacked up on a spree. Doc noticed that the misapprehension didn't entirely displease Millie; he guessed that the idea of having another, clandestine life must've appealed to her. He sat with her over two glasses of iced tea, the blades of a ceiling fan revolving lazily above them. Never before had Doc sensed his parents' unhappiness so acutely.

DOC HAD GROWN TIRED of the hangovers and the bad coffee when he wandered into the Central Plaza, a large ballroom on

111 Second Avenue, just a garbage smell away from the Lower East Side. Two of his Brooklyn "boons"—Art "Trappy" Trappier and Arthur Herbert, drummers extraordinaire—had tipped him off about a jam session that was already in full swing. The place was crowded with beer-drinking college students and the usual Scotch-drinking, Sutton Place jazz buffs. Up onstage, trumpeter Roy Eldridge, pianist Willie "the Lion" Smith, and bassist Pops Foster, each a hot jazz legend, blasted an up-tempo blues. Rock and roll was years away, and the kids still danced to Dixieland. The mood was wildly exuberant and everyone was clapping or dancing or hollering. Cops ringed the ballroom to make sure things stayed under control.

Doc buttonholed one of the guys running the sessions, a pale, thin fortyish Jewish guy named Jack Crystal who wore a shiny old suit and cheap tie. Trappy and Herbert chimed in at just the right moment and persuaded Crystal to let Doc do a song. They promised he wouldn't embarrass him. Crystal nodded. He parted the sea of dancing spectators and led Doc to the foot of the bandstand— the stage was too high and treacherous for crutches. Crystal hushed the audience and introduced a blues-singing discovery making his New York debut. Doc knew what he really meant was that no one in the sea of navy blazers around them was likely to have caught a crippled white shouter at the Cobra Club or the other *de classe* ebony joints out in the boroughs. Crystal stepped away from the microphone. Doc asked Eldridge to play a slow blues in B-flat. He shouted as ardently and loudly as he ever had, ending with a couple of nasty break choruses:

> Well we get home in the evening,
> We turn down all the lights,
> Screams "Daddy, daddy, daddy,
> Everything's all right!"

The musicians followed him sensationally. It was strong medicine for a Manhattan crowd, and when he finished the audience cheered and stomped and whistled. Doc had to do a few encores before they let him walk away from the mike.

Jack Crystal beamed from the other side of the room. He told Doc to come back whenever he had a free Friday. He'd be happy to let him sing. An invitation to perform with his childhood heroes in these relatively tony circumstances, tendered without condescension, was almost too much for Doc to fathom. But then Crystal completely blew his mind when he conspiratorially handed him two bills, a ten and a five, stammering apologetically that it shouldn't be considered a payment, merely reimbursement for carfare and other expenses. Was he kidding? Doc would've happily sung with Eldridge for free, and fifteen dollars—well, that was a ransom. After years of playing gigs for a meal or a couple of drinks, of playing five or six sets a night, nine until three or four in the morning, of toiling in rooms with weak mikes and shitty speakers where waiters seated customers in front of him and served them and argued with them while he performed, Doc could scarcely believe it. He didn't even have to sing long enough to loosen up his pipes.

Doc worked all the Central Plaza gigs he could afford, but rarely made it more than once a month. Showing up more often would have meant breaking up Brooklyn and Jersey dates that paid forty or forty-five dollars for a long, grueling weekend, and he needed the money. But Central Plaza was always on his mind. It wasn't just the incredible band—nearly every living player he admired from the old-time scene dropped by and sat in for a song or two: Max Kaminsky, Baby Dodds, Wilber and Sidney DeParis, Gene Cedric, Zutty Singleton, Freddy Moore, Tony Parenti, George Wettling, Wild Bill Davidson, and dozens more. What made Doc happiest was being on a first-name basis with players he'd idolized since childhood. "Hi, Roy," he'd say to Eldridge, and the trumpeter would reply, "What's shakin', Doc?" He would've happily emptied his pockets and handed over the night's earnings just so Roy Eldridge would talk to him again.

Trombonist Jimmy Archey, a Central Plaza regular, held down a steady gig at a Long Island country club. It was the kind of place that catered to millionaire drunks and their waspy wives and children. They told jokes and loudly ordered sidecars while the band played in the corner. Doc was sure that not a single one of them fathomed the sheer privilege of hearing the musicians they'd hired. Willie "the Lion" Smith—a derby-wearing black Jew who quoted the Old Testament, spoke fluent Yiddish, and claimed to be a rabbi—played astounding stride piano. Louis Armstrong's old compatriot Pops Foster, the owner of the kindest temperament Doc ever encountered, plucked bass. Henry Goodwin had been a soloist with every big band Doc could think of and filled in elegant runs on his horn. Doc got twenty-five dollars to perform three songs every Sunday afternoon in front of this all-star aggregation. With the elder statesmen laying in a rock-solid, mellow groove, he closed his eyes and pretended he was Joe Turner or Little Jimmy Rushing.

Back at the Central Plaza, Crystal, who managed the Commodore Music Shop on West 42nd Street by day, made sure Doc got paid promptly after every date. The cash varied from twenty to twenty-five dollars depending on the take at the door. If Doc was really hurting, he slipped him an extra ten or fifteen on the sly. Best of all, Crystal spoke to him with the same heartfelt respect he showed the others. That alone made Doc feel that he'd been accorded a membership in a fraternity of the privileged few—a kind of musical Mensa Society. Crystal's esteem and much-needed cash smoothed over the rest of Doc's week. Working the Brooklyn and Jersey joints, with their fistfights, cold food, and cheap owners, didn't weigh him down as heavily.

After the Central Plaza gigs Doc usually gave Crystal a ride home. He lived more than an hour from the city in Long Beach, on Long Island. The hand brakes in Doc's Chevy had gotten even more unreliable, and the car lurched to a stop at every streetlight. Crystal pretended not to notice. He behaved as though he was a passenger in Louis Armstrong's Rolls Royce and Doc was according him a great honor. After a couple of conversations and a glimpse of Crystal's modest house, where he lived with a wife and three sons, Doc realized that Crystal's handouts had come from his own pocket.

The jam sessions at the Central Plaza petered out as suddenly as they'd begun, and Doc lost touch with Jack Crystal. He heard of him again in the early sixties when Crystal, still a young man, died of a heart attack. Decades later he watched Crystal's youngest son Billy, a stand-up comic, perform a routine about being a kid and talking to an old jazz musician who plied him with inscrutable philosophical stories. For a while Doc considered tracking him down and telling him about singing for his father at the Central Plaza—the very last time in his life he believed he'd make it as a singer.

DOC MARVELED at an odd paradox. It seemed that whenever he got a taste of the big time he ended up disillusioned, usually worse off than before. There was some Buddhist logic to that, he reasoned, or maybe just the plain meanness of the universe.

It was good old Leonard Feather, the British-born jazz aristocrat, who introduced him to Maele Bartholomew around 1950. She was married to Freddie Bartholomew, the child actor who'd starred opposite Spencer Tracy in *Captains Courageous*. Doc had revered him as a kid. Feather knew that Doc needed a good manager, and Maele's main client was none other than Charlie Parker. The woman was demonstrably legit—she shared a Manhattan office with Duke Ellington. After Leonard made the introductions, Doc, Maele, and Freddie hoofed it to a restaurant. It was a swank, midtown French place with fish forks and decanted Burgundy. Over profiteroles, Maele laid out plans for their lush future. Doc would have a steady run at Murphy's, a club in Elizabethport, New Jersey. And his first big gig would be fronting Ellington's Orchestra. Doc had to squeeze his hands together under the table to keep them from shaking. So he didn't pay much attention when, after the meal, Maele scrounged through her purse with an exasperated expression and muttered an apology. Surely Doc wouldn't mind picking up the tab?

When it came to seediness and pure danger, Murphy's gave up nothing to the Cobra Club and the rest of Brooklyn's roughest honky-tonks. Per custom, a ranked fighter stood at the door. His name was also Doc—Doc Williams—and he, too, had been crippled by infantile paralysis that left one leg atrophied and pitifully short. For hours he hung motionless in the doorway that separated the combination store room and dressing room from the music and bar area. When he moved in any direction he revealed a pronounced limp. But in the ring—his withered leg exposed under his shorts—Williams maintained his balance without the benefit of a boxer's lateral dance and weave. Somehow he still managed to hit hard with both hands. *Ring Magazine* ranked him the sixth light heavyweight in the country. Doc watched him pulverize Henry Hall, whip Charlie Burley and Ted Lowry, and even give champion Archie Moore two vicious fights. Doc saw Williams knocked out only once, by his cross-Hudson counterpart, the Cobra Club's bouncer Bert Lytell.

The show with Ellington was a dream. While Doc sang, the orchestra painted backdrops of fire and silk. After the show he bullshitted with Ellington, even getting their picture taken together. Doc moved into a small room at the hotel above Murphy's, a place patronized exclusively by hookers. The room lay up a rickety flight of wooden stairs. Everyone shared a dirty bathroom at the end of the hall. The weekends were the worst. The johns argued with the girls and occasionally beat them up; then the pimps would run up the stairs and beat up the johns. Every window was cracked or broken. When it rained, the water streamed into the rooms and got into everything, including Doc's books and records.

Despite Maele's assurances, money for the Ellington gig never materialized. Doc kept after her to pay him, but she was practiced at the con artist's psychodrama of alternating self-pity and rage. Eventually she wrote him a couple of extravagant bad checks. One night she came up to his room. Instead of cash, she handed him a packet of heroin. Later, Doc heard that she'd hooked Parker, as well as her only other client, the bandleader John Kirby. He flushed the junk down the toilet and cursed her out.

Doc lived above Murphy's in the summer of 1950 with a dancer in the floor show named Toni, one of those poignant but damaged girls that he met often in nightclubs. One night when she was changing to go onstage, a man from the audience walked into the room and knocked her unconscious. Doc didn't know whether the two knew each other, but he pointed out the attacker to one of the hired enforcers who backed up Williams at the door. From his window Doc watched the bouncer beat the guy nearly to death. Only the ambulance's arrival saved him. A couple of nights later Toni came back to the room drunk, picked up an empty Pepsi bottle, and smashed it over Doc's head. He never asked why.

Later that night an electrical storm blew into town. It tore at the trees on their street and brought down the power lines. Everything went dark. Doc heard the girls down the hallway scream. One of the torn cables kept hitting the window in his room. It sizzled in the rain and exploded in a shower of sparks each time it slapped against the broken pane. Doc couldn't see his hand in front of his face, much less find the way to the staircase. Some part of him had always believed it would end like this, alone at night in some cold, squalid room above a nightclub. Even the moon in the window hid behind black-blue clouds.

From Doc's journal, August 8, 1988:

Pete Brown was kinda short and more than kinda round. He walked and talked real slow and ate real fast and forever. There was always either a deep frown or a huge grin on his face and never no inbetweens. When he spoke, it was mostly in riddles and half sentences. When he was stoned (and that was more than sometimes) the riddles became more obscure and the half sentences became unrelated words. But there was nothing obscure or unrelated about the sounds that came out of his alto saxophone (which, incidentally, was held together by rubber bands and strings and prayers). On the up tempo songs he featured endless staccato bursts played with a nasty tone. The slow stuff was languid blue notes and bends. All the solos kept singing and swinging and building.

Lloyd Trotman usually played bass with him. He was a brown haired, light-complected, mustached soft speaker. Pete brought him to Brooklyn, N.Y. from Boston, Mass. and they both lived in the Bed Stuy neighborhood. Lloyd played with a steady, moving beat and possessed a full tone that was always in tune. He hummed along with his bowed solos a la Slam Stewart. In the late 40's and early 50's they worked places like Farmer John's and the Arlington Inn on Fulton Street and the Putnam Central Club on Putnam Avenue.

One day I was working a matinee dance with Pete Brown at Farmer John's. Now, I'm not certain if Lloyd Trotman was playing that particular gig, but I remember that Reggie Ashby, as usual, was Pete's piano player. The show consisted of Ruth Brown, the great Atlantic Records star, on vocals, George Kirby, the famed comedian, was the MC, and I was hollering the blues. There was a door prize—a huge phonograph and radio combination. When you paid admission to the show you received a stub, and at the end of the afternoon there was to be a drawing and the winner was to receive the door prize.

Well, at the conclusion of the affair, the winning number was announced and when the winner came forward to accept his prize, the huge box was opened and there was nothing inside but rocks and paper. Somebody had "swung" with the "piccolo." Pete and yours truly beat a hasty retreat to the street. We lis-

tened to the sound of the beer bottles breaking, the glasses smashing, and the thuds of the bodies bouncing off the floor and the walls. A bad time was had by all.

Many years later I bumped into George Kirby and I reminded him of the mayhem at the matinee. He cracked up and whispered to me, "you know what really happened that day? Me and my barber buddy from Harlem stole the door prize and sold it for a few coins. This way I had myself covered if I was gonna get stiffed out of my pay when the gig was over. You know how some of those gigs went in those days. And I really was low on loot. Each coin was crucial and I couldn't afford to split with empty pockets."

Well, after all those years I found out what really happened to the "piccolo" at Farmer John's matinee.

I guess a bad time was really had by all, except, of course, George Kirby and his barber buddy from Harlem.

Save the Last Dance for Me

Summer 1956

WHEN HE FIRST SAW HER in the lobby she wore the herring-bone suit. She didn't look like the others who lived at the Broadway Central, those girls from Brooklyn or Queens who promenaded past the front desk and stared down at the carpet, pulling self-consciously at their hems and biting their nails. She looked straight ahead. Not too seriously, but with confidence. And she was beautiful—not the way someone familiar grows beautiful over time, but obviously so, radiantly. Every night Doc watched her from across the lobby. She wore that suit or one of the dresses, her yellow hair up like Kim Novak's in *Picnic*. In a couple of seconds she'd be gone. He began to wonder about her and asked around. She was registered under the name Wilma Burke. An aspiring actress from someplace in the Midwest who shared a room with a girl who painted.

Doc decided he'd meet her.

THE BROADWAY CENTRAL wasn't the Plaza, but at least it was clean. The hotel was populated by long-term elderly residents and NYU undergrads opting out of the dorms, and it had a cheerful, slightly decrepit look. The lobby was furnished with cut-rate loveseats and recliners. Most weekends, the manager rented out the basement ballroom for Jewish wedding receptions. To Bobby Dorr and Willi Burke it seemed impossibly cosmopolitan. When they arrived in New York in early June, their first stop was a Times Square motel. In the middle of the night, after hours of listening

to screaming hookers and a junky scratching at their door, the
girls relocated to the Broadway Central. It was splendid by comparison. Someone even told them Jane Wyman's mother lived in
the adjoining suite.

They had met in a production of *Hamlet* at Catholic University in Washington, D.C. Willi was rehearsing for the part of
Gertrude when Father Hartke asked her to introduce herself to
Bobby, a shy stagehand whose mother had recently died of cancer. Asking Willi made sense. She was considerate, hardworking,
good looking, and popular. She came to CU for a master's degree
after graduating from St. Mary's, the women's college at Notre
Dame; right away she became the star of the drama program. She
sang, acted, danced, and even won a Fulbright to study opera in
Germany. Unlike many of her classmates, she was also devout, and
on Sundays sang solos with the church choir.

Bobby kept to herself, wrapped up in her paintings and day-
dreams. She'd dropped out of college a year earlier and joined the
production mostly to get away from her father's drinking. Willi
could tell she needed a friend, and Bobby appreciated the attention. After rehearsals they confided to one another about
their dreams of acting on Broadway and commiserated about their
alcoholic fathers. With her inheritance Bobby bought an MG
convertible and gave Willi a miniature poodle. They christened
her Lizette *le Chou-fleur* because the tiny dog, with its white fur
and yellow highlights, reminded them of a head of cauliflower.
They spent the rest of the money on a weekend in New York. They
caught the northbound train from Union Station a couple of hours
after Willi's final class. By the time they paid for their sandwiches
at a Times Square lunch counter the following afternoon, Willi and
Bobby knew they weren't going back.

Their room at the Broadway Central had little more than two
beds, a dresser and a sink, but it was plenty. Within a week Bobby
was working as a salesgirl at Anka's Gift Shop at the Plaza Hotel.
Willi lucked into a job as a hostess at Longchamps. The restaurant chain offered "fine dining" at the Empire State Building and

three other high-traffic midtown locations. With starched table-cloths and polished silver, it was fancier than anyplace Willi herself had dined.

Willi worked the split shift—breakfast and dinner with time off for lunch. She got up at dawn, walked to Mass at St. Joseph's on Sixth Avenue, took the subway to work, made the rounds of the theatrical agents' offices in the upper Forties at noon, then walked back to Longchamps in time for the dinner rush. She liked working at the restaurant across the street from the Metropolitan Opera the best, where occasionally she showed Jan Pierce, Robert Merrill, and other famous singers to their seats. Paul Muni, the star of *I Am a Fugitive from a Chain Gang*, ordered vegetable soup. Watching them made her feel as though she wasn't just a tavern owner's daughter from Westville, Illinois. She was a New Yorker now, and it was only a matter of time before something terrific happened to her, too.

In those first months in New York, Willi didn't meet anyone at the Broadway Central. She was too busy. She got out of work around eleven and headed straight to her room, where she and Bobby spent hours talking about their days. Manhattan was limit-less and sophisticated and full of promise, and Willi was willing to overlook its faults. She ignored the hookers who hung out in front of the hotel, the businessmen who gaped at her blatantly on the subway, the catcalls that made her freeze with fear. Bobby noticed early on that Willi made men on the street turn around and stare.

WILLI WAS CROSSING THE LOBBY late one humid July night when she heard someone calling her name. Anthony was a good-looking Italian boy who sold newspapers, coffee, and cigarettes in the lobby kiosk. He'd called a doctor late one night when Bobby came down with food poisoning, and ever since Willi stopped to talk to him before going up to her room. He was grinning more broadly than usual, and told her that a famous songwriter who lived on the sixth floor wanted to help with Bobby's career. The songwriter's cousin was a cartoonist for the *New Yorker*; he could take a look at Bobby's paintings and help her establish some art world connections. Naturally, it was a great opportunity. The whole thing sounded like a come-on, but Willi couldn't be sure. When she asked about Bobby's secret benefactor, Anthony pointed to a man sprawled on a sofa across the lobby. "That's him," he said, "and he'd like to meet you."

The man looked to be in his early or mid-thirties. He was short and heavyset and wore a gray gabardine suit and a faded black tie. It took Willi a moment to notice the steel rails poking out from under the cuffs of his pant legs and the crutches leaning against the sofa. The man had dark, small, questioning eyes that made him look like he was smiling even when he wasn't. He introduced himself as Doc—what a name, Willi thought—and asked her to sit down. On the end table there was a bag of cookies and two cups of coffee; one of them was intended for her. Willi perched on the edge of the sofa and listened to him repeat the improbable story about his cousin Bernard Wiseman, the *New Yorker* cartoonist, who'd maybe help Bobby out with her painting.

Willi was flustered, but something about him made her stay. At first, though she barely dared to admit it, she felt sorry for him and made sure to not let her eyes stray to the crutches. He had, Willi thought, a kind and curious face and spoke in the most fascinating voice—a raspy baritone accented almost equal parts Jewish and black, his sentences full of the kind of hipsterisms she'd heard Steve Allen poke fun at on TV. Doc asked where she was from, and when Willi answered, he hung onto her every word. Soon, she was sipping the bitter hot coffee and telling him about Bobby and Longchamps and Westville.

It felt odd to sit beside the peculiar-looking older man in a hotel lobby, but he was attentive and warm, and at the very least Willi was sure he wouldn't make a pass. Before she knew it she told him about her father's tavern, with its fifty clocks that never told the right time and the potbellied, wood-burning stove and the sunflowers that lined the path to the outhouse. Customers had a habit of throwing pennies behind the bar; every spring her father would move it and sweep up more than ten dollars in change. Dick Van Dyke's father was a regular there, and Johnny Burke was once written up in the *Chicago Tribune* as the singing bartender from Westville because he had a fine singing voice just like Bing Crosby's. Willi told Doc about playing organ at church and getting elected the student governor of Illinois, when she got to deliver a speech and sing at a big hotel in Chicago, and about that first terrifying night in Times Square.

When she finally stopped talking Willi realized it was past midnight, and she still knew next to nothing about the man who sat across from her on the sofa. She said good night hurriedly and, suddenly embarrassed, ran up to her room, where Bobby was already asleep. It didn't occur to her until the following morning that she'd never tasted coffee before in her life.

THE FOLLOWING NIGHT Doc was waiting for her in the same spot. There were two cups of coffee and a box of pastries on the end table. Willi was still apprehensive, but they talked into the night again. This time she resolved to find out more about him. Doc told her he'd been a blues singer and now wrote songs. She asked whether anyone had recorded them, but the names he mentioned— the Tibbs Brothers, Ray Charles, Joe Turner—meant nothing to her. From the way he spoke about it, she could tell he was discouraged. When Willi wondered politely whether she could hear some of his songs, Doc shrugged dismissively. "Nah, they're nothing," he said, and changed the subject.

They saw each other nearly every night. When Willi came back from work Doc was waiting for her in the lobby with coffee and sweets. They rarely made small talk. From the beginning they talked about art, religion, politics, books and especially music. Willi cut their conversations short only when she realized it was getting light outside and nearly time to go to Mass.

She began to look forward to seeing him. It felt good to have a friend in New York besides Bobby, and she had to admit that Doc was the smartest person she'd ever met. In a single night they

debated Mary McCarthy, Adlai Stevenson, Salvador Dali, Irving
Berlin, Ethel Barrymore, and Roy Campanella. Doc talked about
all of them without losing his train of thought or seeming the
slightest bit pretentious. Willi spoke her mind but was eager to
absorb his attitudes and opinions. The only topic that made her
uncomfortable was religion. Doc tread gingerly around Willi's
Catholicism. Whenever they brought it up, Willi began trembling, worried her faith would crumple under the scrutiny of
Doc's intellect. But he could make her laugh almost at will.
When they weren't in the mood for music and books, they sat
and watched the people in the lobby. Doc's asides, delivered in
his Brooklyn brogue, made her laugh until tears streamed down
her face.

Willi never felt the need to decorate the truth around Doc.
She found herself telling him things she'd shared with no one, not
even Bobby. Eventually she told him the truth about her father,
the gregarious owner of Johnny Burke's Breezy Inn, who drank
away his golden singing voice along with the family's savings,
about hiding in the coal cellar with her mother when he came
home, fearing a beating or worse. Johnny had broken her mother's
wrist with a heavy iron door, and Willi was still afraid for her,
the once-proud tavern owner's wife who'd taken her daughter to the
opera and the theater and played piano. Her mother now sewed
five-pound potato sacks at a nearby factory. When she was a
teenager, Willi wanted to be a nun and run away to a convent to
get away from her father. She decided to become an actress instead. She'd never been close—actual friends—with a man. Deep
down, she knew that she was terrified of them. Doc listened to
Willi attentively; she could tell he understood what it felt like to be
scared and humiliated and alone.

In turn, Doc amused her with stories about Otis Blackwell
and Jimmy Scott, about falling asleep onstage during an early
morning jam session at the Cobra Club, about sticking up for a
soused Charlie Parker at Snooky's when the white owner tried to
throw him out. He omitted the disappointments, the violence,

and the women. When Willi probed, he changed the subject and told her about his childhood instead. She was riveted by his stories about contracting polio, meeting FDR at Warm Springs, and entertaining himself for hours in bed by pretending he was D'Artagnan.

One night, they took the elevator to his room. It was cramped, with stacks of books and records on the floor and a small Frigidaire in the corner. Willi sat awkwardly on the edge of the bed while Doc played records on the phonograph. She watched him slide the heavy shellac disks out of their brown paper sleeves, lower them onto the velour-covered platter and drop the needle gingerly onto the record's edge. They were old-fashioned jazz and blues records; Willi had never heard anything like them. The melodies were clanging and strident, the voices guttural and harsh, the words openly sexual and slurred together. Willi was a classically trained singer and couldn't understand why someone would intentionally make his voice sound so ugly. But she smiled and tapped her foot to the music because she didn't dare hurt Doc's feelings.

She was about to go when Doc pulled out a disk with a label covered in handwriting and a stamp that said Atlantic Records. He said it was a still-unreleased recording of one of his own songs. It was called "Lonely Avenue," performed by Ray Charles. Willi thought that for the first time she heard a note of satisfaction in Doc's voice. The song had a rhythm like someone stomping his feet. The singer's voice sounded desperate and hoarse:

> Well my room has got two windows
> But the sunshine never comes through
> You know it's always dark and dreary
> Since I broke up, baby, with you . . .

Willi listened intently but the words made her feel distant and inexplicably sad. She wondered what could have made Doc write something so desolate. Suddenly, she felt as though she didn't know him at all.

NIGHT WAS THE BEST TIME to listen to the radio. Doc preferred listening to records, but when he felt tired or it had rained,
he tuned in to the oldies stations. At three in the morning you
could hear Bechet, Kid Ory, Bix, Lil Green with Big Bill Broonzy
on guitar, Webster blowing with Ellington's orchestra. He lit a cigarette and closed his eyes and let the distant rush of traffic on
Broadway and the laughter and footsteps in the hallway fade
away. The music on the radio, *le jazz hot*, was swell and carefree,
and Doc filled his nostrils with smoke and let his mind drift.

The trouble was that after a while the clubs would come rushing back, and he'd find himself thinking about the Baby Grand
and Aida with her Egyptian eyes and the fiery ribs at the Newark
joint around the corner from Cookie's. The string of memories,
like a night locomotive rolling along familiar, inevitable tracks,
brought him to "Heartlessly." No matter how hard he'd try to shut
them out, to leave them in the past, the verses came blaring back
as though piped in on some infernal jukebox:

> So heartlessly
> You left poor me
> Alone to cry
> In misery
>
> Nobody knows
> How bad I feel
> You gave my heart
> A dirty deal

It was 1955 then, and he'd been playing the Club Musicale on
West Seventieth Street when Johnny Brantley buttonholed him
after a show. Brantley worked for Alan Freed, the hottest radio
jock in the country, and said to Doc that if he ever made a record,
Freed would flip for it. The conversation was on Doc's mind when
he recorded "Heartlessly." He'd heard the new fusion of doo-
wop and rhythm and blues that Freed was playing on the fifty
thousand–watt station WINS. Thanks in part to airtime on *Alan
Freed's Rock 'n Roll Dance Party*, the sides were burning up the

Billboard charts. So Doc decided his new record, a quickie session for Dawn Records, would trade in his usual heavy-breathing innuendo for a sound that was sweeter and lighter and a bit more sentimental. To bust up his streak of rotten luck, Doc decided to record it as Doc Palmer.

Freed not only loved "Heartlessly" but played it on his show daily for weeks. A month later it was a local jukebox hit. Doc was astonished. He knew it wasn't an inspired song, but it was outselling all his thirty or forty previous sides. Doc's calculation was paying off. Freed's clout was confirmed when RCA Victor—the world's grandest record company—swooped in and bought the master from Dawn, the tiny outfit that had released the side, for their new Groove label. After twelve years of hustling dive bars, of singing at Elk's Clubs and fraternity parties and whorehouses, Doc's moment had come.

Poised to break into the charts, "Heartlessly" disappeared. Doc never was sure what happened. All he knew was that someone at RCA decided to pull the plug on the record. It was a weird decision. Doc racked his brain about the executives' rationale. Convinced they'd bought a bona fide black hit, what did they think when they discovered the singer was a thirty-year-old, handicapped Jew? Maybe they pulped it to make room for another rhythm and blues singer on their roster? Paul Levert, the fast-talking manager he'd picked up shortly before "Heartlessly" came out, vanished as suddenly as he'd appeared, and Doc always wondered whether Levert had somehow figured in the song's demise.

Doc supposed he could've gone to RCA to find out what happened to his record. He thought often that he probably should have. But it was 1955, and he'd been a singer ever since he was eighteen—twelve grinding, stoned, vagrant years during which he was lucky to have made two grand. The years had conspired against him. When the prize had slipped out of his hands before, and it always had, he'd managed to dust himself off and head back to the joints. Time and time again Doc emptied himself out for the blues hustle; he'd tied his fantasies to it for too long. Whatever exhilaration

he once felt had collapsed under the accrued weight of penniless-
ness, missed sleep, self-abuse, and the constant near misses. The
desire was gone. Club Musicale would be his last gig.

For weeks after "Heartlessly" died, Doc holed up in his room
at the Broadway Central, so depressed that he shivered and his
teeth chattered until he buried himself under the blankets. In
his mind he lingered over each brush with the big time and each
squandered opportunity like an invalid running his fingers over
imperfectly healed scars. He wondered why he'd never had the
nerve to leave the city. The racially segregated South had always
been off limits. Yet years ago, when Billie Holiday and her husband had invited him for a stay at a club they'd opened in Hollywood, Doc turned them down. He also said no to Jimmy Archey,
the trombonist with whom he'd worked the Long Island country
club, when Archey landed a steady gig in San Francisco and offered Doc a job there. That job made Earl "Fatha" Hines, neglected since his days with Louis Armstrong, into a big-time draw.
But Doc had been afraid to leave New York, not knowing how he'd
survive in California without Millie, the Chevy and the subway.
Had he given in to his fears too easily?

Twelve years of hustling half-empty bars, twelve years of
searching for a taxi and a late-night meal. Had it been worth it?
Doc couldn't stop thinking about Cookie's Caravan and the Cobra
Club, dark rooms packed with black faces and not a single ofay
square in sight, the hollers and the applause, and the working
men who'd fling their wages in the air. In his mind, the dollar bills
still fluttered in the cigarette-smoke haze.

Some nights he thought about Veronica. He'd spotted her in
some Brooklyn dive, a decent-looking blonde in her forties.
They'd begun a fling by the time she told him who she was. Doc
could hardly believe it was Veronica Lake. Just a few years earlier
he'd seen her onscreen in *The Blue Dahlia*, opposite Alan Ladd. A
couple of failed marriages, a foul temper, and a weakness for
booze brought her disgraced back home to Brooklyn, where she'd
been born Constance Ockleman. She was making bit appearances

on TV and traveling with a third-rate theater production when Doc met her. The face of the pristine movie goddess was bloated and lined, the famous mane tangled. She was sad and nearly always drunk. It turned out she wasn't even thirty-five. On his lowest nights at the Broadway Central, Doc tried to picture Veronica Lake as he'd known her and as she'd looked on the screen, her changing face a memento not only of her failure but of his, too.

In his honest moments Doc had to admit that, even if he hadn't quit the stage, the stage would've quit him. The sounds he loved as a teenager were nearly extinct. The city blues he'd sung at the clubs were a music of adult emotions—a knowing, nighttime meditation you could hear in the black section of any large town in America. Like a sliver of quartz it took on multitudes of colors: low-down in the hands of Jimmy Rushing, seductive like Etta Jones herself, or Hollywood smooth and glamorous when sung by Charles Brown or Nat King Cole. Where had it gone?

Sometime in the forties, black music had split asunder. Dixieland had already gone underground by the time bebop, the celebrated jazz of the progressive, upwardly mobile Negro, declared independence from its lowly blues roots. Bebop had grown increasingly cerebral and racially integrated, drifting out of the commercial mainstream into the rarefied world of art. The working-class, dirty traditions Doc toiled in—hot jazz, jump, rhythm and the blues—would remain unchronicled in the pages of music histories but would win over the jukeboxes. By 1956, rhythm and blues had crossed racial boundaries, too, as revved-up dance fodder for white teenagers. Now, the sound that poured out of lunch counters and open car windows was Bill Haley and Little Richard. Doc thought it a lobotomized version of the music he loved and couldn't stand to listen to it for long. "Nowadays they call everything rock and roll," Doc complained to a *World Telegram* reporter writing one of those white-polio-victim-sings-the-blues stories that popped up occasionally in the local papers. "They give it a crazy beat no matter what it is just to sell the records." Once in a while, Doc caught himself thinking a rock and roll lyric was

clever and catchy and passably competent. Sometimes, he thought
he could do better.

NEVER SINGING ON A RECORD for Atlantic was high up on the
list of Doc's regrets. In the midst of the rock and roll onslaught,
the midtown outfit remained a beacon for soulful black music of
every kind. One of the owners was Doc's sweet, mild-mannered
friend Herb Abramson. They'd met out of a mutual love of Joe
Turner, whom Abramson had been producing at National Records.
Abramson's partner was a Turkish-born jazz aficionado who'd
come up with the money to start the company by borrowing it
from the family dentist. Ahmet Ertegun was a sporting, debonair
son of the wartime Turkish ambassador. He sized up visitors with
heavy-lidded, inscrutable eyes and got on amiably with every conceivable type of New York character. Ertegun segued easily from
chatting sedately on the phone in fluent Parisian French to
throwing his arms around a Brownsville trombone player in the
waiting room and shouting, "What's good, home?"

In 1953, after Herb Abramson was drafted, Ahmet brought in
Jerry Wexler, a rambunctious Bronx Jew with a cab driver's voice
and a ten-dollar vocabulary. As a reporter at *Billboard*, it was
Wexler who'd changed the name of the black music chart from
"Race Music" to "Rhythm and Blues." He rounded out a formida-
ble crew. Doc had been stopping by Atlantic since 1947 when the
label first dropped anchor at the Jefferson, the midtown hotel
where he happened to be squatting, and over the years he watched
it evolve into the nation's most exciting record company. Not only
had Abramson brought Turner to the label, but along with
Ertegun, for $2500, he'd bought the contract of a blind Charles
Brown imitator named Ray Charles who reinvented himself as the
most incendiary rhythm and blues vocalist going. Charles was
nearly bankrolling the operation—in 1954 and 1955 alone, he
lofted eight records into the *Billboard* R&B Top 10. Ertegun's in-
tellectual, soft-spoken brother Nesuhi ran Atlantic's jazz division
and built an equally dazzling and eclectic roster, with artists as

varied as cabaret chanteuse Mabel Mercer, balladeer Chris Con-
nor and, later, the avant-garde instrumentalists Charles Mingus
and Ornette Coleman.

In an industry full of characters like Herman Lubinsky and
King Records' Syd Nathan—operators who chiseled and browbeat
their artists, didn't bother with rehearsals, and produced sessions
on miniscule budgets—Atlantic Records stood out for its probity.
The company's business dealings were known to be commendably,
if relatively, honest and its records sounded clean and dynamic, engineered by the shockingly young Tommy Dowd, who'd moonlighted with the Manhattan Project prior to getting behind the
board at National. By 1955, the one-room office above Patsy's Restaurant on West Fifty-sixth Street was bustling. Before a session,
everyone moved their desks against the wall to make space for the
musicians, and Dowd wheeled in the huge Ampex recorder. On
some days he engineered two or even three sessions; it wasn't
uncommon for him to work on a Ruth Brown side in the early
afternoon only to record Mercer singing Cole Porter at dusk.

Whenever he visited, Doc had tested the waters, hoping to
score a session. But Abramson and Ertegun had asked him for
songs instead. Doc had never cared much about songwriting. It
didn't come easily to him, and he hated notating the music. But
writing for others sometimes made enough money to tide him
over between gigs. His first record for another singer had been a
1946 National side for Gatemouth Moore, the blues-singing Bap-
tist minister. In later years, he'd write a bunch of songs in his
room, sing them quietly into a portable tape recorder, then head
to Atlantic where he'd perform the best ones, banging out the
melodies on a piano the best he could. A couple of those songs
would become records for LaVern Baker and Lil Green. Ironically, the man who inspired him to take songwriting seriously was
the same one who, all those years ago, had turned him into a performer: Big Joe Turner.

One day in 1951, Turner was telling Ahmet about a handicapped white guy who'd hollered his heart out the night before at

the Harlem Baby Grand when Doc stuck his head into the office.
"That's him!" Turner shouted. Not only did Doc's childhood idol
prove as personable and encouraging as Doc had hoped, but
when they shook hands and said goodbye, Turner asked, "Why
don't you write me some songs?" Doc took the offer to heart and
for the next three years saved his most inspired ideas for Joe. He
was happiest with "So in Love." He put more effort into writing
the slow, gorgeous ballad than any other song up to that point;
Doc was busting with pride when Big Joe first heard him sing it.
Turner reciprocated by making it one of his most majestic ballad
sides for Atlantic. In November 1955, he recorded Doc's "Boogie
Woogie Country Girl," a dance-floor shuffle driven by the irre-
pressible beat of Harry Van "Piano Man" Walls's piano. It was the
closest the aging shouter would come to embodying the sound
of early rock and roll. Doc gave 15 percent of the song to his
friend Reggie Ashby in exchange for writing the lead sheets for
the band. Throughout, Doc remained Turner's truest fan, whether
or not Big Joe was recording his stuff. Doc made a point of
showing up at the Atlantic office whenever he got wind of a
Turner session. They tended to be joyous and loose. When Turner
recorded "Shake, Rattle and Roll," his signature mid-career
romp, Atlantic's managing partners crowded behind him in their
white shirts and black ties, clapped their hands, and hollered out
the chorus.

In the more lucid moments during the haunted weeks that
followed the demise of "Heartlessly," Doc realized that writing
songs was all that he could realistically do. It wasn't his first love,
but it kept him connected to the music, the only thing he'd ever
cared about. Under the canopy of his melancholy, the one pinpoint of hope and even pride was an unreleased song that Ray
Charles had recorded in May 1956. It was the song he'd played
for Willi. Doc wrote the abandoned lover's lament while driving
his Chevy following an afternoon he'd spent tinkering with his
braces and crutches. He imagined a street inhabited by the crippled, the loveless and the dispossessed, and set his words to a

leaden 2/4 beat he copped from a gospel record by the Pilgrim Travelers. The hand-brake-operated Chevy lurched to the rhythm that pounded in his head:

> Now my covers they feel like lead
> And my head it feels like stone
> Well I've tossed and turned so ev'ry night
> I'm not used to being alone
>
> I live on a lonely avenue
> my little girl wouldn't say I do
> But I feel so sad and blue
> And it's all because of you
>
> I could cry, I could cry, I could cry
> I could die, I could die, I could die
> Cause I live on a lonely avenue

Unlike the baby-honey blues he'd written as a singer just hours before his sessions, this had a piece of him in it, something real. Charles, who knew volumes about being hungry and alone, had felt it right away. When Wexler heard the final take he thought the arrangement too sparse, with too much time between the tolling downbeats. "Don't we need eighth notes or something to fill in between them?" he asked. "No, brother. Trust me," Charles told him. Doc hoped he was right.

Doc had long ago given up on the teenaged fantasy of baring his soul to an audience. He never managed to find that spiritual communication onstage. An attentive, hip audience always sensed the feeling he put over in his singing, and a great set could be thrilling, but so much of it amounted to timing and showmanship and craft. His soul always remained grounded in his body. Doc wondered sometimes whether words sung on a record, like a poem printed on a page, could work as a kind of communion between a listener and a writer. But writing came hard to him, and slowly. If he found a way to work harder, Doc thought he could create something lasting, possibly even commercial. Luckily, he didn't have to do it alone.

IT HAD BEEN the autumn of 1955—nine months before Doc would meet Willi at the Broadway Central—and Doc's little cousin Neysha didn't know what to make of Mort Shuman. They'd been introduced by her boyfriend Phil Sardoff, Mort's classmate at Abraham Lincoln High School in balmy Brighton Beach—Brooklyn's Jewish St. Tropez. Phil and Mort—along with friends Jay Wesoff and Howard Greenfield—sang in an after-school doo-wop quartet and hung out at a Dubrow's cafeteria on King's Highway and Sixteenth Avenue. Rangy and animated, Mortie played the lead in several high-school theater productions but had lately drifted into a moody, rebellious funk. One night Mortie disappeared while everyone was watching a Western on the balcony at the Oceana Theater. After the movie, Neysha found him running back and forth down the hallways and taking drags off an acrid-smelling cigarette. It was the first time she'd seen anyone smoke reefer.

Mort grew up under the BMT tracks just north—on the *goyishe* side—of Brighton Beach Avenue, the only child of two politically progressive immigrants from Warsaw. He didn't know a word of English until he was five and spoke to his parents in Yiddish. His father played the mandolin and gave his son a guitar. Mortie's hard-drinking uncle sawed on the violin and quizzed his nephew about the symphonies and waltzes that blared on the gramophone in his apartment. But Mortie was in love with rhythm and blues. After he got turned on to grass, it became an obsession. He cracked up his friends by talking like a jazz-age hipster and playing Ivory Joe Hunter songs on his guitar.

Neysha told Mort he reminded her of her older cousin Jerome, a rhythm and blues singer who lived in an Upper West Side hotel. So when she heard from her mother, Morris's sister Bertie, that Jerome was dropping by their apartment for a visit, she phoned Mort and begged him to come over. It was an awkward introduction—Doc was thirty, Mort still eighteen. But as Mort galloped through blues changes at Bertie's piano, each saw in the other an opportunity they'd long been searching for.

Mort had never met a white man—someone, no less, from Jewish, middle-class Brooklyn—who lived the kind of life he dreamed about. Mort hadn't even suspected that such a person existed. Doc epitomized the black R&B lifestyle that Mort had constructed in his imagination from listening to T-Bone Walker and Charles Brown records. A playground of honky-tonks and sex and freedom was a door through which he planned to escape his family's stultifying, lower middle-class expectations and his father's ruinous drinking. Doc understood. That escape was something he, too, had pined for when he was eighteen.

As they huddled around the piano, Doc was struck by Mort's knack for the bright, rolling shuffle that he'd heard blaring out of the jukeboxes. Doc didn't quite grasp its appeal but sensed its inevitability. His insecurity ignited an idea. The kid wasn't jaded, had a good ear and a natural feel, and possessed tons of energy—couldn't he be the catalyst that would help him master the new teenage idiom? It was a strange, desperate notion, but what did he have to lose? He figured that if they wrote a hundred songs, at least two or three would stick. Besides, he wasn't getting much done writing alone. Before he left, Doc told Mort to come see his gig at the Club Musicale. He didn't have to ask twice.

BY THE END OF 1955, Mort had become Doc's shadow. Doc snuck him into the Musicale and let him nurse a beer while he sang. The club was located at 117 West Seventieth Street in the basement of the Stratford Arms, a hotel that catered to mid-priced hookers and welfare cases. Before relocating to the Broadway Central, Doc occupied one of the hotel's dank, airless rooms and shared a bathroom with whomever happened to be living next door. The club downstairs was more upscale. The proprietors, Sandy Messina and Morty Jay, hired Doc to perform whenever they opened a music room. The last time around it had been a funky place out on the Coney Island boardwalk. Doc had sung there all summer and every night ate himself sick on Nathan's hot dogs and French fries.

At the Musicale, Doc played four, forty-five-minute sets and emceed everything. He worked weekdays and weeknights and even Sunday matinees. In those days Doc woke up hungover in the afternoons and headed downstairs to listen to the jukebox and hang out with the bookmakers and pimps who made up the club's daytime congregation. The cocktail hounds and cheating husbands flowed in at night. Doc would gorge himself on the chef's cacciatore, head back upstairs to put on his one good suit and a handful of cologne, then come back down for the night's first set. The Musicale brought in a mostly white crowd, so Doc left out the B.B. King material, Jimmy Nelson's "T-99," and other stuff that went over big when he'd played Jimmy's Chicken Shack in Harlem.

The best band he'd ever put together backed him. Guitarist Mickey Baker had been a student of Rector Bailey's. When he wasn't gigging with Doc, he played Alan Freed's wildly popular live shows at the Paramount Theater in Brooklyn, worked sessions as a member of the Atlantic Records house band, and recorded with Sylvia Vanderpool, with whom he formed the hit duet Mickey & Sylvia. Mickey couldn't see out of one eye but backed Doc with buzzing, ferocious solos that sounded more like Chuck Berry than Charlie Christian. His foil was a tenor sax virtuoso from Fort Worth named King Curtis. Capable of everything from the most delicate jazz improvisations to the lowest gutbucket growls, Curtis, too, would become a crucial cog in the Atlantic Records sound. On nights when the band was at its hottest, Mickey and Curtis wailed ten or twenty choruses at a time. The crowd hooted and hollered until it sounded like the Wednesday-night amateur contest at the Apollo Theater. The shows really took off on weekends: aficionados moved out the uptown crowd, and Roy Eldridge brought his trumpet on Sundays.

After the last set, Sandy Messina and Doc usually hung out at a broadcast studio with Stan Shaw, whose resonant, booming voice was heard on the hip, all-night *Milkman's Matinee*. Shaw passed out behind the microphone sometime after midnight, and Doc and Sandy took over the show. They chose records, answered phones and tucked into the free food that local bistros sent over in exchange for plugs.

One afternoon, nursing a hangover over a plate of fried eggs and about twenty cups of coffee, Doc had heard a new record on the jukebox. Someone was singing Junior Parker's "Mystery Train" in a keening, unsteady voice that to Doc sounded like something that came out of the swamps. Sandy said it was a white guy. His name read just as backwoods—Elvis Presley. Doc had never heard anything like it, and something about the record made him uneasy. He knew he had to get to work.

Doc FIRST WROTE with his new partner up in the Stratford Arms. At the beginning, he offered Mort 10 percent of every song just to sit beside him and watch him work. Mort was flattered. Gradually he began to pitch in, mostly up-tempo melodic ideas with a strictly Top 40 sound. They began by listening to the tape recorder, into which Doc had hummed a melody, and looking at some words he'd written; they hashed out the rest. When Doc re-located to the Broadway Central a couple of months later, they went down to the ballroom and wrote around the upright piano. The hotel dick snuck them leftovers from the Jewish weddings, and between songs Mort gorged himself on pastrami sandwiches.

Doc had to laugh. He was going on thirty-one and had performed with Ben Webster and Lester Young, but here he was writing dimwitted songs with a City College freshman who still lived with his mother in Brighton Beach. But his hunch was paying off. Their stuff was becoming more varied and polished; they were beginning to gel. Mort had perfect pitch, and played the piano as fluently as the guitar, but had yet to assert himself fully. When he did, the results were fast, light and sometimes patently silly. In May, the Tibbs Brothers—Doc's Newark buddy Andrew Tibbs and his brother Kenneth—recorded two sides written by Doc and Mort. "I'm Going Crazy" was a raucous wail that captured some of the frenzy that Tibbs had incited at Cookie's Caravan. The second was called "(Wake Up) Miss Rip Van Winkle."

The lyric made fun of a square who wasn't hip to rock and roll—
"You're a Model T in the Atomic Age," the Tibbs Brothers sang—
but Doc and Mortie knew it wasn't destined for the charts. They
still hadn't mastered the formula. At times the work plodded
along or broke down completely. Doc had trouble getting excited
about the teenage material, and Mort could be plain lazy. They
spent too much time bullshitting about any topic that came into
their heads, a pattern that usually culminated in Doc giving Mort
jive advice about women. Sometimes he lost his temper with
Mort for being distracted, but he sounded hypocritical even to
himself. Doc knew the real problem. Most of the time, he just
didn't believe they'd make it.

WHEN HE RAN OUT OF CASH—and he always did—Doc high-
tailed it to 75 Manhattan Avenue. Raoul was home after cutting
short his studies at a Swiss medical school. Medicine definitely
hadn't taken. Away from the cadavers, Raoul spent time studying
German at a language school in the Bavarian village of Kochel am
See. At a tavern there he happened upon a reunion of *Luftwaffe*
survivors and heard them sing "Raise the Banner High," an SS an-
them. When he later visited Dachau, former inmates wearing
their old prison uniforms gave tours of the concentration camp.
Raoul thought the air there still smelled of burnt flesh. He came
back to Brooklyn disturbed by what he saw in Europe and relieved
to be home. He knew he wasn't going to be a doctor. Like his father
before him, he headed to law school.

When Doc visited, Bernard sometimes came for dinner, and
Mort took the subway from Brighton Beach to write around the
living room piano. Doc's parents hardly spoke. Millie prepared
dinner early and ate alone. She'd leave Morris's meal in the Frigidaire, and he'd have it hours later, leave the dishes in the sink and
disappear into the bedroom. Harris hovered around the apartment in his usual ill temper. When he spotted Mort, famished
after his classes and a part-time job, raiding the kitchen pantry, he
loudly muttered *beheimes*. It was Yiddish for "cattle."

They rarely talked about music at the dinner table. When somebody asked about work, Doc replied with generalities. How could he explain the exhilaration of having Joe Turner record his songs? And neither Doc nor his father mentioned the two or three times Doc had spotted Morris sneaking out of a club after one of his performances. Of course, there was never anything upbeat to report about money.

He didn't bring up Willi. Doc was sure it would come to nothing, but he didn't know how to stop himself from falling for her. She wasn't like any girl he'd been with, or any girl he'd known. What right did he have even to hope? Yet something told him Willi was his chance to finally leave behind him the clubs and his bleary-eyed, hungover afternoons. She was just a kid, and not the kind that married paralyzed, broke writers of Negro dance music. In his more sober moments, Doc knew he was setting himself up for heartbreak.

IT WAS NEARLY NOVEMBER, 1956, when Willi found the first poem. It was handwritten on hotel stationary. Doc must have slipped it under her door after one of their late-night conversations in the lobby. The poem was mainly funny, Willi thought, and not particularly personal. Doc must've written it when he couldn't sleep and wanted to show it to her right away. She folded it in half and left it in a nightstand drawer.

After Bobby joined Doc and Willi's late-night conversations, they moved from the lobby up to their room. Most Friday nights they took a taxi to the Old Homestead steakhouse on Ninth Avenue and shared the gigantic porterhouse. Doc always paid. On other nights they ate at one of Doc's favorite places in the Village. Willi and Bobby ogled the street life while Doc regaled them with stories about the music characters and gangsters he'd met at the clubs. The girls threw their first dinner party around Thanksgiving. In the freight elevator, they brought up a discarded door Willi had found on the sidewalk. Propped over two chairs, it made a serviceable table. The main course was two cans of Campbell's soup that Willi heated up with her iron. One of the cans blew up and ruined the iron, but Doc arrived with a couple of steaks, and they talked until three, lingering over Cokes and pastries from Veniero's while Lizette helped herself to the leftovers.

Some nights, Bernard and Raoul joined the party. Bernard amused everyone with stories about the *New Yorker*'s curmudgeonly editors and argued passionately and loudly about everything from the Hollywood blacklist to Paul Klee, gesticulating madly with his hands. Willi thought he was intelligent and handsome, and she adored his drawings, but she loathed his volatile temper. When a stranger accidentally bumped him at the Old Homestead, Bernard took a swing at him before the man could apologize. The maître d' threw them out and told them not to come back. Raoul, on the other hand, impressed Willi as soft-spoken and sweet; she could tell he genuinely looked up to his brother. She found him quiet and ambitious, but he was content to play the straight man to Bernard and Doc, laughing at their jokes along with the girls.

Bobby had liked Doc right away. It felt good to have an older, worldly friend shepherd them around Manhattan. But she couldn't have missed the way he looked at Willi, his gaze always lingering a moment too long. Doc spoke to Willi too softly and tried too hard to make her laugh. When she told him about Mr. Hale—a Nabisco executive who'd held an office party at Longchamps and later thanked Willi by inviting the girls to a matinee of *My Fair Lady* and dinner at the Pierre—Doc scoffed. He thought the old man was trying to pick them up. The way he said it struck Bobby as hypocritical. When she mentioned it, Willi told her she was being ridiculous, that Doc was only being friendly. But the poems now appeared under her door almost every morning.

As Christmas approached, even Willi had to admit that the poems had become unabashedly romantic. She could tell Doc wanted her to mention them, but she never did. Before she drifted off to sleep, Willi began to feel the familiar tinge of panic. She adored Doc, cared about him sincerely, and was grateful for his friendship. But she knew he wasn't the man she'd marry. What could she do? Willi didn't want to hurt him; she just couldn't. On those nights, Willi thought about O. J. Klein, the boy she'd dated back home, a tall, handsome high-school football hero who enrolled at the police academy after graduation. He proposed to her, but she broke it off soon after she went away to college. She knew she'd never be content being a cop's wife in Westville, Illinois.

A few days before she left to go home for Christmas, Willi stopped by Doc's room. For a few hours they talked and listened to records. When she said goodnight, she could tell Doc wanted her to stay. There was something new in his manner, a small but definite directness. It frightened her. She'd finally admitted to herself weeks earlier that his motives weren't strictly platonic, yet it flustered her to have him confirm it.

She put on a painfully serious face and thanked him for the beautiful poems. In a voice that sounded to her stilted and too formal, she told him that though she cared for him as a friend and was grateful for his company, she didn't feel romantic toward him. It took her entire reserve of courage to say it. Doc smiled it away. He didn't deny anything but brushed off her remark, though Willi could tell that his expansive mood had crumpled. Doc thanked her for being honest, said goodnight, and kissed her on the cheek, exactly as he'd done every night before. Willi felt at once awful and relieved as she tiptoed to the elevator. Had she lingered a few moments longer outside his door, she would have smelled a whiff of cigarette smoke and heard the click of a dial and an old Coleman Hawkins ballad come on the radio.

AFTER WILLI LEFT THAT CHRISTMAS, Manhattan looked emptier and more desolate than Doc had ever seen it. Snow fell for four days straight. With its buried cars and iced-over macadam, Broadway reminded him of a scene from "The Snow Queen," the Hans Christian Andersen fairy tale he'd loved as a kid. Doc was stuck indoors. Walking on crutches in snow and ice was treacherous; besides, he felt like he had nowhere particular to go. To get away from the tinsel and Christmas decorations in the lobby, he made an appointment to see Ahmet Ertegun at Atlantic. He took a cab and got there around four.

The tiny waiting room was packed. While Doc waited for Ertegun to finish rehearsing a chart with a session band and Jesse Stone, the house arranger, he said hello to Herb Abramson's wife, Miriam, who scowled at him as usual, chatted with Tommy Dowd, and shot the shit with Jerry Wexler. He also noticed a pair of hipsters in their early twenties perched on a sofa across the room, flipping through copies of the new *Cashbox*. With their smart tweed and leather boots they looked like beatniks with business degrees. Ahmet was taking his time, so Doc struck up a conversation with the shorter of the two. His name was Mike Stoller, writer and producer, just in from L.A. The taller one—he had one blue eye and one green one—was Jerry Leiber. Anyone who'd come within a mile of the record business in the last year had heard their names. They'd written "Hound Dog," a decent blues, for Big Mama Thornton, and had cashed in when it spent eleven weeks at number one after RCA released the Elvis Presley version in July. "Love Me," a ballad they'd written for Presley, was on the charts, too. They said they'd heard of Doc—Joe Turner recorded their "The Chicken and the Hawk" during the "Boogie Woogie Country Girl" session. The conversation was flagging when Stoller leapt from the sofa, pointed at Doc and, eyes wide, yelled, "Alley Alley." He swung his hips side-to-side and belted out the verses of Doc's jingle for the Alley Clothing Company of Bedford Avenue: *Alley, alley, alley, you're so good to me. . . .* He stopped only when Miriam Abramson stuck her head through the door and frowned. It turned out that Stoller had grown up in Queens and heard the jingle on the Symphony Sid show back when it had been in heavy rotation.

Beaming and animated, Stoller told Doc about returning from a summer trip to Europe, where he'd gone to pitch songs to European publishers and spend a belated honeymoon with his wife, Meryl. He was headed back to New York aboard the Italian luxury liner *Andrea Doria* when it collided with a Swedish ship near Nantucket. Panic broke out on board, and Stoller just barely made it onto a lifeboat. When he stepped ashore in New York harbor hours later, Leiber ran up and hugged him, shouting that "Hound Dog" was a smash.

Leiber and Stoller worked with the Aberbach brothers at Hill & Range Music, the company that had an exclusive publishing pipeline to Elvis. Doc made a mental note to try his luck there. After all, the flip side of the "Hound Dog" single was "Don't Be Cruel," written by Doc's old friend Otis Blackwell. Ahmet was finally ready, and Doc played him a demo reel. Doc and Mort had made it on Doc's cheap portable tape recorder in the hotel ballroom. Their voices sounded tinny and distant. Ertegun thought two of the songs—"Love Roller Coaster" and "I Need a Girl," both up-tempo shuffles—might be right for Joe Turner and told Doc he'd let him know.

On the way back to the Village, Doc stared out the cab window at the snow-covered trees and the mud-stained cars wallowing through the sleet. He began to think about Willi. He'd half expected her to turn him down; what reason did he have to hope otherwise? Still, being around her had filled him with heady, ridiculous dreams, and when she cut them down he fell back to earth, back into the body and the life of a thirty-one-year-old cripple. Failure surrounded him. He could smell it everywhere. At times like these, his records and songs and hustles felt like flimsy armor against the world. Doc was used to disappointment, but it strangled him now. He didn't know how much longer he could stand it.

WILLI'S MOTHER came to meet her at the Danville train station in Johnny's beat-up Cadillac. It was already dark, and snow fell around them in large, wet clusters. Willi saw her from a distance in her homemade dress and hat, but when she caught a glimpse of her mother's face, she nearly cried. It was lined and haggard; in the months since she'd last seen her, Lena looked like she'd aged five years. Willi knew her factory job was hard and humiliating, but she never heard her mother complain. Every Easter, Christmas, and birthday her mother still sent her greeting cards with two or three dollars tucked inside.

It was still early when they sat down in the kitchen. Johnny wouldn't be home for hours. Since she'd been a little girl, Willi told her mother everything; sometimes she thought Lena could read her mind. As usual, she told her about New York without leaving anything out and made her mother laugh when she described Bobby, the cigar-chomping theatrical agents, Longchamps, Mr. Hale, and the Broadway Central. Willi had begun to tell her about Doc, a terrific, hilarious character who lived at the hotel on the floor below her, when the phone in the living room rang. Willi picked up the receiver. It was too late for anyone to be calling, something that didn't occur to Willi until she heard Doc's hoarse baritone on the other end.

When he asked about her trip, he sounded choked up and unsteady. It had been fine, she began to say, but he cut her off. "I want you to marry me, Willi," he said, and for the next few seconds all she heard was Doc's shallow breathing. Willi stammered. She managed to tell him she was flattered before he interrupted again. "Don't tell me now, just keep it in mind," he said. She promised him she'd consider it. After another awkward pause, Willi wished Doc a Merry Christmas, a holiday she later realized he didn't celebrate, and said goodbye.

Her mother was waiting for her at the kitchen table. Willi told her what had happened innocently enough and tried to laugh it off. But Lena wasn't smiling. She wanted to know why someone with a name like Doc had proposed marriage to her over the telephone at night. Willi tried to tell her about him—he was heavyset, shorter than her by a couple of inches, and walked with crutches and braces because his legs were paralyzed by polio. She knew it sounded bad, but she wanted to be truthful, so she added that he was thirty-one, Jewish, and wrote songs for colored singers, though he currently wasn't working a lot and had lived the past few years in a hotel. When she was finished her mother was trembling with anger. "How could you even consider marrying someone like that?!" Lena shouted. To her own surprise, Willi began to defend him. "Mama, you don't know him, don't even say those things," she protested. Doc had been nothing but kind to her, and besides, she hadn't decided to marry anyone. Her mother folded her arms. Enunciating every word, she declared, "If you marry that man I will jump out a window."

Arguing was pointless. Willi walked down the hall to her old room. Only a year ago she'd have cried herself to sleep. Instead, she got angrier than she'd felt in years. She'd been a Goody Two-shoes her entire life; Lena once told her that she never worried about her because she always knew where she was. But her mother didn't know a thing about Doc. What right did she have to talk about him the way she had? At that moment Willi felt closer to Doc than to anyone in the world.

Out the window Willi could see Westville's tiny downtown. Her Lithuanian grandmother's tall brick house stood across the street, her grandfather's butcher shop beside it, and several doors down Willi could hear the jukebox in Johnny Burke's Breezy Inn. She knew that in two hours she'd hear her father lock up the tavern and walk up the stairs onto the porch. Willi had heard those footsteps nearly every night for eighteen years. Sometimes Lena lay in bed next to her listening for them, too. When he came home, Johnny could be clumsy and funny and even charming, singing to them or getting entangled in an absurd, long-winded conversation with the telephone operator. Other times he'd barrel into her bedroom red-faced, shouting obscenities. One night when Willi was thirteen or fourteen, he dragged Lena from her bed, tore a lamp out of the ceiling, and beat her with the cord. When Willi screamed and begged him to stop, he tore off her nightgown, leaving scratches all over her body.

Willi thought hard about that night. The house had never seemed more claustrophobic. Just then something in her snapped. Beginning with that moment, she decided that her life would be her own. No one would again tell her what to do. Soon she'd be back in New York and decide whom she'd marry and when, and no one would stop her.

WILLI SPENT HER FIRST NIGHT back in New York in Doc's room, where she told him about her fight with her mother. She was still shaken. She wanted to feel him out, suddenly worried about his reaction. Doc smiled. "She'll come around," he said, and sure enough, Willi knew he was right. Doc had a way of making her crises look like mere misunderstandings.

They sat for a while on his bed, saying nothing, until Doc asked again if she'd marry him. "Yes," Willi said, suddenly. For a moment they both sat there a little stunned. Then they laughed, and Doc took her hand. He walked Willi to his door and, before saying goodnight, they kissed like lovers for the first time.

As she lay in bed, Willi thought about the Catholic retreats she'd sat through as a student at St. Mary's. In a room that looked out on a lake, a priest had talked to them about the various forms of love. Ignoring the titters, he told them that *eros* was love in its most base, physical manifestation, the love known to animals. *Eros* was but a pale reflection of *agape*, divine love, the highest because it was entirely spiritual, devoid of the cravings of the flesh. That, Willi thought, was how she loved Doc—spiritually, on a higher plane. He was the kindest, smartest, most admirable man she'd met, the kind of man her father could never hope to be. He was her best friend and her protector. And if she didn't feel *eros* when she was with him, their love would be all the more pure. Drifting off to sleep she felt the terrible indecision that had weighed on her lifting. She would be Doc's wife until death do them part, and it made her happy to know it.

The weeks that followed were the happiest either of them could remember. They saw each other every night. The awkwardness was gone, and the silences became comfortable. Willi caught herself fixing Doc's collar or brushing his hair with her fingers, and it pleased her when Bobby or Raoul or Mort noticed. When they were alone, Willi began to call him "daddy." She said it first as a joke, but the endearment stuck. Even Manhattan reflected her mood, the snow melting and the plane trees in Washington Square coming to life. When Willi finished her shift at Long-champs, she looked forward to seeing Doc like never before, and hurried down to the subway.

Doc knew his life was taking its sharpest turn since he'd first sung "Piney Brown Blues" at George's. He had assumed loneliness and hard luck were lifelong fixtures, but Willi swept them away more thoroughly than he'd imagined possible. When they were together, her brightness and almost naïve lack of guile made his studied ennui and hipster cynicism seem dull and ungenerous. She made him feel as though nothing was predetermined, as though he could still do and be and have whatever he wanted. Wasn't she proof?

The records on Doc's phonograph changed from sad blues and ballads to the upbeat sides he hadn't heard in years. The bright colors of Fletcher Henderson's orchestra and Dexter Gordon lit up his cramped room and he drummed along on his headboard until the neighbors began to complain. Good news arrived from everywhere. In late October, Ray Charles's "Lonely Avenue" broke the *Billboard* R&B chart and went all the way to number six. It wasn't a smash, but it was the first chart hit with Doc's name on the label. It likely meant more writing work and maybe even a few nickels in royalties. And he'd made a date to play a couple of new tunes for Brother Ray.

He was becoming close with Leiber and Stoller. They checked in on Doc and tipped him about upcoming sessions and new acts. When Doc ran into Mike outside Ahmet's office, he gave him a demo of a song called "Young Blood," thinking it might be a good fit with the Coasters, a vocal group Leiber and Stoller had begun producing at Atlantic. Mike liked the title—Brooklynese slang for a fine young chick—and asked if he could hold onto the tape.

As the snow melted, Willi joined Doc on epic walks around his favorite parts of the Village. He took her to the cafés on MacDougal Street and showed her the picturesque diagonal lanes and alleys near Seventh Avenue. On one of these outings they visited Doc's old friend Leonard Feather, the critic who'd produced his first session back in '45. Willi had never seen an apartment like Feather's. With hardly any furniture, it looked like a Buddhist monk's cell, except for the records and books covering the walls from floor to ceiling. After dinner at a nearby trattoria, they headed back to Feather's apartment to sip espressos and listen to a new LP. The music that poured out of the speakers unnerved Willi. A woman's slurred, haggard voice elongated syllables into anguished cries. The singer was late on the beat and veered dangerously between sharp and flat. Her timbre grated. It was Billie Holiday, and Doc and Leonard listened to her enraptured. Willi hadn't been expecting Gilbert and Sullivan. She was merely amazed that singing so deliberately wretched could be considered sublime. Embarrassed, Willi smiled and said nothing until the side was over and everyone said their goodbyes.

DOC COULDN'T REMEMBER Millie and Morris so jovial in each other's presence, but here they were, dressed up and beaming, looking at Willi with barely concealed glee. Millie prepared a dinner that could've fed twenty and set the table with her mother's English china. Raoul looked at his brother proudly. Even his grandfather Harris seemed interested, his lapel festooned with a white carnation. Millie and Morris asked Willi the usual polite questions about her family and Westville, and she answered them eagerly, not forgetting to compliment Millie's apartment and cooking. Doc was amused at his mother's attempt to re-create Versailles in their cramped Williamsburg living room, but he wasn't in an ironic mood. It made him feel like a sap, but he was bursting with pride at his beautiful young fiancée and his parents' unvarnished pleasure. Basking in Morris and Millie's admiration made him feel like a teenager again. Willi, her blonde hair cascading over a silk crepe dress, looked as exotic in the Semitic environs of McKibbin Street as Grace Kelley at a Harlem fish fry.

Willi had met Millie when she dropped by the hotel to check on Doc and bring him some meals from the nursing home. Willi was impressed by her confidence, smartly cut suit, the chauffeur waiting in the idling company car, and not least by her slight but perceptible British accent. "Hello dear," Millie had said to her when they were introduced and planted a kiss on Willi's cheek. Tonight, Millie and Morris were unmistakably friendly. Willi thought with a pang of bitterness that, unlike at her parents' dinners in Westville, there was no bickering or profanity or screaming.

It was the night of April 27, 1957—Willi's twenty-fourth birthday—and for dessert Millie brought out a cake with candles. When Willi blew them out, Doc took her hand and slipped a ring on her finger. It was gold with rose diamonds and had belonged to Millie. It felt wonderful to get engaged on her birthday, so they decided to have the wedding on Doc's birthday, June 27. With much ceremony, Millie and Morris announced an engagement gift—a catered party on Long Island. Taking the dishes into the kitchen after dinner, Willi found herself alone with Millie, who took her hand in hers and smiled. "You know, dear," she whispered conspiratorially, "we never thought Jerome would marry."

THE FOLLOWING FRIDAY, Doc announced he had a surprise and told Willi and Bobby to be ready to go out at around eight-thirty. Mort was waiting in the Chevy downstairs and drove them for nearly an hour to a small club on the outskirts of Newark. The marquee over the entrance read "Tonight Only—Big Joe Turner!" Inside, the room was dark and drab, with leather banquettes and a cloud of cigarette smoke hovering over the tables. As her eyes adjusted to the dark, Willi noticed that they were the only white people in the room. She studied the couples at the adjacent tables as though she'd arrived in a different country. The men wore high-waisted slacks, angular blazers and pomade. The women wore their hair in large, stiff curls or high-piled bouffants, and their close-fitting skirts were emerald and turquoise and orange and scarlet, colors Willi had never seen in the windows of the Madison Avenue dress shops. Doc and company sat at a table near the stage and ordered ginger ales.

Willi gasped when Turner strode onto the stage. He was a silo
of a man with swept-back thinning hair and suspenders. When he
spotted Doc, he bellowed, "Hiya, Cuz!" and waved. Turner's voice
was so loud and vast it appeared to erupt from someplace backstage. He belted out old favorites like "Careless Love" and "Cherry
Red" and some newer Atlantic hits like "Shake, Rattle and Roll"
and "Chains of Love," drowning out the shouts and applause.
Willi was riveted by his voice. For the first time she thought she
understood Doc's music.

Toward the end of the set, Turner winked at Doc, and the band
struck up a lazy rolling boogie. "Ride on the love roller coaster, my
heart's doing the loop-de-loop," Turner shouted. Willi turned to
look at Doc, and in the near dark she saw him grinning. This was
the surprise he'd been preparing for Mort—Turner was performing
the song they'd written together. Ertegun had given it to Turner,
who liked it and even added a verse of his own. Mortie looked as
though he'd levitate out of his chair with excitement. As Turner
tore through "Love Roller Coaster," Willi felt Doc's hand close
around hers. She shared a proud, knowing look with Bobby, and for
the rest of the night they felt like the four most glamorous people in
the world. As Mort drove them back to the city, they hardly spoke,
lulled by the night breeze blowing through the open windows.

ON A SUNNY SUNDAY IN MAY, Doc asked Willi to come for a
drive to Montauk. Willi had Sundays off; she and Doc sometimes
took Bobby along on day trips to Coney Island, where they
bought hot dogs at Nathan's and watched people stroll up and
down the boardwalk. Montauk sounded like a nice change. They
set off shortly after dawn. For some reason Doc was especially
uneasy. The hand brakes were giving him more trouble than
usual. The halting drive to the end of the Montauk Highway took
nearly five hours. The day was unseasonably cold. After a leisurely
lunch at a café and a stroll spent watching the fishermen cast off a
pier, they decided to head back. As they set off, the sky grew dark
and gave way to a freak May snowstorm.

Doc couldn't see ten feet past the windshield. He cursed until sweat poured down his face. His hands shook on the wheel, and the car took a couple of precipitous swerves before Willi convinced him to take an exit and pull over. Doc sat behind the wheel, panting. Willi had never seen him so helpless. She'd grown so used to thinking of him as her tough, streetwise protector that she nearly forgot he was handicapped. Now, just weeks before their wedding, she saw him panicked for the first time, and it made her sick. She didn't know which was stronger—her disappointment in Doc, or her shame for feeling it. They switched seats and Willi drove the rest of the way. It was the last time he drove the Chevy when they were together.

TWO WEEKS BEFORE THE WEDDING, Willi telephoned her parish priest. She had to tell someone at home, and she was sure he'd keep it secret from her mother. When the Westville monsignor found out the fiancé was Jewish, he told Willi the young man would have to receive instruction. The next day Doc listened gravely, though with much private amusement, to a local priest's commandments about taking a Roman Catholic for a wife. Doc had his doubts about Willi's faith, but he knew the rite would abate her homesickness and guilt. He didn't realize that Willi secretly hoped Doc would convert. Regardless, he didn't have much time to ponder the spiritual counsel. Millie was arriving at the hotel with his tuxedo.

On the morning of June 27, Willi, Doc, Raoul, Bobby and Bernard met in the lobby of the Broadway Central and drove in two cars to St. Joseph's on Sixth Avenue. It was the route Willi had walked to Mass nearly every morning, except on that particular morning Willi wore a wedding dress and Doc held her hand. In the backseat, Willi vacillated between happiness and abject fear. Mort and a couple of Doc's friends waited for them at the church entrance. Everyone walked up the steps slowly to pace themselves with Doc.

On the curb, a middle-aged man walking his dog had stopped and was absentmindedly gawking as Doc worked his way up slowly on his crutches. Willi didn't pay any attention. She was used to people staring at Doc. But Bernard glared at the man and muttered something under his breath. He walked down to the sidewalk, bent down to scoop something out of the gutter and, smiling, extended his hand. The man smiled back and shook Bernard's hand, then recoiled and pulled his hand free. It was smeared with dog shit. The man stood dumbstruck on the sidewalk as Bernard quickly walked back up the steps. Doc missed the incident, but Willi looked on in disbelief as the man, who'd finally come to his senses, ran after them into the church, waving his arms and shouting obscenities, the dog yelping at his feet. It took two ushers nearly five minutes to get him out of the building while everyone stared wordlessly.

Willi was trembling. She was startled, but mostly angry at Doc's apparent indifference to Bernard's outburst. Suddenly, she noticed the vast empty space around them—there were only half a dozen people in the church, and everyone but Bobby was a friend of Doc's. She felt unexpectedly petrified at the idea of getting married in front of strangers. Willi knew in advance that Doc's family wouldn't set foot in a Catholic church, but the front pew, where she always imagined her parents sitting on her wedding day, was empty, too. Everything around her—Doc, Raoul, Bernard, even the city itself—suddenly felt alien.

The man with the dog was gone by the time Willi realized she was squeezing Bobby's hand. Bobby saw that her eyes were filled with tears. Willi wanted to run out of the church and take the first bus home, to confess everything to her mother. Only the thought of Doc, who stood proudly, expectantly, at the altar, stopped her. She knew she couldn't disappoint him. Willi walked up the aisle slowly with a forced smile. By the time she reached the altar and looked up at Doc, she couldn't help but laugh. They were both beaming.

The rest of the day was a blur. After the vows they drove downtown to Gluckstern's Delicatessen, an old-fashioned kosher eatery on the corner of Delancey and Norfolk, where Millie and Morris waited along with the rest of the Felder and Goldstein

clans. Willi's morning chills were swept away by unrelenting hugs
and kisses from strange cousins and aunts who lined up to say
maazel tov to Jerome's pretty shiksa bride. Millie directed traffic,
weaving between tables laden with gefilte fish and challah. When
everyone was seated, Millie announced that she and Morris were
moving to Sheepshead Bay, and were handing over the lease to
the apartment on McKibbin Street to Doc and Willi.

After the meal and an endless procession of toasts, the waiters
moved aside the tables to make room for dancing. A klezmer
band cut loose in the corner. Doc told Willi to go ahead, but she
demurred. "I only want to dance with the groom," she told him.
There was no point in sitting down all afternoon for his sake, Doc
replied, and Willi reluctantly walked out onto the dance floor with
Raoul. She'd nearly forgotten how much she enjoyed dancing.
Bernard cut in after the first number, then Mort, and then, after
much nudging, so did Morris. Doc watched Willi dance. Her
white silk dress shimmered as she moved among women who
couldn't help but seem a little drab in comparison. He felt more
included in the world of men, and less of an outsider, than at any
time except those rare moments on stage when the audience had
hung on to his every breath. But underneath his pride and con-
tentment, the old darkness stirred. Doc knew he'd always merely
look on as Willi danced, another man's hand on her waist, her
hand clasped in his. At those moments he'd wonder what she was
thinking and watch the expression in her eyes.

After Gluckstern's, someone whisked them uptown for Millie's
crowning achievement—a reception at the Waldorf Astoria. Millie
knew the hotel's caterer and wrangled a buffet and a suite. Otis
Blackwell, Tommy Dowd, and Doc's old band mate King Curtis
were already there. Blues friends Doc hadn't seen in years
showed up in droves; Bernard brought a young actor named Peter
Falk. Willi was introduced to so many people she began to lose
track; as midnight approached she could barely keep her eyes
open. The last of the guests said their goodbyes just after two.
Exhausted, Willi and Doc retreated to the bedroom next door.

The room was preposterously large, with gilded wallpaper and a king-sized bed with a mahogany headboard. They laughed at how much nicer it was than the Broadway Central; when she stopped laughing Willi noticed that her heart was racing. Doc took off his tuxedo jacket and walked over to the bed. When he lowered himself onto it, the bed shuddered under him and collapsed. He smiled half-heartedly from the floor. Willi tried to pull him up, but he wouldn't budge. His braces locked up, and he was simply too heavy to lift. Everyone had left, and after pacing the floor Willi called the front desk for help. By the time there was a knock at the door, she was red-faced with embarrassment. They broke the bed on their wedding night—she knew what people would assume. Willi let the two bellboys in, ran into the bathroom, and locked the door behind her. She knew she was being foolish, but she stayed there until a new bed was brought in and they were finally alone.

THE PREVIOUS SUMMER, Willi and Bobby had spent a couple of days in Ocean City, and Willi thought the beach town would make a great spot for a honeymoon. On the morning after their wedding, Doc and Willi shared a room-service breakfast and headed uptown, Willi singing behind the wheel of the Chevrolet. She didn't know the way to Ocean City. When she had flipped through the Rand McNally, Willi discovered it was closer than she thought. They crossed the George Washington Bridge and about two and a half hours later took the Ocean City exit. Willi couldn't understand why the town looked so industrial; it wasn't how she remembered it at all. Maybe they'd entered on the wrong side. But as they coasted down the main street, Willi had to admit that this wasn't the place she'd visited. She paged through the road atlas again, gasped, and raised a hand to stifle a laugh. Last summer she'd been to Ocean City, Maryland; now, they were in Ocean City, New Jersey. Doc and Willi rolled in their seats with laughter.

They stopped at the first restaurant they saw. The steakhouse was empty except for two men having lunch at the adjacent table.

After they ordered, Willi and Doc realized their neighbors were comic Joey Bishop and Julius LaRosa, the dark-haired crooner whose "Lipstick and Candy and Rubbersole Shoes" had been a hit the previous year. They figured it was a good omen. Doc and Willi struck up a conversation with Bishop and told him about the wedding and their misadventures on the road. After lunch, they decided that instead of driving all the way to Maryland they'd find a hotel in the Catskills, an area Doc remembered from childhood family trips. For the rest of the afternoon they drove along narrow country roads and craned their necks to catch a glimpse of ramshackle houses with penned-in hogs and chickens skittering across the porches.

They pulled in at the first hotel they saw. It was a typical Catskills resort with a large main building and cabins that fanned out into the woods. A bellboy led them to a shabby wooden structure with a long stage facing a row of benches. Backstage, there was a tiny space with two beds, a dressing room the management had converted into a spare bedroom. The bellboy said it was all they had; Doc and Willi were too tired to argue.

They were almost asleep when Willi heard a commotion outside. They got dressed, opened the door and walked out onto the stage. More than a hundred people stared at them from the benches below. The night's entertainment was about to begin, and Doc and Willi hunkered down in the front row. For the next two hours they watched a lineup of vaudevillian tap-dancers, magicians, and comics whose jokes would've seemed corny even in the thirties. The audience, elderly Jewish couples from New York and Philadelphia, clapped eagerly, and Doc and Willi chimed in.

When Willi tried to leave their room the following morning, the door wouldn't budge. There was no telephone, and she didn't know what to do. Willi kept pushing until she heard laughter from the other side. The door swung open, and Bernard, Raoul, and Bobby piled into the room. They'd followed Doc's car all the way from the city. Early in the morning, they stuck a bookcase against the door. Bernard had wanted to tie a horse to the door, but

Bobby talked him out of it. Doc and Willi didn't mind the intrusion. Except for the moments when Willi thought unhappily about her mother, she had a terrific time. Everyone laughed when Doc admitted he'd bribed the newspaper boy at the Broadway Central to introduce him to Willi. She'd figured it out a long time ago, Willi said, lying. All five of them had to sleep in the backstage bedroom, but they stayed for another three days.

ON THE WAY HOME Doc and Willi stopped for lunch at a roadside diner. A sign said the town was called Ellenville, New York. When they walked in, a song on the jukebox, a novelty with an R&B feel, caught Doc's attention. The card said it was a Coasters B-side called "Young Blood." Doc pressed his face to the glass and waited for the maroon ATCO label to stop spinning. He could just make out the names printed in tiny letters under the title: "Leiber, Stoller, Pomus." He barely recognized the song he'd given months ago to Mike Stoller—the melody and most of the verses had been changed. Without a word to Willi, Doc walked out to the parking lot, punched a handful of coins into the payphone, and dialed Atlantic Records. Jerry Wexler picked up the phone. "Hiya, Doc," he crowed. "I guess you must've heard it. It's a smash." The record was Top 10 on *Billboard's* pop chart—"the *pop* chart," Wexler repeated for emphasis—and both "Young Blood" and "Searchin'," Leiber and Stoller's flipside, were climbing. Before they hung up, Wexler promised to wire him $1500 as an advance on royalties. Doc took a deep breath. It was more money than he'd made all year.

NEARLY THREE YEARS LATER, Doc found a wedding invitation in a hatbox under a stack of postcards. Doc turned it over in his hands. The moment he remembered best about his wedding day was watching Willi dance with Raoul at Gluckstern's in her white dress. Sitting up alone and smoking as night turned into morning, he wrote on the back of the invitation words to a soaring Latin melody that Mort had played for him that afternoon. It reminded him of a troubadour's song. He wanted the words to sound like a poem translated into English, so he wrote long lines, loading the measures with as many syllables as they could hold. *You can dance every dance with the guy who gave you the eye, let him hold you tight.* Of course it was a love song; he could already hear Leiber and Stoller's Spanish guitar and strings. Doc was writing the second verse when something he suddenly remembered began to intrude. Under his pen, the simple declaration of love he set out to write wavered, giving way to vulnerability and fear. The words pleaded for faithfulness. *If he asks if you're all alone, can he take you home, you must tell him no.* Doc finished the verses. He decided he'd sort it out in the morning with a clear head. He wrote the title—"Save the Last Dance for Me"—across the top, left the words on the coffee table, and went to bed.

From Doc's journal, July 11, 1984:

With someone like you,
A pal good and true . . .

These are the opening lines of an ancient, overly sentimental, tear-jerking ballad called "Let the Rest of the World Go By." It was the only song my father, Morris, knew. And he tortured it with his loud, harsh, unmusical voice on the few occasions my early life found him in a pleasant mood. He scowled constantly— disappeared frequently and disapproved always of my brother, my mother or myself. Mostly he hated us as a group, but once in a great while he disliked us individually, and on those rare oc- currences the individual was usually yours truly.

For many years he ran out of pleasant moods, but then he sang one last time. It was 1957 and I was thirty-one-years-old. The occasion was the long ride on Sunrise Highway, Long Island, New York, coming back from my engagement party. My father was in the front of the car sitting behind the wheel and next to him was Millie, my beaming mother. Wilma, my future wife in a marriage that was to last ten years and produce two wonderful children, Sharyn and Geoffrey, sat in the back with me holding hands. The atmosphere was joyous but quiet.

Suddenly, Morris broke into song at the top of his voice and as usual he sang off key and harshly, ". . . With someone like you, a pal good and true . . . ." He didn't stop for a second— didn't even pause to catch his breath. And at the end reached unsuccessfully for a high note of operatic dimensions. His fail- ure was embarrassing, but we applauded wildly. He sank back panting and exhausted and almost drove the car off the road. When he got himself back together, he forced a stiff, gold-filled, broken toothed smile. It was strangely and appealingly shy and self-conscious.

In 1978, he died in a nursing home. He was eighty-three- years-old and had been senile for years. Up until the very last minute he hurled obscenities to the world in general and to his family in particular.

The funeral services were attended by very few people. His brother Sam showed up, several grandchildren were there, also my brother Raoul and his wife Myrna and my children, and one representative of a senior citizens group that he had once be-longed to. My mother hadn't spoken to him for twenty years and she decided not to come. The eulogy was delivered by a Rabbi who had never met my father. He went on about the fact that my mother was too grief-stricken to attend the services and stated that this was indicative of the feelings of the people who knew him, and that accounted for the sparse attendance.

My father had made out his will many years ago. It re-quested that he was to be cremated. Subsequently his ashes were scattered around the garden of my brother's summer home in East Hampton, Long Island. He left an insurance policy for $10,000, and I was the beneficiary. I gave the money to my brother because he had been taking care of the funeral expenses.

A year later I bought a cassette copy of the latest Willie Nelson album. One of the sides was a touching, tender version of "Let the Rest of the World Go By." I played it over and over again. One day while playing it, I suddenly and unexpectedly began to sob. I went on and on—I couldn't stop until I was raw and empty inside and almost out of tears forever.

This Magic Moment

IF SOMEONE WANTED to turn his song into a record in 1957, all he had to do was walk to Forty-ninth Street and Broadway, a busy corner just north of Times Square that smelled of fried food and exhaust. He'd get a dose of the song business simply by loitering for a while outside the golden Art Deco entrance to 1619 Broadway. The Brill Building was named after the mens clothing store that occupied the ground floor in 1931, the boisterous, democratic year that the commercial, eleven-story high-rise, along with its more famous downtown neighbor, the Empire State Building, was completed. The visitor would huddle there beside the angular, pinched songwriters who cadged cigarettes and strained to overhear news of upcoming recording sessions, or step into the Turf, just off the lobby, where the better-paid contingent mobbed the counter and wolfed down fifty-cent egg salad sandwiches while waiting to buttonhole a certain secretary in the elevator. In truth, not much had changed there since the beginning, when the small-time talent managers, theatrical agents, orchestra leaders, and out-and-out bootleggers and grifters shared a corridor with the blue-ribbon likes of Ralph Peer, the country music talent scout and producer. The vaudeville patina still lingered in the hallways, with handshake cash deals, packs of eau-de-cologned, carnation-lapelled rack jobbers and occasional snatches of Yiddish. The "telephone-booth Indians," as A. J. Liebling had called them in the *New Yorker*—chiselers unable to rent even part of an office upstairs—ran their hustles from the booths inside the Turf and in the building's lobby. "You can reach me at this number from three to four forty-five Wednesdays and Fridays," they'd tell a potential mark. Every Indian respected the others' schedules. If some day-tripper had the bad manners to stand outside his booth, waiting to use the phone, the Indian put the receiver to his ear and moved his lips until the offending party left.

On the other side of the Brill Building's façade, ex-champ Jack Dempsey gazed glumly upon the show folk from behind the plate glass of his restaurant, a nostalgic tourist trap and lunch spot for the older, wealthier leaseholders. Grizzled record men and song-pluggers in fedoras and white-on-black wingtips kvelled over chops at Al and Dick's around the corner; receptionists and typists on their lunch hour dashed up Broadway to Howard Johnson's or Nedick's. Meanwhile, in the offices upstairs, old-line publishers weaned on Harry James and Bing Crosby—middle-aged men in camelhair coats and French-cuffed shirts who looked like Connecticut bankers just off the commuter trains—connived to right the capsizing boat of their business, jolted from its course by an ex-truck driver from the Memphis housing projects and the legion of hollering, ululating, wildroot-oiled hillbillies and blacks loosed in his wake. At their roll-top desks, solitaire cards in hand, they waited out rock and roll.

Willi and Doc, a sheaf of songs and a teenaged Mort Shuman in tow, arrived there every morning from Brooklyn in the tan, two-door Chevrolet. The routine wasn't complicated. Like other hopefuls, they began at the eleventh-floor penthouse and gradually worked their way down, knocking on the increasingly unprestigious doors. The advance against royalties on "Young Blood" was paying the bills. Doc's pragmatic new outlook—and Willi's pregnancy—made him determined to capitalize on the piece of good luck that Leiber and Stoller had handed him.

The doors on the lower floors, where they opened more often, revealed cramped, unimpressive rooms with battered upright pianos and cubicles separated by frosted glass partitions. The better offices had a receptionist; others, just a proprietor with a sandwich or a cigar in hand, playing cards or staring out the window. If the publisher was willing, Mortie slid behind the piano while Doc leaned on crutches beside him. Doc sang if the song sounded more like the blues; Mort took over if it was more rock and roll. Sometimes Willi played, too. She was a game accomplice. Handsome blonde shiksas were in short supply at 1619 Broadway, and if nothing else, she opened doors that otherwise would've stayed closed. More than once, some goon hit on Willi in Doc's presence, figuring the guy on crutches for a patsy, a notion that Doc punctured in staccato fashion with a metallic glare and a ruthless stream of obscenities. Once, while Doc and Mort were filling out a contract in an adjacent office, a sharkskin-suited song-plugger chased Willi around a desk for what felt to her like half an hour before Mortie heard the racket and stepped in his way.

Their hit rate was dismal. When they weren't turned down they'd get maybe twenty-five or fifty dollars. It was dispiriting, and sometimes after an afternoon at the Brill Building they drove uptown to the Atlantic Records office at 234 West Fifty-sixth Street, where at least they were received as friends. Back in Williamsburg, Mortie and Doc wrote around Millie's baby grand. More than anything else, "Young Blood" had convinced Doc that the adult black material he'd written for Ray Charles and Joe Turner was a commercial dead end. White teenagers were the future. He treated it like a job, knowing the "Young Blood" money would soon run out.

Mortie was distracted. He was flighty, in constant motion, showing up an hour late or vanishing for a day, which made Doc furious. Doc leaned on him to stay focused. Still, the kid had a phenomenal ear for rhythm, wrote melodies seemingly without effort, and raved daily about some new record he'd heard, whether R&B or mambo or country. Mortie intermittently attended philosophy classes at City College and held down several part-time jobs. He spent his nights hitting on black coeds, drinking wine, and sleeping on the subway rides back to Brooklyn. His father had died a death hastened by drinking around the time of Doc and Willi's wedding, and Doc became a surrogate father, while Mort tried to support his mother, Esther. Back home in Brighton Beach, he transformed her living room into a jazz appreciation society for teenaged Jewish potheads. Still, in his lackadaisical way, Mort was just as determined as Doc to write a couple of hits or at least make some money.

Since he'd been a kid, Doc felt most acutely alert at night. Sitting up in bed, with Willi asleep beside him, whole lines and snatches of melody blazed up in his mind. He grabbed whatever scrap was at hand—often a napkin or a paper bag—and scribbled them down. He was terrified of losing these notes. In the mornings, when Willi tried to clear the wreckage from his bedside or the coffee table, Doc woke with a start and yelled, "Don't touch it. You're messing up my song!"

Every day, the routine began anew. While Doc waited on the sidewalk, Willi walked two blocks to the lot where they parked the Chevy. The neighborhood had changed since Doc was a teenager. The Jewish families he remembered were leaving, or had already left, for the suburbs of Connecticut and Long Island. Like many of New York's lower middle-class enclaves, Williamsburg housed recent immigrants; the surrounding blocks were now predominantly Puerto Rican. Crime was on the rise, too. Neighbors were mugged; street gangs claimed adjacent blocks and squabbled on stoops and sidewalks. *West Side Story* had just opened at the Winter Garden, just down the street from the Brill Building, but the real-life gangs were a far cry from the Sharks and the Jets.

One day, as Willi walked home after parking the Chevy, a pack of teenagers armed with trash can lids—makeshift shields and clanging gongs—yelled and whistled at her from a stoop. When she ignored them, they chased her down the street. Doc watched from the sidewalk where Willi had dropped him off, bellowing in vain at the teenagers until his throat burned. He'd never felt more helpless than while watching his pregnant wife run toward him through traffic, her face frozen in fear. He wanted to strangle them all, but his arms stayed locked at his sides, holding him up. When they got upstairs, he noticed his palms had gone white from gripping his crutches.

AN OLD GIRLFRIEND of Doc's from the club days saved them
from their door-to-door routine. She ran into Doc on the street
and floated a weird proposal. Her neighbor, a dance instructor at
an Arthur Murray studio, had wed a rich, elderly widow he met in
mambo class. He was desperate to get away from the old shrew
and needed a cover, so he was offering to put up ten grand of her
money to start a fictive record company. All he needed was someone to run it. The setup sounded like an invitation for all kinds of
disaster, but Doc figured the ruse had to beat knocking on doors.
Maybe he'd even make some contacts and a little money.

R&B Records—the name had been Doc's idea—opened for
business at 1650 Broadway, the Brill Building's less glamorous re-
lation two blocks uptown, on the corner of Fifty-first Street. Just
doors away from Irving Berlin's publishing company, it shared a
cramped, bedroom-sized office with a film company's storage
room. Stacks of film cans that rose to the ceiling towered above
their two desks and an upright piano. The company had a staff of
three. The ex-girlfriend's husband—a slick, vapid character poetically named Huckman—applied himself mainly to solitaire and
cashing the hundred-dollar checks he drew every Friday. Mortie
was the shipping clerk, at a weekly take of twenty dollars, while
Doc's title was president—owner of equity shares, promises of future cash, and no salary. The dance instructor never put in an appearance. Doc and Mort's sole job was to cover for him when his
wife phoned about his whereabouts. The arrangement was a definite scam, but Doc had to admit it held promise. He was running
a small label inside the fortress of music publishing; something
could catch. And most of the widow's ten grand was still sitting in
the company's bank account.

Doc and Mortie quickly learned how deadening doing nothing could be, especially around Huckman, who'd nearly inciner-
ated the office before the paint on the door had dried. He had a
habit of tossing lit matches into the wastebasket. One afternoon
he sat mesmerized by the flames while spools of old, dry film
flared into a small inferno. Doc and Mortie came back from lunch

to find their new office crowded with firemen who barely managed to extinguish the rank, smoldering carpet.

Since R&B Records boasted no artists or releases, Doc and Mort had plenty of time to shop their songs, while Mortie made a last stab at being an undergraduate. Mostly, though, he got high, loaded up on egg creams at the Hanson's Drug Store soda fountain on the corner of Fifty-first and Seventh, and spent nights dancing to Machito and Tito Puente at the Palladium, a Latin ballroom two blocks north of their office, at 1698 Broadway. On Wednesdays, Anglo night drew celebrities like Kim Novak and Marlon Brando, but Mort dug the Palladium most on the weekends, when he'd mambo alongside pushers and pimps and ogle the Puerto Rican and Cuban girls from the Bronx and Spanish Harlem.

The tedium at 1650 Broadway had nearly consumed them when a singing quintet from Harlem walked in and asked to audition, unaware the office was a front. The outfit was called the Five Crowns. Doc remembered the name vaguely from his singing days. Their manager was a tall, black Cuban in his forties named Lover Patterson. He couldn't sing, but he loved being onstage; in addition to his main line in promoting fights, he managed every neighborhood singing act he could get his hands on. For his new-look Five Crowns, he recruited two teenagers who happened to be best friends—a talented lead tenor named Charlie Thomas and the shy, soft-spoken Ben Nelson, who'd been bussing tables at his father's luncheonette when Patterson spotted him. The audition astounded Doc and Mort: the group sang with genuine soul, and the members harmonized as though they'd grown up in the same apartment. To Huckman's dismay, Doc and Mortie decided that for once R&B would be a real record company and signed the Crowns—they convinced Patterson to drop the digit—on the spot.

The Crowns hardly left the office, and Doc and Mort loved having them around. At five, when most of the building's occupants stampeded toward the elevators on their way to the buses and trains, Doc sent out for sandwiches. For the rest of the night everyone sat around the piano and sang. A visibly pregnant Willi sometimes joined them. Charlie sang lead beautifully, and Doc got torn up over Ben Nelson, whose voice sounded like it sprang from some private well of feeling. After dark, Ben liked to perform the old sentimental ballads. Doc snuck a look at Willi whenever he sang "Danny Boy." Her eyes mirrored his own rapt expression.

Doc and Mort wrote the Crowns' first, and only, record. It was doo-wop with a bit of The Coasters thrown in. They spent the company's remaining budget on recording, pressing, and trying to promote—the best they knew how—"Kiss and Make Up." The best they knew how turned out to not be very good. Despite a plug from *Billboard* ("Rhythmic meshuga-styled pleaser with a slightly Latin beat. Side has potential if pushed"), the record—which featured Mickey Baker and King Curtis from Doc's old band—never got much local airplay. Everyone was ready to turn the page on the song when they got a long-distance call from a deejay—did they know, the caller asked, that "Kiss and Make Up" was number one in Pittsburgh? It sounded like a punch line to a joke. When Doc and Mort rushed to record a follow-up, they learned the company was broke. Still novices, they didn't know that distributors would only pay for their first record when they delivered the next one, which they now didn't have the money to record, much less press. They were seriously in debt and couldn't even pay the plant to keep pressing "Kiss and Make Up."

R&B Records should've gone bankrupt then and there. But one day a guy stumbled into the office looking like a relative of W. C. Fields—fat, with a three-day beard, dressed in a filthy, ill-fitting blazer and ascot. All he was missing was an empty martini glass. His name sounded familiar. Doc's friend Sandy Messina, who owned Club Musicale, the uptown joint where Doc had made his last stand, used to tell him about Sy Rich, a bizarre character he met in Florida who he said worked as an agent for strippers and supplied local millionaires with hookers. The very same Sy Rich now stood in the R&B office. Doc couldn't have cared less—he was too busy fending off creditors. Rich asked how much he needed to get out of hock. "Ten thousand dollars," Doc replied, mostly to get a laugh. "That's all?" Rich picked up a phone and made a call. Half an hour later, a movie-star handsome stranger named Vinnie Spar walked in and wrote a check for ten thousand dollars. When he left, Doc sent Mortie to the bank with check in hand, convinced it was a fake. The bank manager told Mort that the account held enough money to cash ten checks just like it.

The windfall didn't come in time. A few days later, the dance instructor's wife showed up at the office looking for him. Doc stammered a couple of excuses, but she sat immobile beside the piano all afternoon, waiting in vain for her husband. She may have been gullible, but she wasn't stupid. R&B Records ceased operation the following afternoon. A follow-up to "Kiss and Make Up" never came.

Soon enough, neither the Crowns, nor Doc and Mort, would mind. The Crowns changed their name again. George Treadwell, a trumpet player married to singer Sarah Vaughn, owned the Drifters' name and kept the hit group on a usurious salary. With charismatic lead singer Clyde McPhatter gone solo and his replacement, Johnny Moore, off in the service, Treadwell was casting a new Drifters and offered the gig to the Crowns. For two hundred dollars a week per member—decent money to the hard-up Harlem singers—and the promise that Patterson would become the fifth Drifter and get an extra fifty dollars a week, Treadwell got his new group. The Crowns/Drifters went on the road, armed with a catalog of "Drip Drop," "Lucille," and other Drifters hits that they'd memorized at a marathon one-day rehearsal.

On May 16, 1958, Willi gave birth to Sharon Ruth Felder, an event commemorated in a tiny notice in *Billboard*. Still terrified of hospitals—where he'd spent such a long stretch of his childhood— Doc refused to set foot in one again, so his mother arranged a private phone to be put in Willi's room. Doc called hourly to check on her. They were broke again and he was worried. He had a family now, he told Mort, so their hit had better come soon.

"WHAT'S GOOD, OTIE?" Doc called out whenever his old singing boon from Flatbush wandered into the R&B office. Otis Blackwell hadn't put an iron to another man's pants in years—he was a marquee songwriter. His stuff was red hot thanks in no small part to a contract with Hill & Range, a BMI country and western publisher on the eighth floor of 1650 Broadway that reinvented itself around its exclusive deal with the golden calf of the recorded music field—Elvis Presley. Blackwell's "All Shook Up" and "Don't Be Cruel" had spent a combined twenty weeks at number one, and Otie was excited that Elvis had hewed so faithfully to his demos. Little Willie John's hit recording of Blackwell's "Fever" spawned an even bigger hit by Peggy Lee. Now, Otis was writing for another alumnus of that Memphis rock and roll factory, Sun Records. The lapsed bible college student from Louisiana who recorded as "Jerry Lee Lewis and His Pumping Piano" became a bona fide headliner after shouting Blackwell's "Great Balls of Fire" and "Breathless" through a scrim of pomaded blonde curls.

Blackwell was feeling so flush that he offered to introduce Doc and Mort to Paul Case, the admired professional manager at Hill & Range. By any measure, the publishing company on the eighth floor was an unusual outfit. Founded by Julian and Jean Aberbach, Viennese Jews who'd fled Europe before the war, the company's declared mission was to "celebrate America's folk music." The brothers proved to be uncanny businessmen. By sharing royalties with the songwriters, a radical arrangement at a time when many publishers kept them all, the Aberbachs quickly consolidated a huge country music catalog. Photos of Eddy Arnold, Ernest Tubb, Bill Monroe, Bob Wills and other partners adorned the walls of their office. Before long, the company was branching out into gospel and beyond. In May 1955, an Aberbach operative named Grelun Landon had watched a young Presley perform at the Jimmie Rodgers Festival in Meridian, Mississippi, and immediately phoned the office in New York. The firm rushed out a songbook; in less than a year, they had the industry's biggest meal ticket stowed in their vest pocket.

For all their acumen, the Aberbachs weren't well liked. There were a number of plausible reasons—envy, the brothers' insularity and dislike of publicity, their reluctance to socialize with the trade's rank and file. Julian and Jean spoke with heavy German accents; some among the largely Jewish and considerably less affluent residents of 1650 Broadway and the Brill Building referred to the Hill & Range office as "Auschwitz West." Doc and Mort were bowled over by the luxe spread and the paintings that adorned the walls. The Aberbachs collected modern art. Among framed country song folios by Lefty Frizzell and Hank Snow hung dozens of Bernard Buffet's gloomy canvases, along with a Picasso print of mating doves. Everyone in the office called it "The Fucking Pigeons."

The Aberbachs concerned themselves with business, not music, but knew enough to keep a superb song man on the payroll. Although their younger cousin Freddy Bienstock, who sported Julian's Continental accent and monogrammed shirts, ran the day-to-day operation of Elvis Presley Music, the Aberbachs' secret weapon was Paul Case. Case was brilliant. A Jew from Iowa who'd worked as an advance man for an old-line swing band, he adapted swimmingly to rock and roll. Warm, paternal, and unpretentious, Case was liked equally by the songwriters he nurtured and the record company A&R men with whom he placed their songs. He smoked a pipe, dressed in the slouchy tweed suits of a stylish police detective, doted on a menagerie of plants he kept in his office's every cranny, hosted high-stakes poker games out of the same office on Friday afternoons, and trailed the reassuring, fatherly scent of "Canoe" men's cologne. Unsurpassed as a song doctor, Case could pinpoint a weak line, write a bridge, and pair a song, or a songwriter, with a singer. He liked Otis's friends right away.

Though Blackwell had vouched for them, Doc and Mort had no track record to speak of. Doc's hollers about pot, whiskey and big-legged women sounded as out-of-date as Sophie Tucker; "Young Blood" had been a lucky break; the handful of collaborations with Mort hadn't done anything. And there was nothing recent to suggest that things were looking up. Their tally for 1958 showed nothing even approaching a hit record. Aside from their Crowns side, there was "You Be My Baby," a workmanlike record they'd written with Willi. Ray Charles recorded it only after getting a third of the song. Atlantic also released one of Doc and Mort's earliest collaborations, a maudlin but beautifully performed ballad called "My Island of Dreams" that Clyde Mc-Phatter had cut two years earlier. Their catchiest flop was a riff on Marty Robbins's "A White Sport Coat and a Pink Carnation" sung by Bobby Pedrick Jr., whose high tenor and cloying delivery made him sound a bit like a male Brenda Lee impersonator. "White Bucks and Saddle Shoes" tried hard to be timely, but with lines like "chinos and slacks of course / oh yes, they sure look boss," it sounded like a Harvard Lampoon parody of rock and roll.

Their favorite failure was something that Doc, Mort and Willi wrote with the Coasters in mind. Instead, "Sun Glasses" became a single for new Bigtop Records artists The Shades: Mortie on lead vocal, King Curtis on sax, with backing vocals by the memorably named Knott Sisters—actually Willi and an unrelated theater friend. It was one of a handful of songs that Willi had a hand in writing. On some of the others, the blonde, statuesque Mrs. Pomus was listed as Willie Mae Jefferson, a goof that left Doc and Mortie in stitches. The Shades were a one-flop wonder, but at least everyone had a blast making the record.

Case must've seen something that no one else had noted in the unlikely duo: the round, garrulous, jive-talking bear of a man who opined while leaning forward on splayed crutches and his gangly, nappy-haired twenty-two-year-old partner whose unguarded grin made him look at least four years younger. Then again, in late 1958, several years before the Brill Building's teen song factory was in full flower, a rock and roll writer was still something of a find. So Case took a chance. After he bought several flops—including The Shades record—he offered them a three-year deal. The contract with Rumballero Music, a Hill & Range company, paid Doc two hundred dollars a week and Mort a hundred. Doc had a family to support, and Mort agreed to the split. The contract couldn't have come at a better time. By November, Mort had been expelled from City College and was unloading crates at a minimum-wage job downtown. When Doc phoned him from Case's office with the news, Mort didn't have enough cash for a cab or even subway fare and walked to 1650 Broadway in a blizzard. Hours later, he stumbled into the lobby of the building looking so bedraggled and cold that someone handed him a ten-dollar bill and told him to get something to eat. Mort pocketed the money, rode the elevator to the eighth floor, and signed a contract for his first full-time job.

CASE'S FIRST ASSIGNMENT wasn't exactly flattering. Chancellor Records was looking for material for a fifteen-year-old Italian kid from South Philadelphia. Chancellor co-owner Bob Marcucci spotted Fabian Forte sitting on a stoop minutes after an ambulance carried away the kid's father, a cop who'd suffered a heart attack. His first two records were terrible. Fabian had a reliable range of four or five notes, wobbly pitch and not much volume. But Case had seen him lip-synching at record hops and witnessed the panic he provoked among teenaged girls. Fabian even appeared on Dick Clark's TV show without a single hit record. Case said that a song tailored to his strengths—or rather one that downplayed his weaknesses—couldn't miss. The request mystified Doc and Mort: the kid's records had flopped; he wasn't even a real singer. But as songwriters, they were on the same footing as Fabian. They figured Case was giving them a trial run and preparing them for a shot at Elvis. In the meantime, Presley was driving a tank in Germany; many others, including Otis Blackwell, figured ahead of them in that queue.

At the piano, Doc and Mort rewrote a song inspired by Elvis's frenetic Sun Records, truncating the range and getting rid of the abrupt transitions. Fabian's management demanded strictly wholesome material, so Doc toned down the sexuality, replacing it with mildly suggestive innuendo. "I'm a Man" was a bragging rocker with a vague resemblance to "Blue Suede Shoes." On record, the crack New York studio band made Fabian's voice sound lost and indistinct. Ironically, his labored reading of the macho lyric lent him a vulnerability that couldn't have been missed by his pubescent fans. Doc and Mort had all but forgotten about it when Case showed them the *Billboard* pop chart for the week of February 2, 1959. "I'm a Man" peaked at number thirty-one.

Doc and Mortie presented their follow-up to Fabian onstage following a package rock and roll tour stop in Manhattan. They were surprised by how much they liked him. Fabian Forte turned out to be a sweet, guileless sixteen-year-old who had no illusions about his singing talent and looks. While Mort hammered on the piano, Doc sang "Turn Me Loose," another repurposed Elvis composition, putting some of his old blues growl into the lyric. Fabian was awestruck. "It's so great!" the teenager gushed. "Why don't you do it?"

"Turn Me Loose" had a more memorable melody than its predecessor and more grown-up lyrics. What genuine sexuality Doc had written into it was expunged by Fabian's manager—"gonna have a thousand chicks" became "gonna kiss a thousand chicks"—but some of the swagger remained. Fabian threw himself into the recording session. With Mort agitating at the piano, the record made Fabian sound, if not musical, then at least personable and exciting. Everyone knew it right off the bat. In April, "Turn Me Loose" began its climb into *Billboard*'s Top 10. Fabian flew to Hollywood to take meetings. *Movie Star* magazine ran a photo of the teenaged phenom holding a one-year-old Sharon under the headline "Tiger or Softie?" And the *New York Mirror* printed a staged photo of Doc looming over his doe-eyed interpreter, who was seated at the piano. "A songwriter's job is to write for the market," Doc told the paper. "If the teenagers think that a line like 'I got some change in my pocket and I'm rarin' to go' reflects their feelings, then I'll keep on turning out lines like that." He and Mort, Doc offered, completed three songs a week, "the minimum for survival in this business." The paper made him sound like a dispassionate businessman, which pleased him, and he didn't neglect to let the reporter know that he'd made money. "The result," the article concluded, "has placed both Fabian and Doc in extremely comfortable financial positions." It may have sounded like the big fish stories he'd planted in the papers in his singing days, except this time it happened to be true.

Doc, Mort and Willi celebrated their first rock and roll hit record in Williamsburg. Sharon crawled across the carpet; Lizette slept curled up in Doc's lap. The winter sun shone through the windows, Willi looked gorgeous, and for the first time that Doc could remember there was enough cash in the bank to pay their rent for the entire year. To Mort it was part of the natural order. He assimilated success with the easy faith in his talent typical of a kid his age. The irony wasn't lost on Doc—about to turn thirty-four, he'd been at it for sixteen years. After all the close calls with the big time—had they been close at all?—wailing on stage with Ellington and Lester Young, the dozens of records, the bleary-eyed mornings when he tried to inject every last ounce of feeling into his voice just to cut through the bar banter and clanging dishes, he'd finally won a respite from nomadic poverty by writing a couple of dumb, mawkish songs for a sixteen-year-old pinup boy from South Philadelphia. However he'd gotten there, it felt good. He heaved another piece of pie onto Mortie's plate and downed his champagne.

WHILE RUNNING DEMOS to Ahmet and Jerry at Atlantic, Doc and Mort met a baby-faced singer from the Bronx who was recording a string of flops for the company. Walden Robert Cassotto, who went by Bobby Darin, dreamed of being Sinatra, but for now he was hungry for the smallest taste. He was short, wore a hairpiece, and had an intense, almost malevolent expression that masked an earnest, childishly gregarious personality. They met early in 1958 when R&B Records was still in operation, meaning Doc and Mort still had access to the widow's cash, and they hired Darin to demo a couple of songs. Like the Crowns, he became a fixture at the bogus label's office. Darin sang with almost frightening self-possession—an experienced actor, he could put across everything from Cole Porter to the raunchiest rock and roll—but he was convinced Atlantic was about to drop him. He said a nursery rhyme that he'd written titled "Splish Splash" was his last chance. Prior to his recording session, he spent a frantic afternoon at the R&B office making himself so anxious that he broke out in large red splotches. He clutched his chest and gasped that he was about to have a heart attack. Doc and Mort laughed it off as nerves. They didn't know that a childhood bout of rheumatic fever had left Darin with a damaged heart.

"Splish Splash" became a colossal hit, and soon Darin was back at 1650 Broadway, a game grin on his face, looking for material. Doc and Mortie had written him a ditty called "Plain Jane." There wasn't much to it. It, too, had a nursery rhyme melody—the chorus was lifted from "Buffalo Gals," the nineteenth-century songbook staple—that dovetailed neatly with Doc's silly, appealing lyric about a homely yet sexy chick. As with "Splish Splash," Darin sank his teeth into the job, belting the words with a hot, slightly maniacal edge. Exactly three weeks after Fabian's "I'm a Man" entered the Top 40, "Plain Jane" followed. Doc also offered Darin an up-tempo tribute to his infant daughter. Atlantic held back his recording of "I Ain't Sharin' Sharon" for a year, by which time rockabilly Buddy Knox and James Darren—the male lead in *Gidget Goes Hawaiian*—had already come out with their versions.

Darin often showed up at R&B with a former classmate from the Bronx High School of Science. They'd written a couple of songs and a jingle for a furniture store. Aside from a business degree from Upsala College in New Jersey, Donnie Kirshner didn't have much going for him. He couldn't sing, play an instrument, or read music. While Darin was appearing on TV and touring the country, Kirshner worked as a gopher, delivering lead sheets for Atlantic. When he showed Doc some songs he'd been writing, wondering whether he should pursue songwriting or singing, Doc kindly suggested that he try publishing. Kirshner took the idea to heart. On Fifty-seventh Street, he walked up to Leiber and

Stoller, the best-known writers in the business, and offered them
a piece of a publishing company he was starting. Since they knew
him only as the Atlantic Records messenger, they laughed. He
made the same offer to Doc and Mort, who wanted more money
and were cultivating Paul Case at Hill & Range. Still, they gave
him a try, letting him publish a song they wrote with a writer
named Allen Norman called "Stampede." In the end, Kirshner
managed to find an experienced, well-bankrolled partner in the
much older producer, writer, and lounge music instrumentalist Al
Nevins. Aldon Music—an amalgam of their names—opened for
business on the sixth floor in a cramped office no bigger than that
of R&B Records. It may have closed just as soon as R&B if not for
another good turn from Doc and Mort.

Two stories up, at Hill & Range, they ran into two Brighton
Beach kids whom Mortie knew from Lincoln High. Neil Sedaka,
a bright-eyed, eager Jewish mama's boy, had just performed
"Stupid Cupid," a song he'd written with Howard Greenfield, his
upstairs neighbor from Brighton Beach, at the piano in Paul Case's
office. Case wasn't impressed and had turned them down. When
they ran into Doc and Mort, they looked star-struck—Sedaka and
Greenfield loved "Lonely Avenue" and the rest of Doc's Ray
Charles records. He and Mortie were doing what they only
dreamed about. Mostly, though, they looked dejected. Doc and
Mort felt sorry for them and told them to take the elevator down
to the sixth floor and try their luck at Aldon. That afternoon,
Sedaka and Greenfield became the first songwriters signed by
Kirshner and Nevins; later that year, their "Stupid Cupid" and
"Fallin'" made Connie Francis—Concetta Rosa Maria Franconero
of Newark, New Jersey—an A-list celebrity. Sedaka was still underage; his mother co-signed his contracts. To everyone's surprise, Aldon Music, the fly-by-night publisher on the sixth floor,
was about to become Hill & Range's fiercest competitor.

BY EARLY 1959, Doc and Mortie's three Top 40 records for
Fabian Forte and Walden Robert Cassotto had so impressed Paul

Case that he decided not to tamper with the winning formula. Instead of Elvis, he assigned them to a steady, if unspectacular, procession of doo-wop groups and pseudonymous Italian American crooners that were swarming the charts, many from Philadelphia. Doc didn't mind. The material he and Mortie were writing was ornamental fodder, but memories of writing songs he was proud of for Joe Turner and Ray Charles reassured him, and for the first time he was making real money. When he saw Willi and Sharon at home each night he reminded himself that now he was a bread-winner, a role that he found himself warming to. He was having trouble recognizing his life. The early-morning jam sessions alongside guys who'd gotten high by soaking the cotton from asthma inhalers in their coffee seemed like they'd happened in another lifetime, now faintly remembered. The clockwork rhythm of an office job and a regular paycheck steadied his nerves.

So it didn't faze him when Case appeared at their piano with an assignment for the next Brylcreemed, bronzed, Tony Curtis–visaged Adonis. All through 1959, they supplied songs to the beautiful men of Philadelphia, careful not to overextend their sometimes meager instruments. Each composition was either an adenoidal cry of manhood—a la "I'm a Man"—or a gooey teenage devotional of custard-like viscosity. As the year wore on they hardly believed their success. Every month, they lofted yet another sonic Moon Pie into the pages of *Cashbox*: in August, Jimmy Darren (James Ercolani) struck again with "Angel Face"; in September, Frankie Avalon (Francis Avallone) contributed "Two Fools"; and Bobby Rydell's (Robert Ridarelli's) "I Dig Girls" hit in October.

But none of those months could compare to April, May, and June. It began at a meeting with five high-school classmates from Bensonhurst, a doo-wop quintet named the Mystics signed to Laurie Records, who'd come to Hill & Range looking for songs. Naturally, Paul Case brought them to the reigning masters of Italian American radio operetta. Mortie and the group recognized each other from the neighborhood. The lead, Phil Cracolici, whose brother Albee also performed in the group, sang decently enough, and the group was competent if unspectacular, but what touched Doc was their undisguised youth. They were just kids.

Everyone thought that "It's Great to Be Young and in Love," an upbeat cotton candy wisp of a song that Mort had already demoed, was perfect for the Mystics' simple harmonies:

> It may be raining but the sun is shining in my heart,
> I'm not complaining because I know that you love me
>   from the start,
> Each night I thank the stars up above,
> It's great to be young and in love.

It wasn't any sillier than other lyrics he'd written, yet something about the words struck Doc as phony. Hadn't he once been young and in love? He remembered that it hadn't been great at all, but paralyzing and cruel and sometimes unbearable. It was the subject of his first song, "BB Blues," written all those years ago in 1943 when he was riding the train back to Brooklyn after his first night at George's, and Doc figured being a teenager in 1959 couldn't be much easier. Besides, he was getting tired of writing inanities. Was it really necessary to varnish over the truth just to get a disc jockey to drop your record on the spindle?

Mortie didn't say much either way. Though he sometimes pitched in with a stray lyric just as Doc occasionally contributed a melody, Mort considered lyrics about teenage love—still practically a teenager himself—utterly uncool. So Doc rewrote the words, leaving only "Each night I thank the stars up above," while Mortie changed the melody in the middle section to suit them. When they met the Mystics again, Mortie sang them the new song, accompanying himself on piano while Doc chimed in with the background "ooh-wahs." The group was ecstatic. Convinced they had their first hit, they practiced their parts on the subway ride back to Bensonhurst. The following day, their manager broke the bad news. Laurie owner Gene Schwartz thought the song was too good to risk with an unproven act and gave it to Dion and the

Belmonts, a doo-wop group from the Bronx that had already landed three hit singles on the charts.

Doc and Mort wanted to make it up to the abandoned Mystics. When they offered to write them another song, Schwartz said that it should be something along the lines of "Little Star," a number one hit by the Elegants. Twenty-four hours later, Doc and Mort presented the group with a doo-wop lullaby titled "Hushabye." The chorus, with its cresting harmonies and intricate vocal arrangement, made spectacular use of the group's voices. Weeks later, the unknown Mystics appeared on Alan Freed's Saturday night TV show and "Hushabye," their Top 20 smash, became the show's closing theme.

A few years later, after the Mystics failed to score another hit, each of the former members went to work as an engineer. Meanwhile, up in the Bronx, Dion DeMucci of Dion and the Belmonts had little in common with the domesticated teenagers from Bensonhurst. By the age of fourteen, he'd been in a Crotona Avenue street gang and snorted heroin; unlike Fabian, he didn't need rock and roll to butch up his image. His oiled, lustrous mane framed the delicate face of a criminal. When Dion heard "Teenager in Love," he said the song sounded "faggy." He got on better with its writers. Just like Ben Nelson and Charlie Thomas, Dion could be himself around Doc, while Mort impressed him with his knowledge of the most guttural ghetto jive and with his playing, switching from piano to guitar and from Texas blues to "Guantanamera."

When a messenger delivered the record to Hill & Range, Doc, Mort and Paul Case sat around Case's desk and listened to it in silence. It opened with a jangling guitar and the Belmonts' "ooh-ooh-wah-oohs." At the very moment they gave way to Dion's plangent vocal, the song slipped the bounds of teenage pop and reached for an authentically adult emotion:

> Each time we have a quarrel
> It almost breaks my heart
> 'Cause I am so afraid

That we will have to part
Each night I ask the stars up above
Why must I be a teenager in love?

Dion idolized Hank Williams. Despite the kid's rough-trade exterior, he sang with an arresting, almost feminine emotiveness. His haunting delivery of Doc's revised, minor-key lyric, annunciated with his Alabama-by-way-of-the-Bronx twang, was the closest Dion would come to matching the heartbreak of "I'm So Lonesome I Could Cry."

Even on first hearing, the record left little doubt about its future. It may not have been their very first hit, but Doc and Mort knew it was the first distinctive, fully deliberate song they'd written. The juxtaposition of Mort's lush, deceptively simple, essentially upbeat melody and Doc's tormented, ruminative lyric—a delicious sweet-and-sour dissonance—became a template for their best work. The record's B-side, a terrific ballad called "I've Cried Before," didn't get much attention, but "Teenager in Love" entered the *Billboard* Top 5.

By November, after three versions of the song had simultaneously gone Top 40 in the UK (the other two by Marty Wilde and Craig Douglas), and while a fourth and fifth (by Dickie Valentine and Rikki Henderson) trailed just behind, Doc and Mort received an invitation to appear on British television. Impresario Jack Good planned to devote an entire episode of his television revue *Boy Meets Girl* to British rock and roll acts—many under contract to him—performing Pomus-Shuman hits. All of London, Good promised, was lining up for their material. The Aberbachs said it was a lucrative opportunity, but the trip unnerved Doc. Since he'd taken a train to Warm Springs, Georgia, as a seven-year-old, he hadn't strayed farther from Brooklyn than the Catskills. Mort needed a reprieve from the office, and Willi, too, thought he should go. There was no fighting it—Doc was headed to London.

THE NOTION of sitting strapped to a chair thousands of miles above the earth in an aluminum tube sounded to Doc like something out of one of his old Jules Verne novels. When Paul Case's secretary Elaine made their reservations, Doc insisted that he and Willi travel on separate planes, in case one crashed. Willi couldn't follow his logic, but gave in. Waiting for takeoff on the aisle next to Mort, Doc sweated through his shirt. He pulled his seatbelt tight and nervously eyed the motion sickness bag.

Doc, Mort, Willi and Sharon touched down in London within minutes of each other. They walked into the airport terminal expecting a solitary driver holding a sign with their names. Instead, they were greeted by a blast of flashbulbs. Photographers, newspapermen, executives and fan club reps engulfed them, shouting questions, thrusting microphones, proffering autograph books. For a moment Doc and Mort were tempted to look behind them—maybe they'd arrived on the same plane as Little Richard. It was a full-on rock and roll star welcome, and they were the honorees. With dazed smiles, they grinned for photos and shouted answers at the reporters until a chauffeur led them through the throng of well-wishers and gawkers to an idling limousine. On their way downtown, Doc asked the driver to stop. He'd stayed in his seat the entire flight, unable to maneuver his way to the bathroom. The Rolls Royce pulled over at the first public toilet they spotted. It was coin-operated, and no one had remembered to exchange their dollars for pounds, so Doc had to ask the driver for the change.

The raucous reception at the airport continued after the Pomus-Shuman party moved into the Aberbachs' posh Mayfair suite. In New York, no one ever treated them as anything more than writers of teenage dance tunes—essentially, hacks. But here, visitors and reporters addressed them as though they were cultural emissaries, even artists. It became an endlessly appealing novelty. Every night, Jack Good drove them to another fete. In 1959, London was still a musical province, and all its top attractions—Tommy Steele, Lionel Bart, Anthony Newley—showed up to gaze at the American geniuses. In the afternoons, while Doc and Mort plied the local talent—like Little Tony, the British Fabian—with

authentic, guaranteed-to-sell Brill Building songs, Willi pushed
Sharon's stroller through the city's parks. She wandered through
the British Museum, stopped at Harrods, and took in all the West
End matinees she could. Every night, she went out with Doc and
Mortie, most memorably to a record executive's labyrinthine
country manor. When Willi asked for directions to the bathroom,
a puzzled servant led her along several corridors and up a flight of
stairs to a room with a tub and sink, but no toilet.

The trip was heady stuff for Mort, who'd just turned twenty-
three. On *Boy Meets Girl*—it aired on ITV on November 21—he
followed Marty Wilde's and the Vernons Girls' Pomus-Shuman
renditions by singing Fabian's "I'm a Man" to rapturous applause.
Afterward Jack Good recorded him singing it, along with "Turn
Me Loose," at Decca studios; when Mort heard the amateurish
record years later, he cringed. He also laid down a quick piano
and voice demo of a song that he and Doc had written back in
Brooklyn. Again, Elvis in his rockabilly guise had been the inspiration. They remembered "A Mess of Blues" when they ran into
Lamar Fike, a rotund buddy of Elvis's, in London. Fike, a Memphis friend who was living with Presley near the U.S. Army base
in Friedberg, Germany, asked whether they had any material suit-
able for his housemate. Doc and Mort couldn't decide whether or
not he was full of shit but chose not to squander an opportunity.
Fike promised the demo would get a hearing.

The Brits welcomed Doc and Mortie as though they were
Wallace Stevens and Robert Frost on sabbatical, and Doc wanted
to stay on, but Willi had taken Sharon home and kept insisting that
he come back. After a couple of long-distance arguments, Doc relented. In his absence, Hill & Range had moved from 1650
Broadway to the Brill Building penthouse, the tiniest address in
music publishing, in no small part a tribute to the nearly a dozen
Pomus-Shuman songs that charted in 1959. Only Leiber and
Stoller had more. When Doc and Mort returned, Jean Aberbach
presented his top songwriters with a spacious, outrageously swank
office overlooking Broadway. For days they stared at the panoramic

midtown views and made phone calls. Finally, they asked for some-place they could actually work. Their new office was an eight-by-ten space with two old chairs, an upright piano and an ashtray. It was oppressive and dingy. After an afternoon of Doc and Mort chain-smoking, it felt like the engine room from a turn-of-the-century locomotive. They always got right to work because they couldn't wait to get out of there. The only escape was a small window that led onto a precarious ledge. It was perfect. If he and Mort didn't feel like writing, Doc reasoned, they could jump to their deaths.

AFTER LONDON'S riverfront lofts and calfskin-upholstered car seats, McKibbin Street felt like a latrine. The neighborhood got worse every day. Some nights when he came home from Man-hattan, Doc phoned the local precinct for a police escort. All of a sudden, Doc couldn't bear the idea of his childhood apartment and all of its memories. He and Willi talked often about getting out, and now finally they could afford to.

The final straw was the shattered window in the bedroom. Willi found a bullet hole in the pane; broken glass lay scattered in Sharon's crib. A few weeks later, Doc and Willi signed a deed to a brick ranch house in Lynbrook, Long Island, just off the Sunrise Highway, about a fifty-minute drive from Manhattan. The pie-shaped lot abutted a sleepy, tree-lined street. The house at 190 Surrey Commons—an address they liked after their trip to London—had a spacious living room and several bedrooms, a laundry room, a garage and a huge backyard. It was neither too large nor too small. They walked around their new, empty home in silence. It felt surreal—Doc could never have imagined himself in a house like this, on a street like this one. Manhattan felt a con-tinent away. When they walked out into their driveway, they could've been standing in a suburb of Wichita.

Their optimism brushed away the misgivings. After all, they chose Long Island to get away from the city's clamor and grime and especially from Williamsburg, with its teenaged gangs and howling ambulances and dark, foul-smelling stairwells. They'd raise Sharon on this quiet, tree-lined street, and Willi would make it a home. The quality that impressed Doc most in his wife was her immense energy. In addition to ministering to Sharon and their new house, she scoured the papers for auditions and worked constantly. Willi had a nightly lead opposite Eddie Bracken in a New Jersey production of *Brigadoon*, and in her spare time she sewed curtains, decorated the rooms with Asian-style furniture, much in vogue in 1960, and painted and papered the rooms in clean, modern colors. At Doc's insistence, she hired a live-in governess. Roz, a young girl they met in London, slept in a servants' room off the kitchen.

He'd finally made it. If Doc didn't believe it in his bones, the home on Surrey Commons was proof. Unlike a memory or an emotion, or even the absurdly large Hill & Range checks he deposited on Fridays, the house was utterly palpable. For the first time in nearly thirty-five years, he was a verifiable *success*. It was an unfamiliar feeling. When Doc needed to go to the office, Willi woke early, showered, dressed, made breakfast, and drove him to Manhattan. From the passenger seat, Doc glanced uneasily at the Chevy's old Bendix hand brakes. Just looking at them still gave him a twinge.

One afternoon, Doc wandered into a showroom and bought a brand new silver Cadillac convertible right off the floor. He paid for it in cash.

IN OCTOBER 1959, while Doc and Mort were getting ready to jet off to London, New York's jukebox operators and record dealers took receipt of Atlantic 2040, a 45-rpm single by the Drifters that would sell more than a million copies. The B-side—"Dance with Me"—was credited to five men, none of whom happened to be the song's primary writer. That was Ben Nelson, who now went by Ben E. King. Doc and Mort had written the A-side, "(If You Cry) True Love, True Love." In a quieter but equally pervasive way than Elvis's first sessions, that record disturbed and mutated the manner in which rock and roll songs were written, arranged, produced, and recorded, and rearranged American popular music itself.

After their abortive debut on R&B Records, the former Crowns hadn't fared well on the road. Trotted out in front of chitlin circuit crowds that expected the old Drifters, they got booed off stages all around the country. Fortunately, they'd inherited not only the former group's name but also their contract with Atlantic Records and, consequently, the production services of Leiber and Stoller, who'd written some of the very hits they were struggling to put across on stage, like "Drip Drop" and "Ruby Baby." Knowing a good thing when he saw it, George Treadwell wasted no time pulling his juvenile ensemble off the road and getting them into the studio.

When they heard the new guys, Leiber and Stoller knew that the vignettes they'd written for the Coasters—hip, raucous, juvenile, ironic—weren't going to work. Even the black rhythm and blues sound of their previous Drifters' sides wouldn't suffice. They needed a new approach, and having heard about the group's stint with R&B Records, they recruited their friends Pomus and Shuman. Still, the first two records came from Ben E. King himself. When he auditioned "There Goes My Baby" and "Dance with Me" for the group's Mephistophelian manager, Treadwell unflinchingly bought both songs for twenty-five dollars each.

The Drifters arrived at their first Atlantic date, at Manhattan's Coastal Studio, only to stall in the doorway, dumbstruck. It looked as though they'd wandered into a rehearsal for the New York Philharmonic. A tympani stood in the middle of the room, surrounded by a thicket of Latin percussion. Behind it, a row of cellos and violins lay idle beside stands crowded with sheet music. A Jewish guy in a T-shirt and sneakers handed out charts with complex orchestrations to at least two-dozen musicians. It was a decidedly weird scene for the making of a 1959 rhythm and blues record, but the Drifters would discover that the sessions they were about to embark on had little to do with any rhythm and blues—with any black music, really—that came before.

Overdubs were still years away, and when the light went on, the whole ensemble, strings and all, surged at once. The rhythm section carried a Brazilian beat, the *baion*, that Leiber and Stoller had lifted from the film *Anna*, a 1951 Silvia Mangano tearjerker. The borderline atonal, swirling cacophony emanating behind him—made more eerie by the booming, out-of-tune tympani—so unnerved lead singer Charlie Thomas that on take after take he stumbled over the words. In the control room, Jerry Wexler was getting cagey about studio overtime when Mike Stoller told him that Ben E. King had written the song. "If he wrote it, then let him sing it," Wexler barked, and King never relinquished the lead. When he finally heard the record, Wexler hated it. It sounded, he said, like a radio tuned to two stations at once. "There Goes My Baby," a cut that marked only the second time the Drifters had been inside a recording studio, and released by Atlantic despite the misgivings of its owners, went to number two in the summer of 1959.

Doc and Mort's initial contribution was slated for the A-side of the Drifters' second record. Although King had sung lead on "Dance with Me," Johnny Lee Williams, a high tenor brought in just for the song, took over on "(If You Cry) True Love, True Love." When the tape rolled, the luxurious, strange, heavily orchestrated music staked out an aesthetic space far beyond the genre dialectics of AM radio. The Drifters' vocals were but an element; the recording was a collaboration in the best sense of the word. Stoller's friend Stan Applebaum—the two had met while taking lessons with German-born composer Stefan Wolpe—wrote the arrangement, Pomus and Shuman contributed the words and melody, Richard Wess conducted, King Curtis blew the sax break, honorary Drifter Billy Davis strummed guitar, a group of New York's most capable session musicians filled in everywhere else, while Leiber and Stoller played the Erich von Stroheim role on the crowded set at Bell Studio, demanding take after take until the results matched the blueprint in their collective inner ear.

Doc and Mort marveled at what they heard—Mortie's fine, admittedly conventional melody was exploded like a diorama.

The strings carried the tune, punctuated by bells and background voices, before Johnny Lee Williams's yearning lyric rose above the pulsing Latin rhythm. The record was lush and streamlined at once. Unlike "There Goes My Baby," it didn't rely on the doo-wop model to propel the melody, and the lyric was a coherent narrative. What it wasn't was record hop fodder—Atlantic 2040 was resolutely, even proudly, grown up. The recording sounded as sophisticated, ambitious, lovelorn and knowing as any since rock and roll had taken hold of the radio. While Fabian had made their songs into jukebox hits, the Drifters—along with Leiber and Stoller—transformed them into Tchaikovsky.

For Doc and Mort, the Drifters' sessions sprouted in the midst of the often inane business of rock and roll like lilies in a swamp. In one year they'd gone from running a front for a philandering dance instructor to becoming Hill & Range's marquee songwriting team, with an office in the Brill Building penthouse that they used at their leisure. But none of this meant they'd suddenly become Rodgers and Hart—they still spent most of their time writing pedestrian songs for even more pedestrian singers. They followed up Fabian's first two hits with "Hound Dog Man," a blatant Elvis knockoff. Teenagers still reigned at record store cash registers, record companies continued to lowball their intelligence, and "Hound Dog Man" went Top 10. And Doc never forgot that the company they kept—Leiber and Stoller, along with the Atlantic team—was a happy anomaly in an industry rife with lowlifes. One day, waiting to see the mobbed-up Roulette Records owner Morris Levy, Doc heard a barrage of punches and groans coming from inside his office. When the doors swung open, two goons carried out an unconscious, bloodied man. Inside, Levy sat at his desk unperturbed. "Come in, Doc," he cheerfully told him.

Doc never looked down at the characters or the jobs. He remembered the debacle of "Heartlessly" too well. His taste of abundance was too brief, and too sweet, for him to condescend to the formula. Besides, at nearly every turn, the arbitrary, opportunistic nature of his trade amazed him. When he heard a halfhearted

version of his and Mort's "Go, Bobby, Go" recorded by Philadelphia crooner Bobby Rydell, who wasn't enthused at singing a
lyric with his name in it, Doc took a taxi to Brooklyn's Fox
Theater, where an Alan Freed rock and roll show was under way.
Backstage, he offered the song to a fading New Orleans R&B
singer. "We wrote it with you in mind," Doc explained to Jimmy
Clanton the following afternoon before Mortie sang him "Go,
Jimmy, Go." Pomus and Shuman could do no wrong—Clanton
scored one of the biggest hits of his career.

In the Drifters, Doc found his ideal interpreters. He rediscov-
ered the thrill of pushing himself to write as searchingly as he
could, knowing that Ben and Charlie would reciprocate his effort
in their singing. The group, at their core, radiated the distinctly
black feeling that Doc had loved all along in Joe Turner and the
Tibbs Brothers, yet they remained open and versatile enough to
make the most of Leiber and Stoller's symphonic vision. Though
Ben E. King wasn't yet old enough to drink, he had a native sensi-
tivity to the adult emotions he was asked to enact in his performances. With Leiber and Stoller producing and Atlantic engineering
and marketing their records, the Drifters would soon supplant
Elvis as the Brill Building's dream client, attracting increasingly
ambitious material from the most talented writers. Within a year,
a country club–handsome composer whom Paul Case brought to
Hill & Range—Burt Bacharach, working alongside veteran lyricist Hal David—would tailor his eccentric, angular melodies to
the group. He was followed by two shockingly fresh-faced couples
from Aldon Music at 1650 Broadway—Carole King and Gerry
Goffin, then Cynthia Weil and Barry Mann.

The Drifters reciprocated Doc's admiration. When he taught
them new songs around an upright piano, singing the lyrics in his
throaty, saliva-rich baritone, no one felt as if they were working.
Even in New York's music business, few whites felt genuinely
comfortable around blacks, and Doc's ease put the group at ease,
too. As the fifties came to an end, two days before Christmas 1959
the Drifters gathered at Bell Studio to record the latest song Doc

had taught them. He and Mort repaid "(If You Cry) True Love, True Love" by offering the Drifters their most inspired work yet.

Ben E. King, who in his year-long career had written two hits and sung on three, had nothing except his weekly two-hundred-dollar salary from Treadwell to show for his newfound fame. Shortly before the session he'd decided to quit the group, agreeing to work the date until a replacement was found. He sang the lyric, a story of a first kiss, with tears in his voice, lending it a feeling of foreboding. The eerie portamento Stan Applebaum had written to open "This Magic Moment"—rapidly bowed violins and cellos rising and falling in pitch above a loping bass line—sounded like an inspired fragment from Bernard Herrmann's soundtrack to *Vertigo*. The tilt-a-whirl ended abruptly, giving way to King's ravishing first line, sung a capella before the rest was carried aloft by a swelling tide of strings.

A Spanish guitar, poised just as the third verse took a minor turn, completed the audacious soundscape. The song's opening fifteen seconds may have been the most perfect ever recorded. From that thicket of quivering violins, Doc's account of the revelation of first love emerged imbued with its attendant mystery and terror intact, and its sweetness, too. Mort's melody, stately as an ocean liner, was given Leiber and Stoller's most symphonic orchestration yet. "This Magic Moment" was everything they could ask for. The Drifters, and Doc and Mortie, knew they had their first masterpiece.

Mort celebrated with habitual abandon. Unlike Freddy Bienstock and the Aberbachs, who dressed like trust and estate lawyers, he took to wearing the patterned country suits and kid-leather driving gloves of a British squire, contorting his gangly frame into the seat of a miniature European convertible. He dated a dizzying procession of women, changed apartments every couple of months, continued to dance at the Palladium, chain-smoked Gitanes, and left the country every chance he got. Mort found his favorite Latin rhythms on a trip to Mexico. Back in New York, he played Doc several new melodies that had been coalescing in his head.

Their archaic, faraway sound inspired Doc, too. He used his favorite of the melodies as a backdrop for a lyric about watching a wife or girlfriend dance with another man. To most listeners, "Save the Last Dance for Me" was simply a lilting love song. But someone who listened closely to the words would've heard a more ambivalent story. The very verbs Doc used—"*don't* forget, you *must* tell him no"—demanded but also pleaded, revealing the narrator's trust in the woman, but also his powerlessness to secure her fidelity. The words whispered of suppressed jealousy and anxiety, of emotional desolation. Stirred by the melody, Doc wanted to give the lyric the feeling of a translation, like a Neruda poem rendered into English, and wrote lines like "in whose arms you're going to be" in an oddly foreign locution.

Anyone who knew Doc couldn't have missed the song's meaning. Conferring in the control room before the session, Ahmet Ertegun told Ben E. King that Doc had written the lyric after having watched Willi dance at their wedding. The story haunted the young singer. As he waited in front of the microphone, King fought back tears. Moments later, he laid down one of the most sympathetic and exquisitely soulful performances of his life. Leiber and Stoller surrounded him with an appropriately spare arrangement, all thrumming Spanish guitars and quiet percussion, using strings to accent the melody.

Presented with what would become the biggest-selling record in their company's history, Wexler and Ertegun suffered a lapse. They turned the song down, and Doc and Mort taught it to the ever-reliable Jimmy Clanton. Even when they reconsidered, Ahmet and Jerry exiled "Save the Last Dance for Me" to the B-side, opposite "Nobody but Me," a fairly ordinary Pomus-Shuman R&B-style shouter. It took Dick Clark, who flipped the record over on his show, to make it a hit. A tribute to King's emotive singing, Mort's melody, and the lyric's chameleonic meaning, the B-side surged to number one on *Billboard*'s pop and R&B charts in the fall of 1960. It stayed there for three weeks. Neither Doc and Mort, nor Atlantic Records, nor any lineup of the Drifters had ever scored a number one popular hit. Better yet, Doc sensed that he'd participated in something lasting. "Save the Last Dance for Me" surpassed even "This Magic Moment" as a song that had a chance to endure beyond next week's returns. That record eased Doc's sense—shared by many among his rock and roll cohorts— of being an intruder and a fraud in the Brill Building's venerable hallways. Afterward, whenever he passed the old office of Irving Caesar, who'd written lyrics with George Gershwin before his brother Ira, Doc felt something like camaraderie.

WATCHING A DANCE FROM THE SIDELINES—as Doc described it in "Save the Last Dance for Me"—was an apt metaphor for the day-to-day life of the semi-mobile, and not just when it came to love. Doc and Mort played it out in their cubicle at the Hill & Range penthouse. While Doc sat beside the piano, Mort paced up and down the hallways, sometimes with a lit joint in his mouth. If the executives noticed their star melody man getting high, they pretended not to. Occasionally, he ran out for cigarettes or a sandwich, or just to get some fresh air. He might have returned quickly, or an hour later, or sometimes not at all. Not yet twenty-five, Mort was hungry to travel the world. Doc knew that nearly every moment he spent writing in their smoky garret, Mort would've preferred to be walking barefoot and shirtless and high along a beach in Buenos Aires or Nice. The pattern they established early on— Mort coming in hours late or going missing, Doc chewing him out, and Mort apologizing and promising it wouldn't happen again—persisted. "I'm just stuck here," Doc lamented to Paul Case's secretary Elaine whenever his partner vanished.

It was Elaine's task to scout access to neighboring restaurants and shops. She'd call to see whether the entrance had a ramp or steps, and if so, how many. Doc's biggest obstacle was getting home. He'd sworn off driving, and trains were out of the question, so when Willi or Mort weren't available to drive him the forty-five or fifty minutes to Lynbrook, Doc took a taxi. It was expensive and inconvenient, and eventually Doc and Willi reluctantly agreed that

while he was busy at Hill & Range during the week he'd stay in
Manhattan. The Forrest, across the street from the Brill Building
on West Forty-ninth Street, was the closest hotel. It had a good
steakhouse off the lobby and offered a steep break to residents
who rented by the month.

The most charitable adjective anyone could attach to the
Hotel Forrest was "inexpensive." It managed to register as respectable while edging awfully close to seedy. Its proximity to
1619 and 1650 Broadway and to Madison Square Garden made it
a natural stopover for second- and third-tier showbiz personalities, boxers, and a broad cross-section of the underworld. The
Forrest's roster of regulars included Jack Benny, Duke Ellington's
entire orchestra, Steve Lawrence and Eydie Gorme, and song
peddlers of every strata. The NYPD would nab "Murph the
Surf"— the Miami jewel thief who stole the Star of India from
the Museum of Natural History—at the hotel; mob bosses from
the infamous Apalachin Conference rented entire floors; bellboys
told the story of a famous clown who'd gotten snuffed in his room
during a liaison with a hooker. Tellingly, Damon Runyon, the poet
of Broadway's underclass, once kept an apartment in the hotel's
penthouse; his son, Damon Runyon Jr., an editor at the *Herald
Tribune*, had taken it over by the time Doc moved into his new
digs on the tenth floor.

The heart of the Forrest was the lobby, a dumpy rectangular
space bounded by a collection of upholstered sofas and settees
and separated from the street by a pair of glass doors that opened
automatically whenever anyone approached. Doc had loved hotel
lobbies from his earliest days at the Broadway Central. They at-
tracted the lonely, the crooked and the strange; there was no better
place to observe the unfolding tragicomedy of human striving. The
Forrest was a more colorful venue than most. The couches were
home to an assortment of ancient fighters and fight managers,
world-weary car thieves, Tin Pan Alley has-beens, vaudeville-era
radio personalities, and Ozzie, a vintage bellboy from the Bar-
bados who knew the goings-on of every long-term guest. Doc was

fascinated by all of them. When he wasn't leaning on his crutches and holding forth, he sat on a couch with a notebook in his lap, taking down stray bits of conversation. The ostensible purpose was to find ideas for a song, but he did it mainly because he craved the random brilliance of overheard speech. "His face is asking for brick," he'd hear someone say, or "she loved him into the toilet."

When Doc wasn't at Hill & Range, Elaine sent his appointments to the Forrest lobby. It became his de facto office. On Friday nights, Elaine and her husband, folk singer Fred Neil, dropped by to say hello and have Doc cash Elaine's paycheck, to save her the surcharge at the corner storefront. When Mortie came by, they walked across the street to the office, but just as often they wrote in Doc's room. Doc also befriended Little Johnny, a quiet, troubled Armenian kid from New Jersey whose bouts of paranoia foreshadowed a lifelong struggle with schizophrenia. Before becoming Doc's gopher, bellboy, and scout, Johnny Kabajian was already a Brill Building veteran, having worked for Alan Freed and others. Doc met him backstage at one of Freed's concerts, when he rescued him from an abusive headliner. A too-large nose marred Johnny K's boyishly handsome face. On good days, he was sweet and docile and generally kept to himself. He got into trouble only once at Hill & Range, when he walked out onto the balcony and pissed onto Paul Case's potted plants. It became a joke around the office. "And don't piss on the plants, Johnny," Doc added whenever he asked Johnny to do something afterward.

Doc's most frequent visitor at the Forrest was a short, slight Jewish boy from Los Angeles with thinning hair and a quiet voice who carried a leatherette briefcase that contained a notebook of songs, a comb, a loaf of bread, and a hard salami. Paul Case had introduced Phil Spector to Doc by saying, "I want you to meet this character who's going to be a big, big star in this business." Spector slept on the floor at Leiber and Stoller's office and was canny enough to have ingratiated himself with Ahmet and Jerry at Atlantic, too. He idolized Sun's Sam Phillips and Cadence's

Archie Bleyer, label heads who also had a hand in management and production. Spector's vision included writing, producing, publishing, and owning a record company, goals he'd realize in the space of a few years. For all his ambition, Spector struck Doc as a lonely, precocious adolescent. His childlike stature and obvious strangeness made him an outsider in every room he entered, something Doc could relate to. But Spector was also funny and bright. His intense neediness and hunger for a surrogate father—Spector's had committed suicide—endeared him to Doc. On weekends Spector followed Doc home to Lynbrook, where he slept on a sofa and gorged himself on Willi's cooking, especially her pies and sweets, eating them like a street urchin out of *Oliver Twist*.

The odd-looking pair became a Forrest lobby attraction. Spector showed up in bizarre costumes: capes, rakish hats, and shoes with pointed, upturned noses that played up his elfin appearance. Like Doc, he loved practical jokes. Their favorite target was Artie Ripp, a street kid from Queens who worked for George Goldner, the golden-eared owner of End and Gone Records whose notorious gambling habit had made him an unwitting associate of the mob. Only twenty-one, Ripp was both a braggart and laughably inexperienced. Every night he came back to the Forrest at about two in the morning; on one of those nights, Doc and Spector were laying in wait. Just as Ripp walked into the Forrest lobby, Aggie the telephone operator called Doc over to the front desk to take an urgent phone call. As rehearsed, she announced that the call was coming from a Colonel Parker in Memphis. Doc knew the Colonel from the poker games in Paul Case's office and put on a show of familiarity. He wrinkled his brow and hemmed and hawed into the dead receiver while Ripp stared, transfixed. After Doc had hung up, Ripp demanded, then begged for Doc to tell him what Presley's manager had said. Reluctantly, Doc let it drop that Elvis had come down with laryngitis just prior to a recording session; the Colonel wanted to know whether Ral Donner—an Elvis soundalike under contract to Goldner—would take his place for $100,000. On the couch, Doc and Spector rolled with laughter as Ripp ran to the pay phone and woke Goldner in the middle of the night with the great news.

Up in his room, Doc played his favorite old records for Spector, not just the blues but the jazz ballads, too. The kid was amazed. Their favorite song became "A Cottage for Sale"; Spector played it over and over again on his guitar and Doc sang along. When they got hungry they took the elevator down to the Spindletop, the ruthlessly expensive steakhouse just off the lobby run by a gruff, alleged gangster named Joe Marsh. As far as Doc was concerned, the location couldn't be beat, and the food was better. After their first meal there Spector confessed that it was the first real steak he'd ever tasted. One night, out of the corner of his eye, Spector saw someone in a raincoat and a fedora walk up behind a man at an adjacent table and rapidly fire three shots into his head. The victim crumpled face down into a bowl of bloody linguine. Spector refused to set foot in the Spindletop again. Doc nudged him back: "The place is incredible, right, the salads, I mean how about the service in that restaurant? Babe, you always got to look at the upside." But what about the guy who got murdered, Spector protested. "Well," Doc explained in a bit of philosophy that Spector never forgot, "the murder— that's the down side of the restaurant, you understand, that's the down side."

The action in the lobby really got going after hours. One night, a petty thief who'd just robbed Duke Ellington's van tried to sell the bandleader's snakeskin shoes to the men on the couches. The first Lobbyist—as the Forrest regulars referred to themselves—was Ellington's press agent Joe Morgan. "My boss would love these," he cooed to the car thief, "in fact he's got a pair just like them." When he heard laughter all around him, Morgan finally caught on. Thanks mainly to Doc, the thief managed to make it out of the lobby with only a couple of bruises. And Ripp loved to tell about his double date with Spector. He'd rounded up two young groupies from the Brill Building, taken them to his room, and invited Spector to join them on the bed. Ripp was engrossed in the threesome when he snuck a look over at his co-hort. Spector was in his underwear, curled up on top of the TV with an acoustic guitar, putting the finishing touches on a song he'd written with Jerry Leiber called "Spanish Harlem."

Doc's favorite Lobbyist was John Leslie McFarland, another of Paul Case's wayward songwriting children. McFarland walked with the light tremor of an accomplished alcoholic. Black and six-feet tall, on a good week he weighed 120 pounds. His songs—with titles like "Apple Tangle Tango" and "Pigalle Love"—were as weird as their author. His friends called him Pumpkin Juice, after another of his compositions, or Johnny Jungletree, a pseudonym under which he'd recorded an album of exotic tropical tracks. When sober, McFarland was quiet and nervous and shyly funny. When drunk—he usually was—he'd pick a fight with the largest white guy in sight. Sometimes Doc and Mort managed to rescue him. Other times, all they could do was mop up the damage. One morning, Elaine discovered McFarland lying unconscious on the floor in Paul Case's office. His clothes were soaking wet. She was convinced he was dead, but Case managed to rouse him. It turned out Johnny Jungletree had been running the time-honored scam of selling the same song to every publisher in the building when two Italian guys in black suits shoved him into a sedan and later threw him into the East River.

The Johnny Jungletree stories were legion. In one he stole a mummy from a museum and took it on a bus; in another, he led away a mounted policeman's horse and rode it against traffic down Forty-ninth Street. The Lobbyists laughed about his naked tryst with a local nymphette in the middle of that same street dur-ing a blizzard, and about the time Johnny commandeered a jumbo jet at Chicago's O'Hare airport and gunned it down the runway before cops tackled him to the floor. During a sober spell, McFarland discovered a minister's daughter from Detroit who was living at the Forrest. Johnny borrowed Doc's Wurlitzer key-board and sat up with Aretha Franklin in her room for hours, teaching her "Apple Tangle Tango" and crooning along.

Just once, McFarland managed to persuade Doc that he'd found Jesus and gone dry for good. He'd been wandering from hovel to hovel, so Doc talked the Forrest's manager, a kindly, churchgoing prude named Mac, into renting his friend a room at a steep discount. Johnny, Doc assured him, had turned his life around. On his first night in his new home, McFarland got desperately drunk, stole the axe from the firebox, and methodically demolished every door and mirror in the lobby. Both McFarland and Doc got thrown out of the hotel. It was months before Doc could talk to Johnny Jungletree without fighting a temptation to kill him or at least break his arms. But Johnny wriggled out of that, too. Whenever Doc got mad at him, McFarland threw his arms around his neck and kissed him all over his face. They were friends again before long.

DOC AND MORT had forgotten about "A Mess of Blues" when Paul Case handed them the brand new RCA single. Their song was the B-side. The recording was sexy, knowing, swaggering; Elvis had wrung the salty lyric dry. He sounded like he was cutting loose. Apparently, Presley had flipped for the song when he heard it, and now Case asked them to write a follow-up to the record's operatic A-side, "It's Now or Never."

Elvis had changed. The man-boy from the swamps whom Doc had first heard on the jukebox at the Club Musicale was getting serious about his singing. Since he'd returned from the service, Presley had developed what sounded like another octave of range. He'd transformed the high, adenoidal quaver of "Mystery Train" into a broad, tightly controlled instrument with a plunging low register that he was eager to show off on record. In March of 1960 he even appeared on a Timex TV special called *Frank Sinatra's Welcome Home Party for Elvis Presley*, mugging in a tuxedo with the man who just a few years earlier proclaimed rock and roll the music of "cretinous goons." Now, Presley wanted challenging material that highlighted his range. The rococo "It's Now or Never" was an English-language "*O Sole Mio.*" Besides

contributing the line "my love won't wait" to the collective imagi-
nation of male teenagers, the record erased all doubts about
Presley's post-army career, selling more than a million copies in
France alone.

For a follow-up, Elvis asked Freddy Bienstock for an English-
language version of a turn-of-the-century Italian ballad called
"*Torna a Surriento.*" Sinatra and Dean Martin had already recorded an Anglicized version, "Come Back to Sorrento," but
Presley's version had to be nudged further into the rock and roll
idiom. Mort wanted nothing to do with it. "Why should I want to
write for some redneck idiot who wants to sound like Mario
Lanza?" he fumed. "You write it Doc, you've already got the music." Writing words to an existing melody obviously took less
work than coming up with a whole new song, and in the case of
"Surrender," even Doc's title was just a near-homonym. The
whole thing smacked of mediocrity. By the time the demo
reached Presley, Doc's lyric was dressed up in state-of-the-art
schmaltz that made it onto the record: a James Bond–like introduction gave way to Elvis's arioso, the Jordanaires egging him on
to scale heroic vocal heights.

Though it likely would've bombed in the hands of a Fabian or
a Bobby Rydell, Presley imbued "Surrender" with sly humor and
an almost maniacal ardor, transforming it into a dramatic showcase for his genuinely amazing chops. Neither Doc nor Mortie
thought of "Surrender" as anything but a job. Still, Doc was hum-
bled by the result. He had to admit that Elvis was a songwriter's
dream. He could make a mediocre song distinctive, make a good
one great, and make a great one indelible. When he wanted to, he
sang anything—from spirituals to novelty pop—brilliantly, finding
just the right emotional shading. Presley recorded "Surrender" on
October 30, 1960, in the midst of a marathon session for his first
collection of spirituals, some of which he'd heard at the First
Assembly of God church as a teenager in Memphis. Doc could
hardly believe that Stuart Hamblen's "Known Only to Him," a
sublime performance that inflamed Elvis's voice with what

Jerome gets a puppy from WOR deejay Uncle Don in Manhattan Beach, Brooklyn, 1933. The photo ran in the *Brooklyn Times Union* under the headline "Paralyzed Boy Is Gleeful."

In Manhattan Beach,
Brooklyn, 1934.

Jerome (*left*), Brooklyn, late 1930s.

Jerome, cousin Max
with catcher's mitt,
and Raoul holding the bat,
Brooklyn, circa 1941.

George's Tavern with Doc Pomus and His Blues Men on the marquee,
Greenwich Village, New York, 1943.

Raoul's Bar Mitzvah, in the living room at 75 Manhattan Avenue, Brooklyn, 1947.
From left: Doc, Millie, Raoul, Morris.

Wailing, 1940s.

Doc in action, 1940s.

With Duke Ellington,
Snooky's,
New York, 1950.

Ad for a gig at the
Café Bohemia,
New York Post, 1954.

Onstage, from *Picture Life* magazine, 1954.

At a session, New York, late 1950s.

Mort and Doc in a Hill & Range publicity photo, circa 1959.

The geniuses in London, 1959.
From left: unidentified, Jack Good, Doc, Little Tony, Mort.

The high life, circa 1960.
Willi, Doc, and Raoul with Sharon on his knees.

Mort and Doc at a costume party at Raoul's apartment,
New York, early 1960s.

At home with friends, Lynbrook, Long Island, early 1960s.

The family man, Lynbrook, Long Island, 1962.
From left: Morris, Millie, Willi, Sharon, Doc, and Willi's mother, Lena.

Doc, Sharon, Little Johnny, Geoffrey,
Lynbrook, Long Island, 1962.

A party at the Hotel Forrest, New York, early 1960s.
From left: unidentified, Doc,
the French au pair Bernadette, Raoul, Paul Case.

Willi in a publicity photo
from a production of
The Sound of Music,
1964.

Doc and Scottie Fagan in front of
the house on Surrey Commons,
circa 1964.

Doc and Shirlee at a club,
New York, late 1960s.

With Shirlee, late 1970s.

With Joel Dorn and Jackie DeShannon at the session for
"(If You Never Have a Big Hit Record) You're Still Gonna Be a Star,"
New York, 1973.

SHARYN FELDER

At home with Mac, 253 West 72nd Street, New York, late 1970s.

With Joe Turner, late 1970s.

With Mort at BMI Country
Awards dinner in Nashville, 1984.

With Bob Dylan at the Westover, 1986.

At the Lone Star with Ben E. King, Solomon Burke,
Don Covay, and Peter Guralnick, 1980s.

With Jimmy Scott, late 1980s.

With Otis Blackwell, Maine, 1990.

SHARYN FELDER

At the NYU Medical Center with cards and letters, 1991.

sounded like true religious epiphany, was recorded on the same night that yielded "Surrender's" Neapolitan glitz.

Mort was thrilled that the record was nearly identical to his demo. He'd recorded it at Associated Studio on Forty-seventh Street with a band of jazz musicians recruited by Doc's old Brooklyn pal Leonard Gaskin. It was a welcome change from singing into Doc's Wollensak reel-to-reel. Doc hated studios. They reminded him of the bad old days of "Heartlessly," of the old disappointments and swindles. He showed up to the demo sessions only about half the time, to catch up with Gaskin and the old-time crowd and mainly to partake of the cold cuts. But Mort thrived at Associated. He worked out the arrangements on the spot, moved from piano to guitar, and sounded out ideas with the rhythm section. He made up for a middling voice with a knack for performance. When he listened to Mortie shouting his lyrics into the microphone, eyes closed in abandon, Doc sensed that his partner harbored greater ambitions than being a contract writer of teenage rock and roll.

By the spring of 1961, when "Surrender" rocketed to number one in nearly every market in RCA's global operation, Pomus and Shuman were already anointed as the favorite writers in the House of Elvis. Presley was again the world's biggest act, and Doc and Mort were each earning close to fifty thousand dollars a year, an amount unimaginable even a year earlier. With each passing month, Mort grew more restless. He'd become almost incapable of staying in their penthouse closet for more than fifteen or twenty minutes without coming up with a reason to run downstairs. After each hit, Mort vanished—as though on a long-awaited furlough after having fulfilled an odious obligation—jetting off to Europe or Latin America. The adulation he first experienced in London was still fresh in his mind when he discovered that Paris treated him even better. How could he labor anonymously in a dingy garret above Broadway, when across the Atlantic, in the world's loveliest city, rockers with names like *Richard Anthony et les Chats Sauvages* were singing Pomus-Shuman songs to young, adoring crowds at the *Palais des Sports?*

More often than not Doc celebrated the hits with Willi or Paul Case or Spector, then headed to the office alone. To fill the lulls, Case tried to pair Doc with temporary collaborators, writers like Alan Jeffreys, Jerry Ragavoy, and Ellie Greenwich, a pubescent, Jewish blonde from Levittown, Long Island. Greenwich hadn't yet married Jeff Barry, the partner with whom she'd write a string of classic hit songs, and her biggest success with Doc was called "Who Are You Gonna Love This Winter (Mr. Lifeguard)," which inexplicably charted in Scandinavia. Case also enlisted the help of his poker buddy Snuff Garrett. Barely out of his teens, Garrett was a scrawny Texan who headed up A&R at Liberty Records in Los Angeles. He drove a Rolls Royce and came calling at Hill & Range in bespoke monogrammed suits from Jack Taylor in Beverly Hills, who also outfitted Cary Grant. With Case's blessing, Garrett offered to fly Doc to the West Coast. Doc was languishing in Mort's absence; besides, Garrett wanted material for his moneymaker Bobby Vee and figured that whisking away one of Case's top writers couldn't hurt. "Surrender" was still on the charts. Doc hated the idea of another long flight, but gave in. In Hollywood, Liberty installed Doc at the Roosevelt Hotel. Every morning when Doc arrived at the record company's office on Sunset Boulevard, a crew of guys from the mailroom lifted him, seated in a wheelchair like a rajah aboard a palanquin, and carried him upstairs to Garrett's office.

A few days into the trip, Mortie arrived from New York and joined Doc at the Roosevelt. In their hotel room on Hollywood Boulevard they quickly hashed out a pair of songs. Garrett was disappointed when he heard them. So was Vee, a pretty balladeer who'd just finished the sessions on an album titled *Bobby Vee Meets the Crickets*. Worried they had a dud on their hands, Doc and Mort looked up their friend Bobby Darin. Now a legitimate film actor and a serious singer with Sinatra-scale ambitions, he'd married starlet Sandra Dee and lived in a palatial house in Bel Air. Darin recorded several takes of "(Marie's the Name) His Latest Flame" and "Little Sister" before giving up. He just couldn't get the lyric to gel. His current record was a swinging revival of Hoagy Carmichael's 1932 hit "Lazy River." Rock and roll felt like ancient history. When Doc and Mort returned to Hill & Range empty handed, Paul Case had a client in mind that he was sure could handle the new material.

On June 25, at RCA's Studio B in Nashville, Presley recorded both songs in a marathon session that went nearly until dawn. He loved "(Marie's the Name) His Latest Flame." They were going to get it right, Elvis told the band, "even if it takes us thirty-two hours." In the middle of the night, a phone call from Presley jolted Mort out of bed. How had he gotten the piano to sound that way on the demo, Elvis asked. Doc, too, was woken by a nighttime call from Nashville. Thinking it was a prank, Doc grumbled some bleary-eyed answers into the receiver, not realizing who the caller had been until the following morning. Presley's enthusiasm yielded two perfect recordings. "(Marie's the Name) His Latest Flame," with its itchy, Bo Diddley guitar line, barroom piano and tart, sleepless lyric, was a master class in Brill Building pop. As much as any other early sixties record, "Little Sister" looked ahead to rock. Elvis slowed down Mortie's demo; its sludgy guitar licks and frankly sexual swagger harked back to Doc's earliest rhythm and blues hollers and brought Elvis the closest he'd come in years to the rude dynamism of his Sun Records sides. Not realizing each was a natural number one, RCA released the songs as flipsides. All through September and October, Doc and Mort watched Bobby Vee's castoffs battle each other at the top of the Billboard chart. Eventually, they stalled at numbers four and five.

The single capped two halcyon years for Doc and Mortie. For all of Mort's desertions, they wrote together easily, their songs brimmed with verve and fun, and each record seemed to outsell the one before. Even when they couldn't get the details right, the muse had guided their hands. Doc couldn't come up with a chorus for a song he was writing for the Drifters, and when he taught it to the group, he sang a few nonsense syllables as a placeholder: "nah nah na-na-na-na late at night." The group recorded "I Count the Tears" just as it was, Ben E. King's buoyant lead lofted even higher by Leiber and Stoller's tolling bells and cellos. Following an inevitable showdown with Treadwell, Ben E. King left the group. He was determined to return to his father's restaurant and maybe apply to college when Lover Patterson convinced him to give performing one last shot. He showed up to his first solo session dispirited and broke, he and his young wife just days away from being evicted. In a single afternoon, King recorded enough hits to last a lifetime: in addition to "Young Boy Blues" and "First Taste of Love," songs that Doc had written with Phil Spector at the Forrest, he cut Spector and Leiber's "Spanish Harlem" along with "Stand By Me," which he came up with after hearing the Soul Stirrers sing Sam Cooke's "Stand By Me Father" on the radio. In 1961, a dazzling thirteen Pomus-Shuman songs—more than one a month—entered the pop charts, surpassing Leiber and Stoller along with everyone else. Doc Pomus and Mort Shuman had become the most commercially successful songwriters in the world.

WILLI'S BIG BREAK arrived in 1961, too. After years of summer stock and industrials—complete plays staged for employees of corporations like Coca Cola and Ford—Willi took over the female lead in *Fiorello*, a hit Broadway musical about the New York mayor who'd paid a visit to Morris and Millie's apartment all those years ago. A lead on Broadway was something she'd dreamed about ever since she and Bobby had taken the train to Manhattan back in 1956. Doc watched her on TV when she made the rounds of the morning shows—a three-year-old Sharon on her lap—to promote the role. Willi glowed. When she walked into the house after an evening's performance, she was still singing. There was now enough money for both of them to travel to the city whenever they wanted, and to hire help. Willie Mae Nelson, a friend of Millie's maid, arrived several times a week from Brooklyn to help with the housework. Doc was proud of Willi. When he rolled out of bed on late weekend mornings, he liked to watch her pull the boat-sized, silver Cadillac out of the driveway on her way to a matinee.

A fifty-minute drive separated New York from Lynbrook. Doc wasn't mobile even in Manhattan, so when she wasn't on-stage, Willi brought Manhattan to them. She threw extravagant parties. Willi furnished the house with Chinese antiques she bought from Doc's aunts Bertie and Gisella, who owned an antique shop in Brooklyn. She covered the bedroom walls in grasscloth, and Doc hung an enormous African brass plate—along with crossed swords—on the wall opposite the entrance. He had the garage converted into a music room, with a piano, an electric organ, an expensive hi-fi, string instruments mounted on the walls, and a foldout couch. Surveying their empty backyard one afternoon, Doc decided to put in a swimming pool, which became a focal point for the parties. In the summers, guests basked in the pool while Doc looked on from a chaise lounge. It wasn't fair, Willi thought, and ordered a motorized steel contraption—a small crane attached to a seat—that lowered Doc into the water and lifted him back out.

On weekends they stayed at home with Sharon and waited for caravans of cars to arrive from the city. In the late mornings, Millie and Morris arrived with lamb shanks and rice pudding. Doc's brother usually came, too. Raoul was now a dapper U.S. attorney with the Justice Department and was dating a new girlfriend—Myrna Danenberg, a beautiful Brown graduate from Forest Hills who worked as a dance captain in an off-Broadway production of *Anything Goes.* They met when Myrna needed legal advice, and a friend of Willi's had introduced them. They married in 1963.

By nightfall, the house was bustling. Though Doc had quit drinking, they stocked the house with plenty of alcohol and food; before long, someone picked up a guitar or sat down at the piano. Doc's Brill Building friends—Paul Case, Phil Spector, Dion, Leiber and Stoller, Ahmet Ertegun, Otis Blackwell, Snuff Garrett, Neil Sedaka, and of course Mortie—showed up to take in Doc's lovely wife and their deluxe suburban spread.

Many of the guests were friends of Willi's. On weekends, the house on Surrey Commons was packed with actors and theater people, some cast and crew from *Fiorello.* In the hours before their guests arrived, Doc dreaded the inevitable moment when they'd meet—that brief flash of surprise in their eyes when they'd realize the gorgeous Wilma Burke was married to a short, fat man on crutches. What made the whole thing worse was that the theater folk came from the legitimate side of entertainment. Though many of the songs trotted out nightly on Broadway's stages made LaVern Baker sound like Stravinsky, theater was serious and artistic. Fabian was not. When the guests asked what kind of music he wrote, Doc sometimes found himself embarrassed to answer, convinced Willi's friends laughed at him behind his back. He never could manage to disentangle their snobbery from his own insecurities. On some Saturday nights, he'd hole up in the music room and close the door.

His apprehension surprised him. Didn't he have a palatial home, a Cadillac in the driveway, and a bigger paycheck than either senator from New York? Somehow, none of it made a difference. Like many who'd spent their youth fantasizing about everything they'd ever wanted to buy but couldn't afford, Doc was keenly disappointed in being rich. It failed to transform his life into a serene, never-ending holiday—the old doubts, regrets, and asphyxiating fears lingered. At the parties, his hit records and possessions couldn't insulate him from the perplexed, pitying stares he saw, or imagined seeing, on the faces around him.

He'd hated poverty, but it was easier to handle than success. Back in the club days, a year when he'd been able to afford a pair of new shirts or a suit was a good one. Now, he took a taxi to a swank midtown tailor and ordered ten suits at a time. But he was losing interest. Having just wasn't as satisfying as wanting. Willi was in the dark about their finances. She relied on Doc to balance the checkbook and handle the accounts, but whenever he came home with another extravagant purchase, she fought off panicked thoughts. One night, Doc showed up with a new cart—the kind Willi would use to wheel his breakfast into their bedroom—made of gleaming chrome and upholstered in ostrich skin. When he told her it had cost $500, all she could do was hope their luck held up.

BY THE END OF 1962, the day shift at the Elvis factory was tense and overworked. Presley had made Colonel Parker and the Aberbachs multimillionaires, and they made sure their product never stopped flowing. The more Elvis, they figured, the better. So when Presley, having always dreamed of being a serious actor, became a top Hollywood draw, Parker decided that the best way for his boy to make money in the movies was to make as many as possible. The deal he struck with Hal Wallis—the producer behind the Dean Martin–Jerry Lewis comedies—called for an astonishing three movie-musicals per year, each shot on a modest budget and at breakneck pace, with new songs to be supplied by Hill & Range. The schedule put the Aberbachs, and especially Freddy Bienstock, in a bind—they had to provide up to a dozen songs, including a title song, for each film. That arithmetic didn't include the non-film studio sessions. Even with one of the largest writing staffs in the business, conjuring forty or fifty quality Presley songs out of thin air every year—especially songs anchored in Wallis's insipid scripts, like *Girls! Girls! Girls!* and *Kid Galahad*—was proving impossible.

Hill & Range became an assembly line. Bienstock marked the scripts with placeholders for the songs and handed them out to the writers, who competed with each other to fill as many slots as they could. It was then up to Bienstock and Presley's staff to wade through a dozen versions of "G.I. Blues" and "Follow That Dream." Trying to maximize profits, Parker and the Aberbachs were bleeding their golden calf dry. Thanks to Wallis's screenwriters and Hill & Range's songwriters, Elvis was saddled with performing some of the most inane songs ever devised. Presley would become Hollywood's highest-paid actor, eventually becoming the first to receive a million dollars per film, but his performances reflected a growing exhaustion and boredom. With each film, the conscious artistry that had infused songs like "Mess of Blues" receded farther out of sight.

Doc and Mort chafed at the deadening assignments. The Elvis Tax galled them even more: from the beginning, the Aberbachs had required writers to surrender a third of their royalties to Presley. Still, they played along. Doc co-wrote three versions of a song called "Pot Luck"—with Mort, Phil Spector and Ellie Greenwich—none of which made the cut. When he found out that his and Mort's "Girl Happy" had been rejected, Doc cobbled together another "Girl Happy" with Jerry Ragavoy, an ASCAP writer whose BMI *nom de plume* was Norman Meade. They wrote it in Doc's room at the Forrest in twenty minutes; the result became the film's theme song. Yet Doc and Mort took pride in managing to slip through a few gems that got buried on the Presley soundtracks alongside the likes of "Adam and Evil" and "Fort Lauderdale Chamber of Commerce." Though they wrote the title track to *Viva Las Vegas*, their jazz-hued "I Need Somebody to Lean On," the film's sole transcendent moment, was one of the finest ballads Elvis committed to tape. Adorned with five Pomus tracks, the *Pot Luck* LP boasted the magnificent "Suspicion." Elvis's inspired reading of Doc's short story about a disintegrating relationship, encased in one of Mort's most savory melodies, was a surefire hit. But even their best effort on behalf of the moribund King of Rock and Roll couldn't dent the charts. Though eventually it went Top 10 in England, RCA decided not to release "Suspicion" as a single at home, and it faded away.

TO EASE THE GRIND at the Brill Building penthouse, Doc and Mort decided to branch out. Leiber and Stoller had made a mint by producing the Coasters; Burt Bacharach and Hal David had discovered a teenaged demo singer named Marie Dionne Warrick, who soon added another "w" to her last name. By getting into production, Doc and Mort stood to multiply their incomes and develop a project away from Hill & Range. All they had to do was find a young phenom and then write for, manage, and produce the act on record. They decided their ingénue should be a great-looking teenaged girl, to appeal to the young male record buyer; she'd also have to come across as wholesome, so as not to scare off the female fans. Mainly, she had to have stainless steel pipes and a natural grasp of the rock and roll idiom. MGM Records agreed to cover the initial sessions and offer their discovery a contract. Convinced they were on the trail of the next Connie Francis, Doc and Mort trolled demo sessions, quizzed A&R men and managers, and otherwise spread the word that they were looking for the next female rock and roll star. Their few leads turned out to be no-talent beauties or homely has-beens. After months of duds, Doc decided they'd been overthinking the problem. They'd appeal directly to the public. He had Elaine at Hill & Range phone in a notice to the classified sections of Broadway Bibles like *Show Biz* and *Backstage*:

> We are searching for a young very attractive great female rock and roll singer for a recording contract. Open auditions will be all day Saturday and Sunday, starting at 10 A.M., at the penthouse of the Brill Building at 1619 Broadway.
> —Doc Pomus, Mort Shuman & MGM Records

On Saturday morning at ten, Doc, Mort and Elaine surveyed the throng of hopefuls who'd gathered in the hallway outside the Hill & Range office. There were women of every conceivable age, size and appearance; dozens more poured out of the elevator as morning turned into afternoon. Elaine handed each a number. They decided that Mortie would accompany the hopefuls on the piano he'd dragged into the reception area from their tiny office, while Doc and Elaine took notes. Every girl would perform one song; if they liked her, they'd ask for an encore. At last, Elaine phoned down to the lobby, told the elevator operator "no more," and called in the first future Connie Francis. Girl number one— Jane someone—sang her song. She was awful, the second girl was worse, and the afternoon went downhill from there. At three, Doc, Mort and Elaine gathered in the outer hallway by the freight elevator and closed the door. Their nerves were badly rattled. They hadn't asked for an encore all day.

It was only after Elaine returned with sandwiches and about ten cups of coffee that they mustered the courage to go back into the reception area and call out the next number. The vanishingly thin woman who walked in wore black slacks, a tuxedo shirt, a top hat, and tap shoes. She looked about forty-five, chewed gum, and handed Mort the sheet music to "Bill Bailey, Won't You Please Come Home." She sang the first chorus straight through and tap-danced the next one. She had a keening, unsteady voice and stayed out of meter for the entire song. By the end of the song she and Mort were three measures apart. Doc and Mort stared at each other blankly before noticing that Elaine was hysterical, laughing and crying at the same time. When Elaine's sobs subsided, Doc turned to the singer and said: "Young lady, would you honor us with an encore?"

After about an hour of shoving and cajoling, the three of them managed to empty the hallway of the remaining girls. They quit the talent business then and there. Even if they had to rewrite every song ten times, Doc and Mortie agreed that they were better off writing for the real Connie Francis and Brenda Lee.

WILLI BECAME PREGNANT for the second time during *Fiorello*. She wanted a second child, and the pregnancy offered a convenient excuse to leave the production. After she'd spurned him, a lecherous co-star had turned vindictive and upstaged her at every opportunity. Geoffrey John Felder arrived on June 15, 1962. Willi's water broke while she was washing dishes after dinner; Doc and Mort were writing in the next room. Mort circled Doctor's Hospital on the Upper East Side several times in Doc's Cadillac before he spotted the entrance. The hospital didn't allow fathers into the delivery room, which was fine with Doc, who spent the night with Raoul and Mortie at Café Figaro, an espresso joint on MacDougal Street in the Village. He phoned the hospital every half hour. When he heard that Willi had given birth to a healthy eleven-pound baby boy, he handed the waiter a fifty-dollar bill. Complaining that the tip was too large, the waiter followed him outside and tried to give back the money. Doc finally persuaded him to keep it, hailed a cab, and headed uptown to meet his infant son.

After another long summer of diapers and interrupted sleep, Doc and Willi decided to take a vacation to Florida. Just as the nights on Long Island began turning cold, they squeezed them-selves, the children, and Willie Mae—along to help with the baby—in the car and headed south, Willi at the wheel. Along the way passersby sometimes mistook Doc—with his curly mane and gleaming Cadillac—for wrestler Gorgeous George. They spent a long, lazy week at the Aztec in Miami. Willi practiced songs from *The Sound of Music*, Doc lounged around the pool in a captain's hat and a white terry robe, and five-year-old Sharon suffered her first broken heart at the hands of a twelve-year-old named Russell.

On the way back, Willi took a shortcut along a rural Georgia highway. The Cadillac ran over a beer bottle and got a flat some-where in the night. It was raining and dark, and Willi hadn't changed a tire and didn't know how, so she drove slowly along the shoulder until she spotted a roadhouse. She pulled off the high-way, parked, and walked inside. It was a small room with a few neon signs and a jukebox. It smelled of stale beer and was empty except for a row of men's backs along the bar. Willi told the bar-tender that she was traveling with children and that they'd gotten a flat. Could she use the phone to call for help? He looked her up and down, and said in a low, even voice: "Get off my property." She began to explain again, thinking maybe he didn't hear her, but he cut her off. "You New York Jews think you can come here with your niggers and act any old way you want," the bartender said, louder. "Get the hell off my property!" Willi grasped the edge of the bar and asked whether anyone would help. No one moved. Through the window, she could see the idling Cadillac with its New York plates and Willie Mae holding Geoffrey in the backseat.

Willi stood on the median for half an hour, though it seemed much longer, trying to flag down one of the handful of cars that roared by. The rain made it hard to see, and she was crying. Doc cursed under his breath inside the car. There was nothing he could do to help, and he hated his useless legs more than ever. He wanted to call on some untapped superhuman force to tear the door off the car and rip the roadhouse apart board by board. Instead, he kept looking at Willi from behind the rain-spattered glass. A truck finally pulled over. The driver jacked up the Cadillac, changed the tire, and told them to follow. After he'd taken them to a motel in the next town, Doc offered him cash, but he refused. They talked for a while in their room. The truck driver told them he had five children, and he loved rhythm and blues. Apparently, the roadhouse they'd gotten stranded near had a reputation for rednecks and Klansmen. Before he climbed up into the cab and took off down the highway, he told them that his name was Youngblood.

When they got home, Willi and Doc packed toys, candy, and a stack of Doc's 45s into some boxes and mailed them to the address Youngblood had written in a matchbook. For years, Doc thought about him every time he heard "Rainy Night in Georgia" on the radio.

JUST AFTER WILLI had come home with Geoffrey from Doctor's Hospital, Elvis's "She's Not You" began its climb to number five. Doc wrote the song in thirty minutes with Leiber and Stoller, who'd decided to cheer him up during one of Mort's protracted trips abroad. Mort's absences were becoming the norm. When he was in New York, the two of them fought more than ever; the arguments only drove Mort farther away. His reconciliations arrived via air mail, written on the stationary of Lufthansa or Air France or one of the Aberbachs' European offices:

> Dearest Ol' Pal Doc—
>
> I hope by now you're not mad anymore as it was really not my fault and everything worked out O.K. anyway, except I think you will agree with me that the songs were not up to par, but this of course happens sometimes and we must except [*sic*] it, I guess. Apart from that, I hope you still love me as you know I do you. I guess we get on each other's nerves sometimes, but remember, I've been with you even longer than your wife has so take that into consideration, coupled with the fact that I'm still growing up . . .

If Mort was still growing up, his stay in Israel, where he traveled with his mother in 1963, pulled the plug on his adolescence. Mort was delighted to discover a land where everyone—cops, street cleaners, hookers, even the president—was a Jew. He wandered the countryside like an Old Testament prophet, bedded a kibutznik, stayed high for days, and played and sang Memphis blues at a Jaffa piano bar, inflamed with a newfound sense of belonging. Back in New York, missing the Holy Land and depressed about the prospect of spending weeks harnessed to the upright piano at Hill & Range, Mort headed uptown to a gathering place for Israeli expatriates called Cafe Sahbra. The nightclub in the Westover Hotel on West Seventy-second Street advertised a sultry chanteuse named Esther Thobi, "Israel's Latest Singing Sensation!" Thobi's jet-colored hair framed terrible dark eyes, like the ones in the old Russian folksong, and she was gorgeous. With each sip of sour Israeli wine, Mort fell deeper in love.

Mort forgot the Jewish prohibition against marrying a woman who shared a name with your mother. He wed Esther Thobi in New York on May 5, 1963; they were married again in Jerusalem. They honeymooned at her parents' house in Israel and fought constantly. Their clashes were physical, ugly, and unrelenting; he tried to kill her at least twice. Some nights Mort hid out in Lynbrook where, nursing a tumbler of whiskey, he narrated the chaos in hilarious detail to Willi and Doc. A year of marriage was all Mort and Esther could endure. When Mortie was looking for a lawyer, Doc recommended his brother. Raoul had never handled a divorce, but Mort wanted to avoid attention, and Raoul was family.

It became one of the year's most widely publicized breakups. Egged on by Al Albelli, the legal reporter at the *Daily News*, the papers dissected every twist. Thobi broke down on the stand, complaining of a sexless marriage. Mort's annual income was reported to be forty-five thousand dollars. The scandal's surprise beneficiary was the ordinarily soft-spoken Raoul, who emerged as a courtroom Svengali, as brilliant as he was ruthless. In a gasp-inducing denouement, Raoul somehow managed to get a handsome Dutch waiter who'd been best man at the wedding to admit on the stand that he'd had sex with Thobi before as well as during her marriage. Thobi's seven-hundred-dollar-a-month alimony request was knocked down to a hundred and fifty. "Waiter Spills Piping Dish," screamed the *Daily News* headline. Nearly overnight, thanks in part to Albelli's breathless reporting, Raoul had a new practice and a coterie of A-list clients whose dashed affections merited nothing less than the full remedy of the law.

AFTER THE DIVORCE, Mort grew reclusive and disillusioned. He drifted in and out of love affairs, drank heavily, and stayed away from New York as often and for as long as he could. For years, he and Doc had written three or four songs a week; now they were lucky to write once or twice a month. By February 1964, Doc and Mort's mood matched the pall that hung over the Brill Building after the Beatles made their first American TV appearance just down the street at the Ed Sullivan Theater. At 1650 Broadway, Aldon's young couples were writing songs for the Drifters and others that took on race and class and inequality, but the polite messages of "Up on the Roof" and "Broadway" barely registered, ringing hollow and staid alongside Bob Dylan's assaultive surrealism. The strangled suspicion that songwriting-for-hire had been rendered obsolete haunted the offices at 1619 and 1650. Even the squarest of the buildings' occupants felt the accusing air of tawdriness and political complacency gathering around them.

Hill & Range wasn't about to alter course. Elvis's increasingly pallid soundtracks continued to make millions; when they managed to write together, Doc and Mortie still churned out hits. "No One," which made its initial appearance on the B-side of Connie Francis's terrifically campy "Where the Boys Are," a song written by Howard Greenfield and Neil Sedaka, resurfaced as a record for Brenda Lee and unexpectedly for Ray Charles, who reconnected with Doc after relocating to the West Coast and ABC Records.

Wary to the end, Doc never put himself above the daily hustle of the song business. When Chubby Checker set off a Twist stampede, Doc and Mort hammered together "Queen of the Twisters" for the aging Bill Haley's unintentionally Dadaist *Twistin' Knights at the Round Table.* Nor did they scoff at writing an old-fashioned answer song—an attempt to milk a huge hit for just a little more. They cheerfully concocted Damita Jo's "I'll Save the Last Dance for You," while LaVern Baker's "Hey, Memphis" was nothing but a silly lyric set to the melody of "Little Sister." Mort was exploring writing with others. When Elaine's eight-year-old son kept interrupting them at the Hill & Range office, Mort and John Leslie McFarland wrote "Little Children," a Top 10 hit for Billy J. Kramer and the Dakotas, a group that had been discovered by Beatles manager Brian Epstein.

At home, Doc and Willi drifted apart. After *Fiorello,* Willi took more jobs out of town, traveling with the children to Fort Worth to do *The King and I,* taking a lead in a touring production of *Carousel* opposite Howard Keel, and even getting small parts for Sharon and Geoffrey. Doc stayed at the Forrest for weeks, sometimes months at a time. When they were together, sooner or later Willi steered the conversation to Doc's smoking and, especially, his increasing weight. She hated to nag, but she was worried. Doc had gone from two hundred forty pounds to somewhere in the middle three hundreds, and he was losing what mobility he had. What he'd once done routinely—standing on crutches, taking short walks, even bathing—was becoming an ordeal. Before he knew it, Millie and Raoul were carrying on about it, too. What did they want from him? He'd worked hard, quit drinking, and wasn't about to refuse himself one of the few pleasures he had left. All the talk of diet, exercise, and weight-loss retreats irritated him and made him anxious. When Willi kept on about it, Doc shouted her down.

Doc's parents visited Lynbrook nearly every weekend. A worried Millie lectured her son while Morris kept respectfully silent. But Millie was solitary in her mission. She wasn't about to yield any authority to Doc's wife, as mothers-in-law customarily did, and she kept Willi at a remove. Every week she arrived with bags of presents for the children; Willi complained to Doc that she was spoiling them. Occasionally, Millie phoned the house on Surrey Commons from her office at the nursing home to ask what Willi was making for dinner. "Put that in the refrigerator, dear," Millie would say, "the chef here has made Jerome's favorite dish and I'm bringing it with me." Willi would mutter something in acquiescence. Millie intimidated her, and besides, it would be rude to contradict her. Willi saw Raoul, too, as being firmly on Millie's side. What hurt her most was Doc's reluctance to stand up for her. He was sometimes irritable around Millie and his brother, but no more. Though she said little, Willi couldn't help but feel that Doc's inability, or unwillingness, to defend her constituted a betrayal.

When Willi and Doc felt close, she rested her head on his chest and he stroked her hair. Neither mentioned that their affection now rarely turned sexual. Willi was no longer the naïve refugee from small-town Illinois who'd called him "daddy." Already thirty and a mother of two, she'd realized a girlhood dream of being a leading lady on Broadway and felt more confident than ever. Willi no longer needed a protector. She was becoming dimly aware but hardly dared admit that she was ready for a new love. If he noticed her distance, Doc buried it. A part of him had always been resigned to being alone; if it was coming true, he didn't want to know.

On one of their commutes to the city, Doc heard a familiar melody on the radio. Willi was behind the wheel of a new, gold-colored Cadillac, and Lizette yelped in the backseat. An unknown singer named Terry Stafford had revived a song that Doc and Mort had written for Elvis two years earlier, making "Suspicion" a Top 5 hit. Doc looked out the window while he and Willi listened to the words:

> Every time you kiss me
> I'm still not certain that you love me
> Every time you hold me

I'm still not certain that you care
Though you keep on saying
You really really really want me
Do you speak the same words
To someone else when I'm not there?

IN NOVEMBER 1964, Doc got a call from a kid with a Caribbean accent asking for "Doc Poppas." It sounded like he was calling from a payphone. He said his name was Scott Fagan, he'd come to New York from the Virgin Islands by way of Coconut Grove, and he wrote and sang his own material. He'd gotten Doc's number from a friend of a friend; could he come over and audition some of his songs? The following afternoon Fagan knocked on the door of the tenth-floor hotel room that Ozzie the elevator man had shown him. Inside, he came face to face with a shirtless man sitting up in the middle of the biggest bed he'd ever seen. The man had long, curly black hair, a beard, powerful shoulders and arms, an enormous belly, and stunted-looking legs that he kept folded under him like a Buddha. He wore a sheet around one shoulder, toga-style, and looked up at him with small, dark, sparkling, curious eyes. He was at once leonine and homely; something about him made the teenager feel safe.

Fagan was eighteen, almost girlishly pretty, and sang with a strong, clear baritone. He did a couple of originals, okay teenage ballads, but he performed them emotionally, with real guts. When Fagan was done, just like that, Doc said that he and his partner Mort Shuman would manage him. He gave him some cash and told him to get a room at the front desk and charge it to him. Doc said he'd be the first artist signed to Pomshu Productions. In the meantime, Fagan went to work singing on Doc's demos—Mort was in England—and joined the flamboyant retinue that gathered nightly around Doc in the lobby of the Forrest Hotel.

Fagan had read Damon Runyon's stories. Sure enough, the Lobbyists struck him as the remnants of those glorious 1930s Broadway characters. He felt as though he'd discovered a pocket of nearly extinct aborigines. Their names—Freddie Future, Jackie Winston, Johnny Jungletree—fit the part. There was Broadway Johnny, a professional poker player who dressed like a mobster out of a hardboiled *film noir* and smoked five, five-dollar cigars every night. The cadaverous, goose-faced Damon Runyon Jr., the son of Broadway's famed chronicler and a capable prose stylist in his own right, sat beside him. Every day Runyon snapped dozens of photos with the Nikon that hung around his neck but mostly haunted his father's old penthouse apartment, where he staggered through bouts of copious drinking and intense depression. The lobby jester was a touching, homely kvetch who'd left his suburban home and job as an aluminum siding salesman in middle life to become a working comedian. Rodney Dangerfield had since bombed on nearly every stage in New York.

Doc sat majestically among the lobby's plastic flowers, surrounded by his court along with a sprinkling of aged has-been actresses and radio stars, failed bookies and retired boxing promoters, like the director of a surrealist play. He had time for all their hard-luck stories, conspiracy theories and memories of long-gone heists, and they repaid him with adulation. Sometimes, mid-conversation, Doc's head rolled down onto his chest and he dozed off. All night he'd drift in and out of sleep, never losing his place in the conversations that percolated around him. Doc was devoted to all the Forrest regulars, but Fagan sensed that for Doc the alternative to the lobby was a night alone in his room in front of the TV.

The landscape inside Doc's tenth-floor room was just as rich. A steady procession of visitors included Little Johnny, who'd arrive with sandwiches or Filipino take-out, and Ozzie, who brought fresh sheets and updates from the lobby, and a whole panoply of local hucksters who showed up to hip Doc to some strictly confidential, semi-legal merchandise that they always happened to be carrying on their person. Doc kept a hearty roll of cash in the room because he couldn't say no to the steeply discounted shirts, watches and jewelry. He stockpiled these treasures in the room's corners. As a goof, he'd bought a couple of chunky rings inlaid with turquoise and fake gems and wore them in bed, every day looking more like a tribal chieftain.

Around the Forrest, Doc had a reputation as a fixer. Residents came needing a dispute settled, or advice, or sometimes just a handout. Johnny Jungletree, whose drinking and manic spells were getting worse, came to dry out. Doc sent Scottie upstairs to check on Runyon, whom he often found on his bed blue-faced and near unconscious, the windows in the apartment thrown open and the curtains billowing as snow or rain poured into the room. Esther Phillips, the terrific, vinegar-voiced R&B singer who recorded for Atlantic, showed up at odd hours looking strung out and terribly thin and curled up across Doc's bed in nothing but a bra and panties. There was plenty of room on the bed; Doc had told her to come and go as she pleased. One morning while it was still dark, a tremendously stoned Phillips staggered into Doc's room. "Hiya, Doc baby," she slurred before climbing atop his huge belly and passing out. No matter how hard he shook her, she snored louder. Pinned, Doc couldn't reach his crutches or the phone, and finally gave up and fell asleep.

On a few occasions, the crew from the lobby relocated upstairs. When Doc finagled Dangerfield a break—a live spot on the Jerry Lewis telethon—everyone gathered around Doc's small black-and-white TV. No one made a sound as the Lobbyists watched Dangerfield deliver the familiar routine to a packed theater. Everyone waited for the big laugh, but not a soul in the audience even snickered.

All through 1964 and 1965, Doc spent most of his days in bed. He talked on the phone for hours with Paul Case, discussing demos and the latest sessions. When he left his room now, it was most often in a wheelchair. Some afternoons Fagan pushed him around the corner to the restaurant at the Loew's Midtown Motor Inn, where he met with A&R men or singers on the make like Sal Mineo and Bobby Goldsboro or talked boxing with Emile Griffith, the welterweight and middleweight champion whom Fagan knew from St. Thomas. Fagan and Doc listened to records for hours, old blues and R&B sides as well as recent ones, like the Beach Boys' joyous cover of "Hushabye" and the glorious booming records Phil Spector was making with the Crystals and the Ronettes. Doc also chanced upon a second Pomshu act—a trio of Jewish girls from Brooklyn named the Lovelites. They went on to join Spector's disintegrating empire but made only a single record before the Tycoon of Teen shunted them aside for another girl group.

Doc scrambled for co-writers during Mort's long absences. The hits already seemed like a memory. Their most recent Top 5 had been a song that ten acts passed on before it landed in the lap of Andy Williams, the former house tenor on Steve Allen's *Tonight Show* and the star of a maudlin variety series. Williams hated the song, too, but his producer persuaded him to make the record. "Can't Get Used to Losing You" sounded nothing like the middle-of-the-road stuff he was known for—the B-side was "Days of Wine and Roses." In the spring of 1963, "Can't Get Used to Losing You" became his biggest hit in years and revived a fading career. Mort's playful melody lightened the lyric's bitter goodbye:

> Guess there's no use in hangin' 'round
> Guess I'll get dressed and do the town
> I'll find some crowded avenue
> Though it will be empty without you
> Can't get used to losing you
> No matter what I try to do
> Going to live my whole life through
> Loving you . . .

It was only after spending a few weeks with Doc and Willi at Surrey Commons that Fagan began to understand the meaning of those words. Later, watching TV back in Doc's room at the Forrest, Scottie and Doc chanced across a popular commercial. A strapping Nordic man with a square jaw and a billowing coat smoked an Erik cigarillo aboard a Viking longboat that pulled into New York harbor. "Erik is Here!" the legend on the screen read.

The actor in the commercial, a Norwegian named Erik Silju, had starred opposite Willi in a touring production of *The Sound of Music.* "I think that's the guy Willi likes," Doc said quietly.

When Mort returned from England, the trio headed to Bell Studio to make Fagan's second single. Watching both halves of Pomshu Productions in one room, the eighteen-year-old singer began to wonder whether the lyric of Andy Williams's hit had really been about Doc's writing partner rather than his wife. In London, Mort had befriended Rolling Stones manager Andrew Loog Oldham and spent time with Mick Jagger and Marianne Faithful. He showed up at the studio with an English runway model on each arm, dressed in a Teddy Boy's Edwardian drape jacket and brocade waistcoat. Fagan could tell Doc disapproved. It hadn't helped that, in Lynbrook, Mort had bedded Doc and Willi's young governess, Bernadette, who sailed back to France brokenhearted. The unease between Doc and Mort was palpable, and the contrast unsettling. Like Fagan, Mort was infatuated with the British Invasion, with Europe, and with a new generation of singer-songwriters like Dylan. But Doc, Scottie could tell, wanted to turn him into a new Bobby Darin.

One afternoon, Paul Case brought Andy Williams and his manager by the Forrest. Doc felt sentimental about his and Mortie's last hit and told Case he wanted to meet the singer. "I don't have time for that," Doc overheard Williams say out in the hallway. Doc looked hurt for days afterward. He stayed in his room and played the latest Pomus-Shuman record that the tenor from Wall Lake, Iowa, had recorded. It was called "Wrong for Each Other," and it captured Doc's mood perfectly. "And one day you'll thank me for saying so long," Williams sang over Mort's swirling waltz. "For making an end to a love that was wrong."

AT NIGHTS, before his vigil in the lobby, Doc liked to see the lights on Broadway. Scottie Fagan pushed his wheelchair past the Ed Sullivan Theater and the bright movie marquees. He slowed down in front of the store windows, letting Doc take in the mannequins, the pyramids of books, the lit-up cars in the empty showrooms. Each was engrossed in private thoughts on one of their nightly trips when a wheel slipped off the curb. Doc tumbled out of the wheelchair onto the pavement. He didn't wear braces in the wheelchair, and when he fell his legs crumpled awkwardly under the weight of his upper body. Doc bellowed in pain on the sidewalk. It felt as though someone was scraping a long, dull saw along the sides of his knees. Fagan couldn't lift him on his own; it took four or five men to get Doc back in the chair.

An ambulance took him to Doctor's Hospital on the Upper East Side, near Gracie Mansion, where his son had been born. Doc tried to protest but the pain shut him up. The only vacant room was on the cancer ward. The doctor who examined him said the ligaments in both knees were torn and would take months to fully heal. Later that night, Doc was glad to see Willi and the kids, but he could sense the months of estrangement that lay between them. He was suddenly scared. When Mort came to visit, Doc implored him to take Willi to dinner and put an end to whatever thoughts of leaving she may have been entertaining. He told Mort to tell her that when he got out of the hospital he'd change, take better care of himself, be more attentive.

Over dinner, Mort and Willi reminisced about the Broadway Central, back when they'd been little more than teenagers, directionless and broke. The last ten years had been good to both of them. Weren't they roughly where they'd dreamed of being all those years ago? Mort's halfhearted attempt to persuade Willi to stay stalled. Instead, the two began to commiserate. They'd always liked each other, and over the course of the meal both of them discovered that their minds were already made up. While Doc was still recuperating at Doctor's Hospital, Mort told him that he was leaving. A few days later, Willi asked for a divorce.

For Doc, the weeks that followed were a great unfolding funeral. The last scaffolding of hope—or had it been denial?—crumbled away. The torture of memories and remorse began in earnest. He was confined to bed for the first week, and the four white walls of his hospital room, like the bleak soundtrack of his thoughts, began to drive him crazy. He'd begun to count the cracks and spots on the ceiling by the time he got permission to wander the halls in a wheelchair. One day, while exploring on another floor and wheeling himself down a hallway, he saw an elderly man in a wheelchair being pushed toward him. As he drew closer, Doc realized it was his father. Doc hadn't spoken to his parents in weeks. It turned out Morris had been in an elevator that fell several stories, and he had suffered a minor heart attack. Doc couldn't believe it when Morris told him that Millie was recovering on a floor above them from a broken hand she'd suffered in a traffic accident. All three were patients at Doctor's Hospital that week in the fall of 1965. It made Doc feel like a ghost.

To get away from his room, Doc lingered in the reception area where the cancer patients spent time with their families. He got to know a young couple whose daughter, a skinny twelve-year-old named Carol, was dying. They owned a stationary store, and when they found out Doc was a lyricist, they brought him bags of pencils, pens and endless reams of paper. Like most parents on the ward, they refused to face that their child was nearly gone. Every day, they recounted her progress to Doc. They always said she was looking better, convinced she'd turn it all around.

They were saying just that in Doc's room—their daughter hadn't been able to take solid food for days but they swore she was feeling better—when they mentioned that Carol had been talking about her favorite singer, Bobby Darin. When they left the room, Doc dialed Darin's number in Bel Air. It took him a day and a half to track him down. It turned out Bobby was rehearsing a television show with Steve Lawrence in New York. They talked for a couple of minutes, and Doc asked whether he'd send over an autographed copy of his new record for a sick friend. Darin promised he would. He burst into Doc's hospital room three hours later. He and an assistant staggered in under the weight of toys and packages tied with ribbon. Darin said he didn't want anyone to know he was coming and turn the visit into a publicized celebrity

photo op. It took Darin three trips to carry the last of the packages into Carol's room, then he closed the door and spent the rest
of the afternoon with her.

Six weeks after the accident, Doc returned to his room at the
Hotel Forrest. He'd never felt more alone. A couple of days after
he was discharged, Doc got a call from Carol's mother, who told
him that Carol had died in her sleep.

From Doc's journal, November 23, 1982:

The year was 1960 when Philadelphia's beautiful singing and non-singing young men ruled the kingdom of rock. It was Frankie Avalon and Fabian at Chancellor Records and Bobby Rydell and Chubby Checker at the Cameo label. Bernie Lowe was the music director and half-owner of Chancellor. He never smiled and always looked as though he had a permanent case of advanced dyspepsia. One day he approached Mort Shuman and myself about writing some songs for Rydell. His class way of doing it was to call up and say "write songs" as though he was sending us to the grocery store with an order. He was not exactly on familiar terms with respect or filled with the milk of human kindness. Mort and I came up with two songs; one entitled "Go, Bobby, Go" and the other was "I Dig Girls." After Lowe heard the songs he nodded vaguely, which meant that he liked them enough to record them, and soon afterward, in a neighborhood Philly studio, Bobby put down his versions on wax. They came out good but not great. Lowe mumbled that they would make active and interesting "B" sides, but he had an "A" side that he thought was an instant hit called "We Got Love." After more than a little prodding from yours truly, Lowe relinquished "Go, Bobby, Go." I convinced him that "I Dig Girls" had more to do with Bobby's image, and I said it in such a nonchalant way that Lowe never realized he was being handed a little bit of New York Con. . . . I think part of me did it because Lowe treated New Yorkers like they possessed a highly infectious fatal disease. He would never let them near the artist or the recording studios. Even the musicians and engineers were all home products and the session food was a Philly steak sandwich and Bassetts ice cream.

Later on that week I went to an Alan Freed show at the Brooklyn Fox Theater. I hung out backstage playing poker with Dicky Doo of Dicky Doo and the Don'ts, Dale "Suzie Q" Hawkins and Thomas Wayne, who had one hit called "Tragedy." We were joined by that sweet and lonesome-voiced New Orleans rock and roller—handsome Jimmy Clanton. After winning a few bucks I went down into the basement to press my luck shooting craps with some dude who broke me with dice

*that not only were loaded, but seemed to chatter "sucker" as
they rolled along the cold stone floor. I sadly went back upstairs
and watched the show from the wings. Clanton did his thing
and afterward I cornered him before he had a chance to sneak
out with a groupie or two. I told him I had just written a song
for him called "Go, Jimmy, Go." He was thrilled! I told him to
meet me the next afternoon at our office at 1619 Broadway, better known as the Brill Building. I had, of course, realized that
all I had to do on "Go, Bobby, Go" was to substitute any two
syllable name every time "Bobby" was mentioned in the lyric.
Now I had a brand new song specially written for Jimmy
Clanton entitled "Go, Jimmy, Go."*

*Jimmy showed up the next afternoon with his manager,
Cosmo Matassa, a legendary New Orleans studio owner. Mort
played and sang the song for them. I contributed to the back-
grounds and general conversation. Jimmy and Cosmo both
flipped out. Paul Case, the professional manager of Hill &
Range Songs, hired a great New York arranger named Bob
Mersey (who later became the head of Columbia Records) to
conduct and arrange the session. It came off great and Jimmy
had a smash hit with "Go, Jimmy, Go."*

*We didn't tell him the real story until years later and by
that time Jimmy was only too happy to remember only the
good times. . . .*

The Real Me

I write for those who stumble in the night.
—Doc

ON MORNINGS when Doc woke alone in his room and it was still dark out, he wondered where he was, and when. He lay in bed surrounded by shadows, and in the moments just before he'd cleared the last shreds of sleep from his eyes, he sometimes believed he was at the Broadway Central and it was 1956. When he realized he was at the Forrest and it was a decade later, he felt the familiar stab of disappointment. He'd traveled all this way only to find himself back where he'd started. At forty, he was living the way he had when he was twenty. Mort and Willi were gone; the house in Lynbrook was off limits; he was broke. The homeless cripple with a rattling tin cup who haunted his singing years had reappeared in his dreams. Doc sat up, squinted at the dull ache in his knees, and pissed into one of the plastic urinals that hung along the headboard. It was the late autumn of 1965 and the old acrid smell of failure hung in the air.

THERE WAS AN AIRY SUITE with a picture window overlooking midtown next to Doc's room at the Forrest. Doc rented it when Sharon and Geoffrey came to visit from Lynbrook and he enlisted Ozzie the elevator man's daughter to babysit. He considered the suite part of his tenth-floor domain. When someone new moved in for more than a few days, Doc sent his protégé Scottie Fagan to check them out. The suite's most recent occupants had been a

five-piece, all-girl bagpipe troupe from Scotland called the
Dagenham Girl Pipers. When they weren't gigging, the girls spent
weekend nights in Doc's room, listening to records and helping to
polish off the heaping trays of fried chicken. Doc headed up a
Forrest delegation to see them at a club called the French Quarter,
and later one of the Pipers took up with Scottie. They left in the
late fall, and the suite was briefly taken over by two hookers and a
pimp. The next occupants were a pair of coeds from the Midwest.
Doc sent Scottie to investigate.

THE GIRLS WERE ONLY EIGHTEEN. They'd been roommates at
a girls' college in Illinois and dropped out after their freshman year.
Fran was a slender redhead who wanted to study piano at Julliard.
The aspiring actress was named Shirlee Hauser. She was a cute
blonde from Darien, Connecticut, who'd done some modeling for
Lord and Taylor while in high school. Her first job in the city had
been at *Candid Camera* as an assistant to the show's host, Allen
Funt. When she kept dashing off to afternoon auditions, Funt
fired her: "Sugar Plum, we have only one star here, get it?" Shirlee
lucked into another CBS job, a children's program called *The
Captain Kangaroo Show*. After work, she'd managed to bomb at a
dozen auditions, get nosebleed tickets to *Funny Girl* at the Winter
Garden, and get hit on by Joe Namath at a Chock Full O' Nuts.
  Shirlee and Fran's first stop in Manhattan was a small hotel
that catered to older lesbians—something they didn't realize until
years later—near Gramercy Park, then the Hotel Warrington on
Madison Avenue across the street from the American Academy of
Dramatic Arts. The only distinguished thing about the Warrington was the name. The girls shared a bathroom with an old drunk
who had a habit of throwing his empties against the door. After
they happened across a rat skittering around in the closet, they
packed their bags. The hotels in the Yellow Pages looked identical, so Shirlee decided to poke a finger at the listings and leave it
to fate. The Forrest, on West Forty-ninth, wasn't too far from the
CBS studios and sounded just as good as the others.

The day manager showed them a spacious, clean suite with an uptown view on the tenth floor. The rent was laughably cheap. Shirlee fed him a line about recommending the Forrest to co-workers at CBS. As it turned out, she didn't have to. Shirlee and Fran soon realized that they were among a handful of legitimate women staying at the hotel. In fact, most press notices about the Forrest involved run-ins between celebrities and hookers. Shirlee heard that cops routinely dragged out a handcuffed Richard Pryor for beating up prostitutes. In the lobby, she'd noticed a number of B-list showbiz personalities wander in, buy a newspaper and ciga-rettes, and slip into the elevator to visit "a friend" upstairs. One of the friends lived on their floor. Sherry was a tall former showgirl who promenaded past them in the hallway in a full-length fur. When Shirlee found an envelope full of hundred dollar bills stuffed under her door by mistake, she knew who to give it to.

The Forrest came to life after ten. A jazz club called Embers West opened just off the lobby, and at night the music wafted into the hotel. The first Lobbyist Shirlee met was Rodney Danger-field. He called her "K.O.," for knockout, and sat her down on the couch to try out new material: "Only the clean stuff, kid." The group of men—some reticent and neatly tailored, others done up in gangsterish wide lapels and braying jokes—who gathered on the sofas and chairs among the potted palms and sand-filled ash-trays fascinated Shirlee. The cast changed nightly, but at the cen-ter sat a bearded, heavyset, animated character of about forty with an ironic baritone and laughing eyes. Shirlee had watched him for hours before she noticed that he used a wheelchair. Minus the beard, she thought he looked like the actor John Garfield.

It took her weeks to connect the guy in the wheelchair to the night noises coming from the adjacent room. Shirlee complained about the loud music and the opening and closing of doors to the manager, who ceremoniously told her—as though it was some kind of honor—that she lived next door to a famous songwriter. He rat-tled off a list of hits, but Shirlee recognized only Terry Stafford's "Suspicion," a song she hated. Now she was seriously annoyed.

She didn't think about him again until a knock on the door a few days later. Two guys—a boyish one with long hair and an island accent who introduced himself as Scott Fagan, and an older one with horn-rimmed glasses named Joe Kookoolis, Fagan's songwriting partner—invited Shirlee and Fran next door to meet their famous neighbor. His name was Doc Pomus. He wanted to apologize for the noise, Fagan said, and to ask them for a favor.

The Garfield look-alike sat in bed wearing a pullover sweater from Leighton's and blue polyester pants. He was picking at a robust portion of fried chicken. Doc offered it to the girls, and they ate and talked until morning. Fran left first, but something about the man made Shirlee linger. Doc talked to her as though they'd known one another for years—he told her he was separated from his wife, described his children, and rhapsodized about Joe Turner, who was a blank to Shirlee. She tried hard to sound sophisticated, but in truth she felt as square and tentative as the suburban eighteen-year-old she was. Still, something important was happening. She felt strangely excited talking to the much older man—half-pirate, half-Buddha—whose dark, amused eyes saw through her airs but remained kind. Before saying good night, Doc asked whether he could store some hi-fi equipment in their room when he visited his kids in Lynbrook over Christmas. Shirlee said sure.

HILL & RANGE dissolved an eight-year relationship with Doc by declining to renew his 1966 contract. When Paul Case told him, Doc felt like the floor under him was tilting and he was about to slide off the edge. But like the breakup with Willi, he later realized that he'd been half expecting it. Mortie was gone and he was missing a melody man; it had been nearly two years since he'd had a song in the Top 40. And just to walk the hallways of the Brill Building and 1650 Broadway was to witness the slow demise of an entire generation of popular music. Rock and roll was officially deceased. The Drifters, the Shirelles, the Ronettes, Connie Francis, Fabian, even Elvis—where had they gone? They'd been carted off and replaced with over-amplified rock bands and spiritual folkies and surrealist singer-songwriters with tapered-leg trousers and empty eyes. These cold-blooded new kids made the record hops and bull sessions and lead sheets and Twist knockoffs that preceded them sound irredeemably banal. The Beatles, the Stones, and Dylan had swallowed them whole. "I'm hot for you and you're hot for me—ooka dooka dicka dee," was Dylan's appraisal of the rock and roll records fashioned over Broadway. "Tin Pan Alley is dead," he told a reporter. "I put an end to it."

A raft of hope arrived in the guise of Donnie Kirshner. He'd sold his song factory to Columbia/Screen Gems, and Aldon relocated from its homey digs on the sixth floor of 1650 Broadway to a sleek new corporate office at 711 Fifth Avenue. Donnie returned Doc's old favor and brought him along, offering him a one-year staff writer contract. The new office was as cozy as an operating room, and Kirshner's composing couples—Goffin and King, Weil and Mann, Sedaka and Greenfield—were demoralized and up in arms. Kirshner was now an executive at a massive conglomerate and wasn't available to stroke their egos. None of it mattered. Before Doc could get entrenched at the new job, Kirshner was fired in a conflict about the management of a group called the Monkees. With Kirshner gone, no one knew what to do with the bearded guy in the wheelchair, and Doc wasn't about to stick around.

THE HOLIDAYS HAD PASSED, and Shirlee was talking to Doc in his room. He told her the stay in Lynbrook had been awful; he and Willi began to argue the moment he'd come through the door. Doc asked Shirlee about her Christmas in Darien, and gradually, she found herself telling him about her parents. Her father was a vice-president at Pitney Bowes; her mother, a tense, unhappy housewife who was uncomfortable with being touched. Shirlee's parents hardly ever raised their voices, but their marriage was miserable. Doc could relate. The way Doc described his own parents' marriage made Shirlee laugh out loud. She glanced at Doc from time to time as she talked. He sat up in bed and bantered with her casually, but when she answered his questions he listened carefully, maybe too intensely. She knew he was trying hard to charm her, and she liked it, because she was trying just as hard to impress him. Shirlee found Doc, twenty-two years her senior, oddly wholesome. He was everything that Darien hadn't been. After the Gregory Peck film *Gentleman's Agreement*, which was set there, the town became best known for its anti-Semitism. At twelve, Shirlee had already looked voluptuous, three or four years older than her actual age. She learned that in the hermetically sealed world of white, upper middle-class Connecticut, with its cocktail party manners and WASP politesse and secrecy, married men in their forties and fifties—men with respected surnames and yachts and eight-bedroom "hideaways" in Cape Cod—thought nothing of making a pass at a teenaged girl. By the time Shirlee left high school, she'd grown wary of older men. But she'd never met anyone like Doc. He was more at home in his enormous, broken body than any able-bodied man she'd known. He didn't hide a thing. Doc wasn't full of judgments and deferred malice—when it flashed, his anger stayed on the surface. And though even she, still a virgin, could tell that he was flirting with her, she was flattered rather than scared. While they talked, Doc got a phone call from Ray Charles. She'd heard the black singer's name before, but her taste in music ran toward the Broadway show tunes she'd performed onstage in high school. Shirlee pretended to be impressed.

They began to see each other more often. Shirlee preferred not to intrude on his nocturnal lobby scene and kept the Runyonesque characters at a distance. Occasionally, they intruded on her. One night, she and an actor friend shared an elevator up to her room with an emaciated, bug-eyed black man Shirlee had seen in the lobby talking to Doc. Her friend, a handsome, well-built boy who stood a few inches taller than six feet, was bantering with her and let loose a few phrases in an Al Jolsonesque black southern patois. When the elevator doors opened, the black man let out a chilling holler, tackled Shirlee's friend to the floor, and began punching him in the face. He'd broken the boy's glasses by the time the actor managed to run into Shirlee's room and lock the door behind him. "That guy is crazy!" was all he could muster. When she looked through the peephole, Shirlee was surprised to see the black man shuffle into Doc's room next door. Doc later explained that Johnny Jungletree only picked on bigger white men when he drank.

Sometime during that late winter of 1966, while Doc and Shirlee were winding down another hours-long, rambling conversation, Doc leaned in and kissed her. Shirlee didn't pull away. He was a great kisser, though she didn't have much to compare him with. She told him good night, her head still buzzing from the kiss, and walked next door. Somehow she never questioned the strangeness of what had happened. Shirlee knew she was pretty; men had hit on her ever since she'd arrived in New York. But she found Doc genuinely sexy—he made her feel original and smart in a way she'd never experienced, and unlike most of the young actors who made passes after rehearsals, Doc was never banal. What must have appeared strange to everyone else wouldn't strike her as remarkable until years later.

Scott Fagan, who'd lived with Willi and Doc in Lynbrook, watched the unfolding romance with disbelief. He thought Shirlee was the squarest girl in Manhattan. And the similarities between her and Willi were uncanny. It was as if Doc had discovered another Willi—as she had been in 1956—living next door to him at the Hotel Forrest. Heartsick about his marriage, it was as if he'd molded Shirlee out of thin air, Pygmalion-like, with an exertion of his will.

DOC HAD BEEN CASTING ABOUT for Mortie's replacement ever since he'd returned from the hospital. He'd tried writing with former Brill Building regulars like Helen Miller and George Fishoff—who'd worked on *Georgy Girl*, one of the shortest-running shows on Broadway—and even tried a few songs with a guy he'd heard playing piano at a nearby restaurant who turned out to be Louis Prima's cousin. Nothing seemed to take. Doc was beginning to think that Mort was irreplaceable. For an afternoon he even teamed up with Neil Sedaka. Like everyone from the old scene, Sedaka was scrambling to re-invent himself. Before they sat down to write, Sedaka nestled behind Doc's Wurlitzer and galloped through nearly every one of his old hits. When at last he looked up from the keyboard, Doc was snoring.

Doc finally stumbled across his new partner in the Forrest lobby. Broadway Johnny had never written a note of music. He was bright and plainspoken and carried himself with an unflappable dignity that distinguished him from most of the other Lobbyists. His real name was Johnny Mel. He'd been a war hero in Korea and came from somewhere in Rhode Island. Johnny's dream had been to open a cigar shop in his hometown after the war, but after the Veterans' Administration refused to help him secure a loan, he swore that he'd never work a legitimate job again. Every day Johnny wore a freshly pressed suit, smoked a handful of expensive cigars, and played poker. He was the best card player Doc ever met and prided himself on being strictly honest.

Doc sat in on some games at the Forrest; he knew he was pretty good, and Johnny told him so, too. Over the course of 1965 and 1966, Johnny taught Doc the rudiments of high-stakes poker: how to read an opponent's face, how to keep him from reading yours, how to bluff, when to fold, when to settle up. Broadway Johnny played all over town and occasionally on Long Island and in New Jersey, too, and began to bring Doc along. They split the take. They never lost much, and on a good night each made a couple hundred dollars. Doc didn't particularly enjoy the games—it meant spending sleepless nights at some dingy apartment around chain-smoking, addicted gamblers and occasional gangsters—but he liked the strategy and he liked winning and most of all he needed the money. The rock and roll muse had hidden her face from him. Without Mortie and Hill & Range, he was out of options. For the moment, poker was going to be his secret.

SHIRLEE LOVED NEW YORK with the deliberate affection of a transplant, and she couldn't imagine a hipper, more in-the-know guide than Doc. He took her to restaurants and delis hidden from the busy avenues, strange, dark rooms where a manager or waiter came out of the woodwork to hover over their table and shoot the shit. After dinner they'd head to the Americana to see Tony Bennett or Buddy Greco, or over to the Riverboat. The first time Doc took her to the Riverboat, Dusty Springfield was sharing the bill with Buddy Rich, and the headliners had a drag-out fight backstage. Springfield had punched Rich in the jaw. After her set, Dusty sat at their table, all soaring eye shadow and platinum bouffant, and complained about Rich upstaging her. When she left, Buddy Rich sat in her chair and told his version. Both of them cursed like Marines. Shirlee took it all in. It wasn't like anything she'd experienced while performing Gilbert and Sullivan with Trooper's Light Opera Company in Darien.

After the clubs, Doc and Shirlee returned to his room and listened to Aretha Franklin or Morgana King on Doc's hi-fi. Shirlee began to notice cracks in the presentation as the nights wore on. Sometimes, when they disagreed or she reminded him of something once too often, he'd snap and begin screaming, his face contorted into a dark, hostile mask. Shirlee was getting to know the flipside of Doc's Don Quixote persona. Behind the hickory-smoked baritone—Brooklyn accented, with a thick black undertone and a surprisingly literary locution—there was a weary, angry pessimist beaten down by wave upon wave of fear about encroaching middle age, an increasingly burdensome body, a lapsed career, a broken marriage, and a future he was convinced he'd spend broke and alone. It was harder, Doc told her, to deal with poverty at forty than it had been at twenty-five. Shirlee had met Mort when he'd stopped by the Forrest during some last-ditch attempts at writing, but the visits were doomed by awkwardness and mutual, mostly unspoken recriminations. Doc felt abandoned, and Shirlee thought that he resented Mort at least as much as his wife. Conversations about Willi filled her with apprehension. Shirlee doubted that Doc still believed he could save his marriage; more likely, his forty-year-old ego simply couldn't let go of the life he'd been living only a few years earlier.

In the spring of 1966, Doc moved out of the Forrest. Twice, while he was away at poker games with Johnny Mel, someone had burglarized his room. The thief took a gold ring, a pair of favorite cufflinks and a lot of cash, and Doc figured it for an inside job. After a string of tearful goodbyes from his Forrest flock, and with the help of dozens, Doc moved his possessions all of two hundred yards to Loew's Midtown Motor Inn around the corner on Eighth Avenue. Loew's was far more prosaic than the Forrest. As far as Doc was concerned, the one plus was its location directly across the street from Madison Square Garden. The fighters walked through the lobby and ate at the restaurant. After hundreds of nights spent in hotel lobbies and twenty-four-hour diners, Doc was adept at buttonholing people he wanted to talk to. He hit it off best with heavyweight Cassius Clay—since 1964 a Muslim named Muhammad Ali—whose love of gab matched his own. He opposed the war in Vietnam on religious grounds but had just been reclassified 1-A, fit for combat, by the Louisville draft board. Ali was hugely unpopular with the press and soon would be stripped of his heavyweight title and sentenced to five years for refusing the draft. In a booth off the Loew's lobby, Doc spent hours arguing with Ali about pugilism and race and Lyndon Johnson over massive portions of Yankee pot roast. At night, many of the Lobbyists stopped by to visit. Damon Runyon Jr. took dozens of grainy, black-and-white photos of Doc reclining in the neon twilight of the Loew's eatery, Ali grinning photogenically from across the table.

Doc moved out of Loew's a few months after he moved in. He'd enjoyed watching the fights and the Knicks' games at the Garden, and his occasional tableside interviews with contenders had been a blast, but the hotel was dead, an anonymous midtown stopover for sightseers from Omaha and St. Louis. Doc's friend, the comic Nipsey Russell, recommended the Henry Hudson Hotel on

West Fifty-seventh Street between Eighth and Ninth avenues. Russell took Doc and Shirlee to his penthouse apartment there, a huge, well-lighted loft lined floor-to-ceiling with books. The Henry Hudson was quiet and nondescript. Nearby theater companies rented most of its meeting spaces for rehearsals; the building stood amid a two-block stretch of restaurants and clubs. Shirlee began to understand that, for Doc, the details of the surrounding block—the location of the steps, the height of the curbs, the proximity of food, coffee and cigarettes, and other things able-bodied men rarely noticed—determined his days. Doc now went out only in his wheelchair. He got around his room on crutches, but one day he told Shirlee that he was through with them. The muscles in his arms had atrophied during his stay at the hospital, and he'd gained even more weight. Using the crutches was now simply too painful. Shirlee encouraged him to keep trying. "Don't you want to face the world standing up?" she asked. "Forget it, baby," Doc told her. "I just can't do it anymore."

When her roommate Fran gave up on Manhattan and went home, Shirlee moved to the Winslow, another anonymous hotel, on Madison Avenue. The distance only made her want to see Doc more. She still wasn't sure how deeply her feelings ran; it had taken nearly a year for their kisses to evolve into sex. Still, she visited him at the Henry Hudson nearly every day. Their favorite place on the block was Johnny Desmond's. It featured a few lounge acts and decent food brought by a thin, sallow Romanian waiter of about sixty. Every time they saw him he was completely stoned. Doc asked whether he was flying above Pittsburgh that night, and the waiter always grinned and nodded. Back at the hotel they spent nights listening to the record player or just talking, and if Doc was in a particular mood, he held Shirlee in his arms and sang to her.

One night at the Henry Hudson, after some friends had left, he turned to her and said: "I'm really over my wife. We're getting a divorce. I want it to be us now, baby. I really, really love you." When he told her before that he loved her, there was always a

whiff of stagy sentimentality that Shirlee mistrusted. This time he
was crying. Shirlee told him she loved him, too. When she said it,
she realized it was true. That night, after Doc had dozed off, she
began to sense his life pulling her in like a riptide along a deceptively calm break. She thought about his wife and children, his en-
tanglements and resentments, the flashes of raw anger that she'd
already experienced. For the first time she felt scared.

IN THE SUMMER OF 1967, Willi got the call from her agent that
she'd been expecting for weeks. After an audition and two call-
backs, she'd landed the lead in *Happy Time*, a Kander and Ebb
musical. The production promised to be a blockbuster: produced
by David Merrick and directed by Gower Champion, with Robert
Goulet in the male lead and Charles Durning rounding out the
cast. She'd taken over an existing role in *Fiorello*, but this was a
chance to *create* a Broadway role. Rehearsals began on September
19 in Los Angeles, and the play opened on the first of November
at the Ahmanson Theater before traveling to New York, so there
wasn't much time to get ready. With Raoul's help, Willi put the
house on Surrey Commons up for sale and rented an apartment on
a particularly seedy block of New York's Upper West Side on West
Seventy-ninth Street, where hookers patrolled both sides of the
street. The house sold for an early offer of $38,000. Doc thought
they should've held out for more but was leery of another argument. Fair or not, thirty-eight grand was still a useful sum.

When the sale went through, the realtor told them the IRS
had placed a lien on the house. It turned out that Doc hadn't filed
a tax return in five years. No one bothered to figure out whether
Doc had been misled by his accountants or, more likely, had assumed that the accountants were working magically behind the
scenes and never took much interest in his finances. It didn't matter. Nearly all the proceeds from the sale of the house went directly to the Internal Revenue Service. Doc hadn't saved, and
now the house was gone. He realized that in six years he'd managed to burn through a quarter of a million dollars. After the hits

and BMI dinners, the bespoke suits and the Cadillac convertibles, the lavish tips and the nighttime taxi rides to Long Island, he was utterly, completely broke. Willi hadn't fared much better. She'd let Doc handle the money, never signing a check, and now all she had to rely on was a promise of a good payday in Los Angeles.

There was one last thing to take care of before Willi left for the West Coast. New York was the last state to grant divorces solely on the grounds of adultery, a charge that was notoriously difficult to prove in court. Like hundreds of other Manhattan divorcees, Willi booked plane reservations. On July 8, 1967, ten years almost to the day after her wedding, Willi obtained a divorce in Juarez, Mexico, on the grounds of "incompatibility of character." It was nothing like Mort's acrimonious front-page split. Willi asked her brother-in-law to handle it; Raoul, already a top divorce specialist, filed the papers.

Weeks earlier, Millie had come to Lynbrook and implored Willi not to leave her son. It was the first time Willi had allowed herself to call her mother-in-law by her first name. They sat together and cried. Then they embraced. Of course, it was too late. Willi realized that the bucolic suburban house had suited her as poorly as it had Doc. The marriage, for reasons right or wrong, was over. There was a new start awaiting her and the children in California. After a day in Juarez, Willi joined her boyfriend Erik in Dallas for a brief run of *The Sound of Music*, then flew back to New York and began to pack her things.

The divorce papers were proof that a chapter of Doc's life was closed. Everything he'd once taken for granted—family, home, job, money, respect, even the ability to walk on crutches—was gone. The worst of it was that he wasn't sure what had happened. Wasn't he still the same man? Whom had he pissed off in the celestial front office? He was jobless, broke, and afraid, living alone with his wheelchair in a cramped hotel room. There weren't any answers.

THE ONE HAPPY VESTIGE of Doc's old life were his kids, and he wanted a place where Sharon and Geoffrey could stay when they returned from California. In October 1967, Doc and Shirlee found a spacious one-bedroom in a bland white apartment tower at 888 Eighth Avenue, just off Fifty-third Street. The rent was almost twice as much as it had been at the Henry Hudson, but Doc was tired of feeling like the prodigal husband hiding out in hotel rooms. He was making a go of it with Shirlee now, and he wanted to live like a family.

After a few dinners with Raoul and Myrna, it was Shirlee's turn to meet Millie. When Doc signed the lease to their new apartment, Shirlee and Millie spent a day at Bloomingdale's and Macy's picking out lamps, a sofa, a rug and end tables for the new space. Millie turned out to be tiny. She wore a tailored brown suit with stylish shoes and a purse and had the air of someone accustomed to being in control. They got along surprisingly well. Millie was relieved that Jerome had found someone so quickly, and after shopping she took Shirlee to a small, English-style teashop for lunch. She may not have been the catch that Myrna was, but Shirlee thought that she passed the test.

One morning, while zigzagging between the three daily papers, Doc came across an item in a gossip column. It said that the female lead in *Happy Time* had been replaced. Willi and the kids were staying at the Hollywood Landmark, and Doc dialed the number. Willi answered. She said it was true—a few weeks after the show had opened, producer David Merrick decided he wanted another girl for the lead. Doc could tell she was depressed about it, so he tried to be kind, biting his tongue for once about wanting the kids back in New York. Willi said she planned to stay in L.A. for a while longer. In fact, she was working more than ever. She'd made TV appearances, met influential people, and was sharing a manager with actress and singer Kaye Ballard. She thought she could make it work.

Doc didn't hear from Willi until three months later, in early February, when he got an urgent call from a surgeon at Cedars of Lebanon. Willi was in critical condition. She'd checked in on February 2 with acute peritonitis that she'd neglected during rehearsals. She was scheduled for a hysterectomy just as soon as they could bring down her fever. Her chances, the surgeon said, were fifty-fifty. Shirlee and Doc caught a redeye to California. Doc was almost as scared of flying as he was of needles and blood. He'd hated it since the trip to London and hadn't been aboard a plane in six years. Days earlier, he'd gotten a rush job to write the words to a prerecorded instrumental for a Dino De Laurentiis picture called *Anzio.* It was due the following day. Doc brought a tape recorder and headphones to his seat, and during the flight Shirlee watched him listen to the music over and over. He bobbed his head, eyes closed in concentration; he tapped the beat on the fold-down table and mouthed the words as they came to him, writing down the lyric in a spiral notebook. It was the first time Shirlee had watched him write. She could hardly believe it. She knew Doc was torn up about Willi, scared for the kids, and worried about money. But he worked in a trance, calm even during turbulence. The song was done by the time the jet touched down at LAX. Singer Jack Jones recorded it—a schmaltzy, overproduced thing typical of late-sixties Hollywood—three days later.

They ran into Frankie Valli in the Hyatt lobby. He'd been on the same flight and was frantic about his eardrums; he was scheduled to play the Hollywood Bowl but still couldn't hear. Doc phoned a delivery service to pick up the lyrics for transcribing, then called the hospital. Willi was awake and wanted to see him. In the taxi, Doc handed Shirlee a set of silk pajamas that he'd bought her in the lobby gift shop. "I think you better give those to Willi," she said. While Doc was in Willi's room, Shirlee sat alone under the fluorescent lights in the empty reception area. What was she doing there? She'd never felt younger or more exhausted. She decided that, if the trip brought Doc and Willi back together, so be it. They did have two children, after all.

Doc looked relieved when he finally came out. The surgery had been a success, and Willi was recovering. She'd been grateful to see Doc; when things had gotten really bad, Willi told him, it was Doc she'd wanted. He hadn't mentioned Shirlee because he didn't want to upset her. And there was one more piece of news: "Willi said she wants to get back together. Don't worry, baby," he added, catching the expression on Shirlee's face. "That was the morphine talking. It's all going to be different tomorrow." Sure enough, it was the last time Shirlee heard about it. They picked up the kids, who were waiting for them at the Landmark with their governess Pat, and spent the next two weeks taking in Los Angeles. Bobby Hart and Tommy Boyce, songwriters Doc had known in New York who wrote for the Monkees, shepherded them around town. Phil Spector showed up, too, on fire about a group called The Checkmates. Doc tried to get Spector to write: "Why don't you and me sit down and write some shit! Come on, man!" It was a line Shirlee had heard Doc lay on many of the players, stars, and even rank nobodies who'd shown up in previous months to pay their respects. It rarely worked, she thought, probably because it sounded so desperate.

Willi returned to New York at the end of February. L.A. had been rough on her. After she'd lost *Happy Time*, Desi Arnaz offered her a role alongside Kaye Ballard and Eve Arden on a TV comedy he was producing called *The Mothers-in-Law*. Willi agreed, only to learn the job required going to bed with the married, fifty-year-old Arnaz. Willi told him to beat it, and when he sent seven-dozen roses to her hotel room, she told the girl at the front desk to route them to the nearest hospital. After she checked out of Cedars and convalesced for a few weeks, Willi had had enough. She took a role opposite Erik in a four-week run of *Carousel* beginning in May in Johannesburg, South Africa, and headed back East.

She wanted to take the kids to Africa, but Sharon and Geoffrey were back in New York and didn't want another adventure. They had gotten used to new teachers and friends they'd made at the school for the children of the *Happy Time* cast on the Paramount lot. They missed the hotel pool and spending Christmas at Jimmy Durante's, and ten-year-old Sharon had fallen in love with Robert Goulet's stand-in, a soap opera heartthrob named John Gabriel, and later with Goulet himself. February in New York was cold and wet. Still, Sharon and Geoffrey got along with Shirlee right away. She was more like an older sister than a mother, and Doc had never been one for discipline anyway. Besides, the Cowsills—the band that became the model for *The Partridge Family*—lived a couple of floors above them at 888 Eighth Avenue.

Shirlee adored the children. Geoffrey was an exuberant, imaginative and utterly trusting kid with a Beatlesesque moptop. Freckles covered Sharon's face like confetti. When Shirlee had first met her at the Forrest, she'd been wearing one of the ensembles Millie bought her—a sleeveless, curly mohair dress, a white patent leather handbag that doubled as a wind-up music box, and white patent leather shoes—and looked like a miniature Doris Day. The four of them—along with their aged poodle Lizette, who'd taken to hiding in the closet—shared the one bedroom apartment. The children enrolled in the Professional Children's School near Lincoln Center, where they reunited with some of the friends they'd made during *Happy Time*, since the musical had already moved to Broadway. At nights Shirlee told Geoffrey bedtime stories, and after he fell asleep, she and Sharon painted their toenails and talked. On other nights everyone gorged on huge spaghetti dinners at Mama Leone's and afterward, mostly at Doc's urging, spent the last hours of the night whooping among the blazing, cacophonous pinball machines at the arcades on Broadway.

SHIRLEE DIDN'T GIVE MUCH THOUGHT to the poker games. All she knew was that a few nights a week Broadway Johnny came over with Walter, a sweet old black guy from Georgia who'd once worked at the nursing home for Millie. Walter owned a van with a ramp. The three of them took off in Walter's "handicap van" around six or seven, and Doc didn't come back until early the next morning. Shirlee knew he played cards to pay the bills and left it at that. It didn't bother her until Doc decided that the games weren't bringing in enough cash. Sure, on a good night he could win a couple hundred bucks, occasionally more, but on more than a few nights he barely managed to break even. There was only one sure bet: whoever hosted got a piece of the pot, and Doc decided that one night a week he'd run a game at 888 Eighth Avenue. The money was guaranteed, and he could stay at home.

Before a game, Doc's valet Little Johnny or Shirlee, sometimes with Sharon in tow, stocked up on supplies: salami, ham, a few loaves of pre-sliced white bread, mayo, mustard, cartons of Chesterfields and Marlboros, and oceans of coffee. They picked up fried chicken at KFC, and Doc had a case of liquor delivered from the corner store. Sharon and Geoffrey were packed off for the night to stay with Millie and Morris, who'd moved to the Bancroft on West Seventy-second Street. Before the players began to arrive at eight, Doc threw a blanket over the seven-sided mahogany table he'd brought from Lynbrook and pinned a sheet on top of it. Everyone played gin rummy until the last of the regulars had arrived.

The card players were a sadder, more desperate breed than the Forrest Lobbyists; for all their peculiarity and color, everyone was a stone addict. Each played several times a week and gave the impression that they'd paddle a rubber raft across a lake of fire before they'd miss a game. Roughly a third of the regulars were career gangsters and swindlers of various degrees of cunning. The rest were merely hooked; their only crime was gambling on the premises of a private residence in New York State.

A numbers guy named Harry the Horse took bets on the phone between hands of seven-card stud. The ancient Lillie Train arrived with a bowl of chopped liver. Johnny Mansey, a magnificently dressed gentleman mafioso and loan shark, dispensed inside dope on the latest tabloid crimes. Willie Wald, another small-time numbers guy who fancied himself a Brando look-alike, bragged about sharing a girlfriend with Englebert Humperdink and contemplated his cards with a hypochondriac's thermometer in his mouth. The best player was an intense, wiry sixteen-year-old in loud print shirts and polyester slacks named Stuey Ungar—a future gin rummy and poker world champion. His mother brought him to his first game. Win or lose, he never smiled, his face stony under a mop of greasy, straight dark hair. Mary, Chico Marx's still-pretty, platinum blonde widow, showed up with her much younger boyfriend. If anybody at the table cracked wise about Mary's departed husband, they didn't do it twice. Mary let everyone know that his name was pronounced "Chick-o," not "Cheek-o," and that she wasn't about to tarnish his memory with the likes of them.

Frankie and Kiki always arrived together. Frankie was scrawny and short with a huge beak nose and thinning hair. He wore cheap suits and shirts with collars two sizes too big. A head taller and plump, Kiki clung proudly to Frankie's arm. She wore lots of rouge and dark red lipstick and kept her dyed black hair in a flapper-style bob. In her bright print dresses and tiny high-heeled shoes she looked like a slightly mad, elderly Kewpie doll. From the moment Frankie and Kiki sat down next to each other, they launched into interminable Pinteresque bickering that drove everyone at the table crazy. Poor Frankie didn't win a single argument.

The Greek chorus was a revolving cast of occasional gamblers. There was License Plate Benny from the Bronx, who never showed up without a hand truck and a contraption that reset used car odometers, and melancholy, kind-faced Red, who kept his last name a secret from the other players, and some big mafia guys who looked like central casting clichés. Everyone hunched under the cover of cigarette smoke until dawn broke through the blinds. Someone was always taking a catnap on Doc's bed or hogging the phone. "The hostess" was usually a girlfriend or a wife. She ferried sandwiches and drinks and coffee to the card table in exchange for tips. It wasn't long before Doc asked Shirlee to hostess. She laughed, but he persisted. It wasn't like she'd have to leave the apartment, and they both knew she could make four or five hundred in a single night. When Shirlee finally relented, she told herself she was doing it for Doc.

Her first night was a disaster. The game had barely begun when a knock came on the door. Someone looked through the peephole and hissed, "Shit, it's the cops." Doc grabbed Shirlee's arm. "Quick, you got to flush the pot," he whispered. He kept a large bag of fresh, aromatic weed in his cufflinks box in the bedroom. Shirlee shook it out into the toilet, flushed, and ran to the door. The officers were in a good mood. They made a show of disapproval but were more interested in the gold records and music photos on the walls. When they found out the guy in the wheelchair was a famous songwriter, they let him off with a warning. The game picked up where it had left off.

In general, it wasn't hard work—making roast beef on Wonder Bread sandwiches, refilling coffee and emptying the ashtrays, mixing whiskey and soda and G&Ts—but Shirlee despised it. She hated it all—smelling the cigarette smoke mixed with body odor around the table, hearing the muttered obscenities of the acne-scarred heavies, passing some snoring, shellac-haired guy passed out on their bed, a Smith & Wesson poking out of his waistband. After each game she gave her tips to Doc and promised herself she wouldn't do it again. But somehow he managed to talk her back into it: "Please, baby, you got to work the game."

Doc told her he did it for the money, but Shirlee thought there was something more to it. The man she'd met cared only about music and his friends. She knew the card games were a cosmic fuck you to both the muse and to the business he now resented. The life he'd once had was trickling away. Shirlee couldn't help but think that every night Doc spent behind the card table was a rejection of everything he loved and wanted to be. After working seven or eight games, Shirlee told Doc she'd had enough.

In the early spring of 1969, to get away from the apartment and clear her head, Shirlee flew to a friend's wedding in Palo Alto and afterward decided to spend a few days in San Francisco. She was watching a war protest in Golden Gate Park, where she'd played as a little girl, when she noticed a stranger standing beside her. He was slim and handsome with shoulder-length brown hair, probably in his late twenties. When he introduced himself he spoke with a lilting Irish accent: John Moriarty, professor of literature at McGill University in Montreal. He was headed to a coffeehouse to read from a recent collection of his poetry, and invited Shirlee to come along.

It felt good to walk down the street with a man beside her again. When they passed a group of sailors who catcalled Shirlee and made some cracks about the poet's long hair, Moriarty put his arm around her shoulder and guided her away from them. Then he walked up to them and said, "I presume you have better things to do on your leave than get into a fight with me." To Shirlee's surprise, the sailors walked away. She wouldn't remember much about Moriarty's poetry, but when he read she liked his beautiful voice, his long legs and open collar, and the way he unself-consciously ran his fingers through his hair as he bent his head over the pages of the book. They spent six days together. They walked, read to each other, talked until dawn. On a few nights Shirlee came close to being unfaithful but always pulled away. She told Moriarty everything about Doc. He asked her to spend the rest of the spring with him in Montreal, and Shirlee daydreamed about it. In the end, she returned to New York.

Doc had asked her to marry him before, but Shirlee had always said no. Something about it sounded so complicated and final. Soon after she returned from San Francisco, Doc's proposals took on a new urgency. He became more considerate and attentive. Later, she found out that John Moriarty had written her two letters; Doc had opened, read, and hidden them away. Shirlee was furious. But she realized that she was in too deep. She couldn't let Doc and his children go. The four of them were bound by love and by Doc's ongoing predicament.

PHIL SPECTOR CALLED and asked whether Doc had enjoyed the two-dozen steaks from Lobel's he sent a couple of weeks earlier. Doc was nonplussed; he never got them. Soon after, the building manager at 888 Eighth Avenue wandered over with a malignant glint in his eye, bent down to Doc's ear, and whispered, "I sure loved those steaks." Doc got it right away. The manager wanted a piece of the games for keeping his mouth shut. He was the one who'd phoned the cops. Doc knew they had to leave— they could barely afford the steep rent anyway.

They found an affordable one-bedroom apartment on the eleventh floor of the Westover—an old hotel in the midst of being converted to a rental—at 253 West Seventy-second Street, between West End Avenue and Broadway. It was the same hotel where Mort had met Esther Thobi. Shirlee, Doc and the increasingly erratic Little Johnny moved their things there on a windy winter day in 1969. The place was smaller than the previous one, but the location was ideal: they were down the street from Morris and Millie's apartment, a short walk from Willi's, and oddly enough just a few doors down from the office of Doc's old friend Paul Case, who'd moved to Seventy-second Street along with the rest of Hill & Range Music.

The kids had moved in with Willi after she returned from Africa. For Geoffrey and Sharon, the contrast was severe. Compared to Doc, Willi handed down more curfews and rules, behaving more like a parent than a friend. The kids also got to know Erik. He was nothing but kind to the kids, but the situation was awkward on all sides. One day Sharon snuck a glimpse of Erik admiring his physique in the mirror wearing nothing but a pair of bikini briefs. When Willi toured or spent late nights at rehearsals, Sharon and Geoffrey stayed with their grandparents or headed back to the Westover.

Shirlee had met Willi at the old apartment on Eighth Avenue. Her first impression of Doc's former wife startled her. They looked remarkably alike. Each had blond hair, brown eyes, and stood roughly the same height. Later, Shirlee learned about a host of other similarities: both happened to be only children, were born in late April, and shared the same blood type. One thing they didn't share was confidence. Tentative and shy, Shirlee was not yet twenty-one, and Willi, who was in her thirties, struck her as remarkably self-assured. They got along surprisingly well. When Willi visited Doc, Shirlee left them alone. The two fought incessantly. Doc accused Willi of being theatrical and selfish toward the children; Willi said he withheld child support payments and let Sharon and Geoffrey run wild. Each was struggling, and money was the topic that ignited the loudest arguments. Their phone calls often ended with one of them slamming down the receiver. Shirlee felt for Doc but empathized with Willi, too. She'd learned firsthand how infuriating Doc could be when he was stewing about something. He sometimes shouted her down or, even worse, simply fell asleep mid-quarrel.

Doc never stopped writing. His bedside was piled with composition notebooks, the kind with the black-and-white mottled covers, and when he went out to restaurants and clubs he scribbled in matchbooks and on napkins. At home he turned his pockets inside out, careful not to lose the scrap of brown paper bag that held a few lines from the song that might finally turn his fortunes around. The quarterly royalty check was the only reminder of the old days. Doc would tear open the envelope and toss it aside, invariably missing the wastebasket, and bury his nose in the long rows of numbers. "Those bastards! I don't believe this," was the usual response. Occasionally, when the news was better, he'd announce to Shirlee, "Well, baby, tonight I'm buying you a steak dinner." The steak dinners got less frequent and the checks got smaller, an exception coming in 1969 when a white quartet from Belle Harbor, New York, named Jay and the Americans charted a Top 10 hit with their version of "This Magic Moment."

Always on the lookout for partners, Doc had learned how tough it could be for two writers to gel. So many things could go wrong—chemistry, taste, style, personality. The chances grew worse as the potential collaborator got older. With Mort, after all, Doc had gotten a chance to mold an inexperienced kid. He got the opportunity again in 1970 when he received a call from a Queens College student named Kenny Hirsch. After a stint in a rock band called The Sound Solution, Hirsch decided he wanted to be a songwriter and, in the time-honored tradition, began to troll the offices in the Brill Building. Someone there told him that Doc Pomus, the old-time rock and roll lyricist, was coming out of retirement. Hirsch wrote down the telephone number and dialed it as soon as he got home.

Hirsch had never seen an apartment like the one at the Westover. It was cramped, dark, with stacks of records and books everywhere. He found the famous lyricist in his enormous bed. Propped against the bed stood Doc's new possession—Mr. Bidet. Doc's wheelchair didn't fit through the bathroom doorway, and the new contraption was a portable toilet inside of which an evil-smelling solution disintegrated the contents. The chemicals' sweet, acrid odor permeated the bedroom.

The eager kid turned out to be Mort's polar opposite. Methodical, punctual and hardworking, at first he struck Doc as not particularly funky. But for the first time in years, Doc had a melody man to write with every day. He handed him a lyric and told Hirsch to see what he could do with it. Their first song was titled "We Got a Good Thing Going"; by the time they'd written four, Doc took Kenny to see Paul Case two doors down on Seventy-second Street. Hill & Range was a sliver of what it had been during Elvis's prime, and Case's influence had diminished. But now that Doc was working again, Case wanted to give him a push. He signed the twosome to a six-month deal. Doc would get $250 a week; Kenny, $75. Doc was thrilled—the rusty wheels of his career were again turning.

Right away the pair hit a wall. Writing songs was one thing, but getting them recorded was something else. Doc thought that the business had changed more in the five years since his last Top 40 hit than in the twenty before it. Kenny was green and didn't have many connections, and Doc no longer had the ears of A&R men and label heads. Nearly everyone he'd known from the old days had relocated or retired. Paul Case barely had enough work to fill his afternoons; Ahmet Ertegun was courting Led Zeppelin and the Stones. Doc and Kenny floundered. A song they wrote for

Elvis never reached him. They sent another called "I Hate Myself for Loving You" to Janis Joplin just weeks before she died. Roberta Flack promised to record "Sometimes It's Hard to Be a Woman," but somehow things never came together. It was the usual music business bullshit, except that Doc was on the outside now, plugging along with the other wannabes and has-beens. Kenny and Doc labored on, hunched over the Wurlitzer on West Seventy-second Street. They knew their break had to be waiting right around the corner.

THE HOTTEST young comics and singers performed at Bud Friedman's Improvisation on West Fifty-third. It was there that Doc found his old friend John Leslie McFarland staggering drunk among the tables. Johnny Jungletree looked worse than ever. "It's just the same old shit," he confided to Doc, steadying himself against a table and pointing at the stage, "except for this white chick named Midler. She's gonna be a big fucking star." Doc had never known McFarland to let him down in the talent depart-ment, so he stayed for the show.

The following morning Doc was wound up. "Shirl, you gotta come see this broad," he raved. "She's really not a great singer, but she's got that crazy energy, and she's so fucking original!" They ar-rived at the Improv late. The lights were down, and Jimmie Walker was already onstage in the middle of his monologue. Danny Aiello, a bouncer with whom Doc had gotten friendly, moved some tables to make room for Doc's wheelchair, and comic Robert Klein, scheduled to go on last, came over to sit with them. After Walker took his bows, the house lights went up and then down again, the drums began to pound, the music swelled, and finally the headliner sashayed to the stage, bowing over and over in mock humility. Bette Midler had a head of wild, reddish brown hair, had on hardly any make-up, wore a low-cut halter—showing considerable cleavage—and a short black skirt. Someone cracked that she looked like a Jewish parrot. Midler adjusted the mike, looked out over the foot-lights, and said "Weeeeeell!" rolling her eyes with pleasure, a coy grin spreading across her face. She followed some surprisingly raunchy patter with "Great Balls of Fire." She screamed, shouted, sank down to the floor and shimmied back up, skirt flying. She didn't have a huge voice but made for a riveting sight. Every pair of eyes followed Midler around the stage, and she thrived on the attention. After a couple of encores, she walked straight to Doc's table. "Hiya Doc," she said, sweating and out of breath, motioning the waitress for a drink. "Great show, baby," Doc told her.

Shirlee had never met anyone like her. Midler's last job had been a gig at a gay bathhouse in the basement of the Ansonia Hotel, but she carried herself with the confidence and ambition of Mick Jagger. At the table she watched everyone at once, soaking up every bit of information from the buzz that surrounded her. Offstage, she turned out to be sensitive, well-read, bright, and easily wounded. And Doc was right about one thing. She was a phenomenal performer. As soon as they got home from the Improv, Doc began to make plans for his new discovery. The following morning he was on the phone with Ahmet Ertegun asking, begging, him to see Midler that very night. "You got to, Ahmet, she's a star!" Doc pleaded. Ertegun promised he'd try.

After he hung up with Ahmet, he dialed a young producer at Atlantic named Joel Dorn. Having mainly produced instrumental jazz, Dorn took a vertical leap within the company when he brought in the young vocalist Roberta Flack, whose first record would soon go platinum, and was on his way to becoming Atlantic's youngest VP. He'd met Doc the previous year in the office of his boss, Nesuhi Ertegun, the head of the jazz division and Ahmet's older brother. Dorn had worshipped Doc's Ray Charles records as a kid growing up in Philadelphia, and when he heard that Nesuhi was in a meeting with Doc Pomus, he barged into the office and introduced himself. Doc had come looking for a writing partner, so Dorn paired him up with David and Eddie Brigati from the Rascals, a mix that definitely didn't take. But the two remained friends. Doc talked on the phone with Dorn nearly every day. He knew that if Ahmet didn't take the bait and go see Midler, Dorn definitely would.

In the meantime, Midler became a constant presence at 253
West Seventy-second Street. Doc offered suggestions about stage-
craft, timing, even her costumes. He advised her to tone down the
raunchy stage persona and concentrate on the songs. With Kenny
Hirsch at the keyboard, she practiced Doc and Kenny's songs and
even cut a few demos at a studio. Every day, Doc became more
convinced that Midler was the dynamite girl prodigy he'd been
looking for all along. They signed a contract naming Doc Midler's
musical director in exchange for a small cut of her gross. But
Midler was no ingénue. She took what advice she considered useful and kept her own counsel. When Doc tried to push through a
song she didn't like, or hammered on about a suggestion she'd already vetoed, she told him that he reminded her of her father. It
didn't sound like a compliment. Things got more tangled when
Doc discovered that Kenny and Midler were having a fling. He
disapproved, wary of the potential fallout, but Bette was a liber-
ated seventies woman. One sweltering afternoon at the Westover,
when everyone was crowded around the iced tea, bagels, and lox
laid out on Doc's poker table, Midler mopped her brow with the
hem of her T-shirt. She wasn't wearing a bra. Geoffrey was standing beside her. The following morning Willi was on the phone
wanting to know why Doc's buxom protégé had exposed herself to
their eight-year-old son.

When Midler gigged she sometimes took Kenny along as her
pianist. Together they worked the Hamptons and got a job opening for comedian George Carlin at the Playboy Resort in Lake
Geneva, Wisconsin. When the audience attacked Carlin after a
string of particularly cutting jokes, the three hid out in Carlin's
dressing room. Midler didn't have to play dives for long. Joel
Dorn finally caught her at Upstairs at the Downstairs in midtown.
There was hardly anyone in the club, but Dorn was riveted by
what he heard. He was taking it all in with his eyes closed. "Wake
up, schmuck!" Midler yelled at him from the stage. He signed her
to Atlantic Records over objections that her stage act wouldn't
translate to LP.

With Dorn at the board, she recorded an album of retro songs that captured her panache and wit. She slowed down "Do You Want to Dance" to ballad tempo, cut a swinging version of the Andrews Sisters' 1941 hit "Boogie Woogie Bugle Boy," and surprised Doc by recording Dion's "Teenager in Love" a cappella, backed only by the harmonies of the Persuasions.

But Midler's break had come months earlier, when she had gotten booked on Johnny Carson's *Tonight Show* without even a single to her name. She made the first trip to NBC Studios at Rockefeller Center in August 1970, with Doc and Shirlee. They watched her utterly charm Carson—Kenny accompanying her on piano for "Am I Blue"—from the green room. Incredibly, Midler was back only two weeks later. During her second appearance, Doc and Shirlee shared the couch with aging comedian Red Buttons, who was scheduled to go on next. During the commercial break it became clear that Carson had invited Midler to stay on for another segment and Buttons jumped up, outraged, and began to pace from one end of the green room to the other. "Come on, come on," he muttered. When he'd had enough of watching Midler vamp for Carson, Buttons grabbed his manager by the lapels and pushed him against the wall. "What the hell is going on here? Who is this fucking broad? Who the hell has ever heard of Bette-fucking-Midler??? Look at her! A vampire sucking up my goddamned spot! Go get Freddie or a stage manager! Someone!" He finally let go and threw up his arms: "I just fucking don't believe this!" Eventually he got the signal to head backstage and get ready for his cue. Red Buttons stormed out toward the wings, his suit tails flying. Midler, Doc, and the rest drove to an Italian restaurant on West Seventy-second Street to celebrate.

No one remembered Carson so smitten with a guest. Before the year was over, Midler made four more appearances on the show. On one of her segments she sang "Teenager in Love" while Carson, co-host Ed McMahon, and bandleader Doc Severinsen crooned the "ooh wah oohs" behind her, playing the Belmonts to Midler's Dion. In the space of a few months she'd become a household name. Doc's protégé had broken through spectacularly, but Doc felt as though he was losing touch with Midler. He read the interviews and profiles in magazines searching for a mention of his name, but never found it. And he worried about money. After all, while Midler chatted with Carson on TV, he still laid out the corned beef and baloney for the weekly card games. He confronted her about it one night when Doc, Shirlee, and Bette were about to head out to dinner. He wasn't hostile, but was direct. As she listened to him Midler looked crestfallen and tired. She covered her face with her hands and began to cry. Then she walked out.

Shirlee had grown to like Midler. At that moment she guessed that Doc must've appeared to Midler like another handler wanting to ride her coattails to the big time, while Doc suspected he'd gotten used and was being thrown away. After she left, Doc and Shirlee sat together for a while in silence. In the summer of 1972, while Dorn vacationed in Europe, Midler decided to re-record tracks from her still-unreleased first album with an Atlantic engineer named Jeff Haslam, and then re-recorded others with her new accompanist Barry Manilow. Only five of Dorn's original tracks made it onto the eventual record. "Teenager in Love" was deleted. Within months of its release, *The Divine Miss M.* was certified gold.

Doc saw her perform again someplace in Maine a few years later. He sat in the front row, and Midler acknowledged him from the stage, and after the show they briefly talked. But Doc never managed to put it aside or make sense of what had happened. He wondered about it after paging through Midler's book, and her subsequent biographies, only to learn that his existence had been expunged. It was like the disappearance of "Heartlessly"—one of those weird junctures where, despite his best efforts, the door was slammed in his face for no discernable reason. For years afterward, whenever he heard "Teenager in Love," he racked his brain about Bette Midler all over again.

THE MONTHS THAT FOLLOWED were even worse. The songs Doc was writing with Kenny weren't selling; the royalty checks got ever-smaller. The only steady income came from poker. Paying the bills was a high-wire act: each month Doc had to scrape together child support payments, tuition for Sharon and Geoffrey's school, rent, utilities, and supplies for the games. When his driver Walter retired, Doc shelled out for his own ramp-equipped van and kept a driver on call. It was the only way he could get to the games and to clubs. But it was almost impossible to find somebody willing to wait around, someone who was strong enough to occasionally lift him and broke enough to do it for the chump change Doc paid. Even when he found them, the drivers never stayed long. Over the years, they formed a gallery of psychotics, neurotics, sociopaths and the merely strange. There was the rabbinical student/baker who kept selling Doc on sure-fire get-rich schemes, the failed cop, the burnt-out hippie active in NAMBLA. A Swiss driver told Doc that his mother was a notorious kidnapper. A woman he'd hired complained about anal warts. Then there was Big Harry. Once, while driving on the Long Island Expressway with Doc and Joel Dorn in the back of the van, Big Harry began shouting something in the direction of a tiny MG convertible coupe in the adjacent lane that was occupied by a tweedy, middle-aged couple. Before Doc could figure out what was happening, Big Harry was leaning out the window and swiping at the MG with a machete.

A typical day at the Westover began whenever the first phone call jarred Doc awake. If it was a bill collector, Doc barked "wrong number" into the receiver and hung up. Otherwise, he took the call. On many mornings Doc greeted Shirlee with, "I'm up! Some knucklehead woke me up just to tell me he got my name from the phone book and he loves my songs." Doc usually told the caller to meet him in the afternoon at the Copper Hatch, a nearby diner. When Shirlee asked him why, Doc replied, "Aw, he sounds like a poor shlub. Some lost soul trying to get ahead writing songs."

Shirlee emptied the urinals and made breakfast. Sometimes they ordered in from the Star Coffee Shop across the street or the

Famous Dairy Restaurant down the block. If Shirlee or Little Johnny hadn't already picked up the three dailies and the unfiltered Chesterfields, the delivery boy brought them. Doc scoured the headlines and the club listings, picked at breakfast, answered the phone, smoked, and watched TV all at once. Then he'd use the bidet, take a bath—accomplished with a basin, two washcloths, and a towel—and brush his teeth, rinsing with water from one glass and spitting into another. After a shave with an electric razor and a small mirror, Doc got into the clothes Shirlee had laid out the previous night. He accomplished all of this himself, sitting up in bed. He called out for help only when he was ready for the wheelchair. Shirlee or Sharon or one of the drivers held it steady for him while Doc maneuvered himself in. Even with the wheels locked, if the chair slipped even an inch, he'd end up tumbling to the floor.

Most afternoons Doc had a visitor—someone from the old Brooklyn club gang, or Carole King, or the Japanese owner of Sony who wanted to meet the writer of those old Elvis hits—but mostly Doc headed out to a nearby café or just up the block for a breath of fresh air, pushed by Little Johnny or the driver of the moment. He tried never to have Shirlee push his wheelchair because it hurt his pride. For the rest of the afternoon he'd sit in the lobby, chat with the doorman, and watch the passing parade on Seventy-second Street. Sometimes he dozed off. When the sun set, he went back upstairs to order dinner or prepare for another game.

On nights when Doc got the kids, he liked to take them shopping. He'd buy Sharon a pair of silver earrings; Geoffrey might get a couple of 8-mm reels of Abbott and Costello. For dinner they'd go to Patso's for burgers or to El Faro for Geoffrey's favorite, chicken Villa Roy, or just order in and watch a movie on TV, everyone huddled on the bed with Solon, Doc's new border collie. When the kids were over, Millie often stopped by with lamb shanks and fried chicken. Sometimes they went to the Embassy right around the corner for a movie. Doc would park his wheelchair in the handicapped space behind the last row and promptly fall asleep.

In 1972, while performing in a production of Abe Burrows's *The Cactus Flower* in Dallas, Willi fell in love with an actor named Bob Brooks. They decided to marry as soon as his divorce became final. In the meantime, he moved in with Willi and the kids. The years following her stay in Los Angeles had been as hard for Willi as they'd been for Doc. Sharon and Geoffrey kept her busy, money was scarce, and auditions were harder to come by than they'd been when she was twenty-two. A Korean war veteran from Brooklyn, Bob decided that Willi's chaotic life needed structure. The obvious place to start was with the children. When he first met Doc, Bob tried to discipline the kids in front of their father, something Doc hated. Things got even worse at Willi's.

Sharon was already a self-possessed fourteen-year-old experimenting with boys, cigarettes and the occasional joint. She'd even changed the spelling of her name to "Sharyn." One day Shirlee found her at the door to Doc's apartment in tears, carrying a suitcase and her schnauzer, Beatlebaum. Sharyn said she'd argued with her mother, who told her that if she couldn't abide by her rules, she was welcome to leave. Shirlee dialed Willi's number but heard only the slamming of the receiver. Accusations flew back and forth for days. Doc was heartsick about the children and not sure what to do. Sharyn moved in with him and Shirlee, but Doc worried most about Geoffrey, who remained at Willi and Bob's.

In those days Doc found it hard to imagine that ten years earlier he'd been living with Willi and the kids in the suburbs, a Cadillac in the driveway and a hit song always on the charts. That life appeared absurdly remote. Now he shared a small, two-room apartment with Shirlee and Sharyn around the corner from the junkies in "Needle Park" and survived on card games he'd grown to loathe. Willi had remarried. And he could tell that the darkness around him was gradually driving Shirlee away, too.

On New Year's Day 1973, Doc's neighbor and friend, a schoolteacher named Roseann Quinn, was found stabbed to death in the Westover, a murder that inspired the novel *Looking for Mr. Goodbar.* That's how the year began. Doc never thought of himself as a depressive, but in those days he struggled to hold on to the better memories. The bills and the bill collectors were a daily anguish. The deadening hours at the poker table—Frankie and Kiki's bickering, the mobsters with their bulging sidearms, the smell of roast beef and smoke, all tainted with an undercurrent of dread—were wearing him down. Doc was nearing fifty, and the sleepless nights were getting harder to spring back from. He kept a loaded gun in a nightstand drawer. Even the landmarks of his former self were slipping slowly away: The Broadway Central, which had become a welfare hotel, collapsed suddenly in August, submerging lower Broadway in debris and dust. Damon Runyon Jr. jumped into the Potomac. Big Maybelle, just forty-two, died of diabetes and dope in her mother's house in Cleveland. And on a frigid winter night, Johnny Jungletree staggered drunk into an unheated tenement basement and fell asleep. They didn't find his body until the spring thaw.

ONE OF MILLIE'S CO-WORKERS was married to a teacher who ran an art academy in a small town in France. Millie wanted to get her sixteen-year-old granddaughter away from the poker games, her parents' arguments, and New York's sweltering, crime-ridden summers, and Sharyn wanted to go. Doc didn't have the money to send her, but Millie did.

Saint Germaine les Belles turned out to be as rustic as its name. The art school occupied a part of the Chateau de la Grilliere, Simone de Beauvoir's childhood summer home. The other Americans were mostly older, so Sharyn hung out with a twenty-year-old Queens College student from Jackson Heights who was renovating the building. At nights, Will Bratton liked to play the theme from *Last Tango in Paris* on his alto sax. He had long hair and a beard and raved about Elmore James and Howling Wolf. Before Sharyn left, he got her number.

The next stop was Nice, where her host was none other than Mort Shuman. Doc had tracked him down, and Mortie said he'd be delighted to look after *petit* Sharon. Mort was doing better than ever. After his split with Doc, he'd flipped for the Belgian chansonnier Jacque Brel and begun to translate his lyrics into English. *Jacque Brel Is Alive and Well and Living in Paris*, the revue he wrote with poet Eric Blau, became a sensation and played at the Village Gate for more than four years. In 1973, "Le Lac Majeur," sung by Mort in Brooklyn-accented French, became a number one hit across Europe and one of the best-selling French-language records of all time. Mort picked up Sharyn at a desolate motel and drove her in a tiny convertible to a villa in the hills overlooking the beach. His skin was tanned a dark umber. Passersby on the streets of Nice greeted him with cries of *mon Mort!*

For Sharyn, *chez* Mort couldn't have been stranger. Tanned, topless bathers sauntered around the house. Her father's old partner spoke English with a heavy French brogue and existed in a nimbus of cigarette smoke. "Watch your nipples, bay-bee!" he advised her before she headed off to sunbathe by the pool. Everyone dined on squab, then watched a Yorkshire terrier run across the table and eat the leftovers right from their plates. When Mort headed into town, he stopped every couple of minutes to sign autographs. He questioned Sharyn about Doc with grave concern. "I hear things there are so bad," Mort cooed, shaking his head wistfully and exhaling the aromatic scent of Gitanes.

ONE VESTIGE of the old days that Doc always enjoyed was the annual BMI award dinner. Way back when, he used to be an honoree; now he showed up because someone remembered to invite him. It was no different than any other awards banquet—long speeches, forced applause, chicken Diane with overcooked vegetables, and sometimes, depending on the table he was assigned to, a chance to catch up with some of the old characters. Just before the 1973 dinner, Doc got a call from BMI. A girl on the other line told him that John Lennon had requested to be seated next to him. On the appointed night at the Statler Hilton Hotel, Doc picked at hors d'oeuvres, resplendent in a tux, when he spotted John and Yoko making a beeline in his direction. Lennon stuck out his hand excitedly at Doc. "It's such a pleasure to finally meet the legendary Doc Pomus," he said in his famous Liverpudlian cadences. Then he offered his hand to Shirlee, but Yoko slapped it away and offered hers instead.

Ignoring the gladhanders, dignitaries, and Beatles business manager Allen Klein, Lennon and Doc talked the entire night— about Phil Spector, who'd been producing John and Yoko's records, about how Lennon and Paul McCartney had used part of the melody from "Save the Last Dance for Me" in "Hey Jude," but mostly about politics. Lennon pointed out two men in dark suits watching them from near the door and said that they were FBI agents who shadowed him and Yoko everywhere they went. They wanted to stay in the United States and reunite with Yoko's daughter Kyoko; the BMI dinner was their attempt to appear as respectable members of the establishment. They didn't know how long they could keep it up. Lennon was no longer the wisecracking presence Shirlee had remembered from watching *A Hard Day's Night* with her high-school friends in Darien. He looked intense and a little frayed. While he and Doc spoke, Yoko took turns carefully watching everyone at the table and doodling on the tablecloth. Before the speeches ended, Lennon made plans to see Doc again; he was moving to the Dakota on Seventy-second Street, and they were going to be neighbors. He also told Doc that the first song the Beatles had rehearsed together was "Lonely Avenue."

It had been a dismal year. Still, Shirlee hadn't remembered Doc as happy as he was that night, a warm breeze blowing through the van's open windows on their way home. Doc felt more surprised than flattered. He didn't believe in nostalgia. He'd left the old songs in the past, along with Mortie and the Brill Building and everything else that was useless to him now. What was he now besides a broke, middling poker player? But Lennon had made him think that maybe the best of what he'd done was more than just jukebox sweetener knocked off on spec, dated like a copy of last week's *Daily News*. He'd known it once and now remembered it again. It made him want to write more than ever.

ON ONE OF DOC'S VISITS to Atlantic Records, Joel Dorn introduced him to a strange character. According to Dorn he was a genius and the world's greatest session musician, having played with
everyone from the Stones to B.B. King, and Doc already knew
that he made intensely weird records of his own. The man who
shook Doc's hand was a huge, bearded frontiersman in a lizard
jacket and Old Testament sandals who carried a carved wooden
cane. He spoke in a self-made dialect—a mix of Creole, street,
and sheer insanity—that in comparison made Doc's Brooklyn jive
sound as staid as Cronkite. He'd named himself Doctor John, after
a nineteenth-century voodoo practitioner, and onstage appeared
in wooly Mardi Gras costumes. The guy hailed from New Orleans's
Third Ward and knew everything about Louisiana music down to
the name of the drummer on Eddie Bo's most obscure single. He
also knew all about cooking, gris-gris religion, extraterrestrials and
drugs. Doc liked him immediately.

Joel had an assignment for a movie soundtrack and suggested
that Doc and Mac Rebennack—his Christian name was Malcolm—
write one together. By the time they finished, the movie assignment had dried up, but they liked the song enough to try to write
again. Mac played the keyboard with the elegant skeletal funk
New Orleans was known for, and sang in a gravel-and-molasses
wheeze that sounded the way Memphis barbecue tasted. After
Doc figured out the vicissitudes of his vocabulary, he realized that
he and Mac had lived parallel lives. Mac, too, had spent his youth
imagining he was black. He'd been one of a mere handful of sig-
nificant white performers on the New Orleans R&B scene, and
when the time came to get his union card, he joined the black
musicians' local. By the end of Mac's first visit to the Westover,
when he sat on Doc's bed and improvised a slow blues figure on
the Wurlitzer, both of them knew that it could work.

They spent a few nights out on the town. Mac took Doc to the
Brooklyn Academy of Music to hear The Band record their *Rock
of Ages* album, arranged by Mac's New Orleans friend Allan
Toussaint. Doc remembered the group, who'd first recorded for

Morris Levy's Roulette label as members of Ronnie Hawkins and the Hawks, from the Hotel Forrest. Mostly, Doc and Mac got together late. The phone at Doc's apartment had stopped ringing, Shirlee and Sharyn had gone to bed, and both were at their sharpest at night. They'd order Cuban takeout and iced tea and write around the keyboard, passing a joint back and forth until their eyes ached from the smoke. In between songs they consumed cases of A&W diet root beer and watched Doc's boxing films. They liked best to regale each other with jive stories from the past, and one night, Doc shared with Mac a story that he'd kept to himself, his family, and a handful of his closest friends for more than twenty years: in 1951, Doc had been so broke that he sold "Chains of Love," which became Joe Turner's first Atlantic Records hit, to Ahmet Ertegun for fifty dollars. Mac grinned. He'd already heard the story from Van Walls, who'd sold his half of the song to Ahmet, too.

Mac loved to talk about the old R&B characters they both happened to know, in particular a New Orleans belter named Mr. G who in his heyday in the late forties worked Cookie's Caravan in Newark as Mr. Google Eyes. One night they decided to phone Google Eyes and spent a stoned, three-way long-distance conversation laughing about the Tibbs Brothers, Big Maybelle, and the famous barbecue pit just down the block from Bill Cook's nightspot.

Inspired, sated, and fully juiced, Mac and Doc would reach a hard-boiled near-telepathy, where just a few phrases stood in for entire sentences. "He's putting some weak shit on some strong people," Doc would say. "It just ain't right," Mac responded. While Mac talked about the "karaktuhs" he'd known in New Orleans, or expounded on his personal "musicnology," his fingers careened across the keyboard as though guided by a disembodied ghost, wringing the most inventive arpeggios Doc had ever heard out of the Wurlitzer. They usually wrapped when a neighbor began knocking on the wall. Mac gathered up the spent soda cans, said "so long," and headed home.

What Doc couldn't abide were Mac's spells in the bathroom. Sometimes he was in there for half an hour or more, and when he came out his face registered something between bliss and coma. The bathroom door stood behind the headboard on Doc's bed, and he had to twist his body to get a look, but he'd seen plenty of junkies. It worried him and pissed him off. Doc chewed Mac out, called him an asshole, threatened, offered to help. But he'd known addicts and he knew it took more than that to kick heroin. Sometimes Mac's old lady, a slim, striking singer and songwriter named Libby Titus, called looking for him. She, too, struggled with dope and pills. One night at a club Doc watched Libby and Mac stand with their arms around each other, teetering and weaving in place, each propping the other up. Playing the bad cop was a drag, but Doc couldn't lose Mac before they'd even begun. They had a bond now. As Mac liked to say, they were now "podners."

DOC GOT A REPRIEVE from the card games when a Los Angeles music publisher signed him to a trial contract in 1976. The company put him up on El Camino Real, not far from Melrose, in a comfortable suite overlooking a swimming pool, and furnished him with a twenty-four-hour driver. The publisher paired him with a writer named John Durrill. They didn't connect but managed to grind out one record, "Love the Devil Out of Ya," for Cher. Doc hated it. But he was grateful to get away from the gambling and for once wasn't too worried about things back home—Shirlee had just gotten a job she liked at CBS Records, Geoffrey was doing well at the Bronx High School of Science, and Sharyn had begun her freshman year at NYU. So Doc lounged by the pool, read Raymond Chandler paperbacks, and scoped the tanned California beauties. At night he made the rounds of the clubs, looked up Bud Friedman at his new West Coast Improv, stocked up on Western shirts at Nudie's Rodeo Tailors on Lankershim Boulevard, but mostly hung out with Phil Spector.

Their friendship was preserved in amber. Doc saw through Spector's worsening paranoia and erratic behavior to the winsome, brilliant kid he'd known at the Hotel Forrest. To Spector, Doc was still the benevolent father figure who'd housed him, nurtured him, and tipped him off about the business's shylocks and con men. It helped that they'd never gotten involved in a joint business venture. Still, each chose to see the other in the best possible light. Doc sent Spector's kids letters and gifts on their birthdays—he'd once mailed them a near-life-sized gingerbread house—and when Spector found out that Doc was broke, he mailed him a blank check, which Doc made out for four thousand dollars and cashed.

When Shirlee arrived to stay with Doc in L.A., they decided to spend an evening at Spector's mansion. After dinner at a favorite Jewish deli, Spector volunteered to show them the city. Doc's driver followed Spector's white convertible into the Hollywood Hills. As Spector gunned his car around hairpin turns, his bodyguards wincing in the backseat, Doc's van tried to keep up, the wheelchair rocking precipitously side-to-side. "Enough of this shit," Doc barked finally and told the driver to head back to Spector's. Everyone arrived at the mansion in tandem. As they neared the gate, Spector floored the gas. He tore ahead of Doc's van into the driveway, slammed on the brakes and spun the convertible sideways, showering everyone with gravel and dust.

Spector's fortress was an adult playroom stocked with recording equipment, pinball machines and odd statuary. Spector insisted that his bodyguards lower Doc in his wheelchair into the sunken living room. Doc protested, knowing it would be a hassle to lift him back out, but gave in. The night began pleasantly enough. Spector played piano and guitar. The conversation meandered. They talked about a recording session with Lennon and about the time Doc, during a previous visit to Spector's, mistook a suit-and-tie-wearing Leonard Cohen for Phil's accountant. Spector rambled about Darlene Love threatening a new lawsuit, his children, the Kennedy assassination, Paul Case, "River Deep, Mountain High," Sonny Bono, Lenny Bruce.

To get away from the cigarette smoke, Shirlee ducked into a bathroom and opened a window. An alarm blazed up around the house, and a pair of Dobermans snarled at Shirlee from the other side of the glass. A servant reset the security system. Spector's people seemed to think it was funny. By the time Shirlee came back to the living room it was nearing morning, and Doc was antsy to leave. He dropped hints but Spector kept talking. He was drinking wine straight from the bottle and decided it was time to show Doc his gun. He waved it above his head and pantomimed shooting. Doc had had enough. "Phillip—cut this shit out. Now!"

"Aw, Doc, baby! I'm just kidding around," Spector laughed, taking another swig from the bottle. He cocked the pistol and aimed at one of the statues.

"Phillip, fucking behave yourself and cut this sick shit out. I want your guys over here now to get me out and I mean it!"

Spector kept laughing but put away the gun and gave Doc a hug, telling him how much he loved him. The bodyguards lifted Doc out of the sunken living room. Back at the hotel, Doc tried to convince Shirlee that he knew how to handle Spector. "He likes me to talk to him like that sometimes," he said. After Shirlee returned to New York, Doc called her every day and told her about the good times he was having with Spector. It sounded great, Shirlee replied, but she wasn't sure she believed him.

ON JUNE 9, 1972, before his four-day, sold-out stand at Madison Square Garden, Elvis Presley held a press conference at the Hilton, and Doc decided to go. He was determined to finally meet him. Shirlee was standing near the podium, and when Presley appeared, tan and supremely gorgeous, he winked and said, "Hi, honey, you look just like my girlfriend Linda." Doc wheeled his chair toward the podium, but Colonel Parker blocked his way. The Colonel feigned small talk; Doc realized later that Parker had simply wanted to keep him away from his boy. By the time he got away from Parker the press conference was over. Doc made his way back to his table only to realize that he and Sharyn were sitting next to Elvis's father, Vernon. Sure, he'd take him to see Elvis, Vernon promised, but when they went backstage Presley had already left.

Doc thought about that afternoon—and about the bungled phone call that had woken him in Lynbrook—while watching Elvis's funeral on TV. A eulogy in some L.A. paper quoted one of Elvis's producers: "It's like someone just came up and told me there aren't going to be any more cheeseburgers." Doc knew just what he meant. The era of American pop he and Mort had belonged to—at once more innocent and more cynical than the one that followed—died in 1977 along with Elvis. Doc was convinced that the royalty checks were now gone. "Well, that's the end of the Presley money," he told Shirlee. But Elvis, whom hipsters and journalists had long scorned as a parodic, grandiose has-been, rose larger than ever from the public outpouring of grief. Reissues inundated the record bins. Doc's checks—helped along by a change in copyright law—were suddenly larger than they'd been in a decade and only kept growing.

It wasn't just Elvis. Everything around him was changing. Shirlee had moved out in the summer of 1974. She'd just turned twenty-seven and needed to figure out where her life began and Doc's ended. She'd begun to date, and couldn't stand the idea of hurting Doc with her comings and goings. He pleaded with her not to leave. They argued, then sat together and cried. Shirlee was about to sign a lease on a three-storey walk-up down the street when Doc wrangled her a studio apartment upstairs, on the seventeenth floor. He knew he wouldn't be able to visit her at the other apartment, and now she was just an elevator ride away. Shirlee couldn't bear to move away completely. She told herself it was a compromise. Still, when she brought dates home, somehow Doc always turned up in the lobby. Shirlee later figured out that the doorman tipped him off. In the end, she spent nearly as much time at Doc's as she had before.

Shirlee leaving put Doc's bullshit into perspective. For years she and the rest of the family had been begging him to stop smoking, arguing about his health as well as secondhand smoke and the

kids, to no avail. When she left, he tossed the last of his Chesterfields into the wastebasket. He didn't have much stomach left for
the card games, either. They'd turned dangerous. At a tense, late-
night game at someone's house on Long Island, two men had
burst through the door with drawn guns, flashed police badges,
and robbed everyone of their jewelry and wallets. "Don't look at
their faces," Doc hissed at Shirlee. She hadn't wanted to be there
in the first place and was suddenly shaking with anger. When she
defiantly stared at the robbers she thought they looked apolo-
getic. Before they left they warned everyone not to call the cops
and took along a hostage to make sure—Doc's hapless valet Little
Johnny. Doc thought he was going to have a heart attack, but
Johnny walked through the door ten minutes later. He said the
robbers had let him out at the corner.

It was a preview of things to come. A game at the Westover
was held up and cleaned out at gunpoint. Real cops raided Doc's
apartment, too, and this time took him down to the precinct.
Worse, organized crime was taking over gambling in the city and
took an unwelcome interest in his games. He knew he had to quit
when a made man who was a regular at his poker table went missing. A week earlier he'd been offering Doc a cut in a loan-sharking
operation; now he was a headline in the *Daily News*, fished out
dismembered from the East River. When Doc realized he didn't
need the money anymore, he was relieved to say goodbye to the
poker-night regulars for good. The last of the games petered out
by the early eighties. Doc felt like he was waking from a long,
bad dream.

WHEELCHAIR BE DAMNED, Doc tried to take in as much live
music as he could manage. With the games no longer monopo-
lizing his nights, he started to go out nearly every evening. And
he decided that he had to look the part. Doc hit the clothing
emporiums that catered to what was left of the Alley's clientele. He stocked up on extra-large cowboy hats, Western shirts,
loud pony-hide shoes and boots, and dusted off his old collec-

tion of big chunky rings that he'd bought off the Forrest shylocks. He haunted a store down the block that specialized in
turquoise jewelry; the store had two steps going down, so the
owner brought the merchandise out to Doc on the sidewalk.
The new look was a conscious decision. Doc had gotten used to
people staring at him wherever he went. Let them look and remember, he decided. He was going to go down fighting, go out
a "karaktuh."

Doc's driver whisked him up and down Manhattan to the
Fugue, Tramps, the West End, Mikell's, and two-dozen other
clubs. His favorite joint was the Lone Star Cafe on Fifth Avenue
in the Village, a long, two-storied space that trafficked in country
and blues. Spruced up in his finery, Doc rolled in through the
service entrance in the back and parked himself at his usual table
to watch Charley Rich, Roy Orbison or Delbert McClinton. He
could begin a conversation in a loud bar better than anyone; his
table was always full. Of course there was never a shortage of
posers and hangers-on wanting to hype themselves or talk shit
about others, but Doc cut them off with a well-practiced stare
that telegraphed street danger from underneath furrowed eye-
brows. But he enjoyed the young singers, songwriters and comics
who approached him looking for advice or a connection or who
just wanted to slip him a tape. Kris Kristofferson or Johnny
Paycheck sat down with him to talk or just to ask how he'd liked
the show; John Belushi dropped by to share a dirty joke or ask
about an obscure blues record.

Doc's van usually next took him down to Kenny's Castaways
on Bleeker, where Doc held court all over again and waited for
Mac to finish his show across the street at the Village Gate. He
had a swarm of regulars there, too: musicians, waitresses, writers,
young singers like Marshall Chapman and Shawn Colvin—it
never hurt if the singers happened to be good-looking broads.
Doc had time and an ear for anyone with an entertaining story,
anyone with a good joke or talent or even a decent face. They
whiled away their nights at Doc's table because he had the ability,

so rare in those touched even lightly by fame, to genuinely listen. Inevitably, he pulled in a share of "lames." He was, Doc liked to say, a mark for every asshole in the music business. In all those years spent in hotel lobbies and clubs, he figured that he'd heard every lousy hustle, every excuse, lie and boast there ever was. At a local stationary store he ordered business cards that read:

Doc Pomus

I'VE GOT MY OWN PROBLEMS

DOC LIKED TO INSIST that he hadn't been born gregarious. It came about as a result of being paralyzed. A shy cripple was always alone, so Doc devised ways—just as he'd learned to walk on crutches, or to move onstage—to befriend anyone in just about any situation. The wheelchair and his weight weren't about to hold him back. From his bed at the Westover he relied on the telephone to make introductions. If he read an article that riled him up, he'd get the author on the phone and tell him what he thought, good or bad. More than a few of those initial conversations turned into lasting friendships. At home, the receiver rarely came unglued from Doc's ear. "Can you believe this shit?" was how he began most conversations. He'd spend his nights on the phone communing with Gerry Goffin, whom Doc had met at a hospital while visiting Little Johnny, catching up with Herb Abramson or Ben E. King, or dishing about some industry troglodyte with writer friends like Peter Guralnick or David McGee. Kenny Hirsch was now based in L.A.; when he and Doc needed a new bridge or a better intro, they spent hours on the phone humming and reading lyrics into the receiver.

McGee, whom Doc had phoned out of the blue to say how much he liked his article on Merle Haggard, took Geoffrey to baseball games in Central Park and for a time shepherded Mac to Doc's apartment for writing sessions. Mac needed the help. McGee helped him get onto the cross-town bus that dropped

them off at West Seventy-second Street. On weekday afternoons it was packed with elderly women terrified at the sight of
Mac, who sometimes boarded the bus in full Dr. John regalia,
wearing what looked like a shrunken human head on a rope
around his neck. Mac was too gone to notice. When he was in a
talkative mood, he wanted to talk about football. "You catch the
Cowboys game on Monday?" he'd ask McGee in a sleepy, strung-
out voice.

DOC WAS SCOURING the concert listings when he noticed an ad
for Big Joe Turner at the Cookery. It was 1976. Onstage Joe
looked shaky and even larger than Doc remembered, but he
hollered as powerfully as ever. It was great to see him again.
Turner was booked at the Cookery for four weeks, and Doc was
there for every single performance. But the schedule was wearing
Joe down; he was getting winded by the second set. He was sixty-
five and must have weighed close to four hundred pounds. Doc
complained to the Cookery's owner Barney Josephson that Turner
was being overworked. When Josephson blew him off, Doc had his
driver walk across the street to a phone booth and call in a bomb
threat. The cops evacuated the club, and Joe finally got a day off.

Afterward, Doc and Turner rarely went a day without talking
on the phone. Doc's old hero was close to broke. Through some
amateur sleuthing Doc found out that for more than a decade
Turner's royalty checks had been mailed to the address of an ex-
wife in L.A. A battery of phone calls and a couple of threats later,
Doc recovered more than twenty-five thousand dollars in back
royalties for Turner. And he became determined to get him on
record once again. By the summer of 1983, he'd worked it out.
Joe Fields, the owner of the jazz label Muse, agreed for Doc to
produce a Turner session backed by Roomful of Blues, a band
from Rhode Island whose first record had been produced by Doc
and Joel Dorn. All Doc had to do was agree to work for free and
pay for the rehearsals. He said sure. Doc would've paid fifteen
times the money to work with Joe again.

They rehearsed at Doc's apartment, Turner sprawled in a chair, the Wurlitzer manned by Doc's neighbor Stuart Hemmingway. Doc and Turner had picked out some ancient favorites for the record; for the closer, Doc volunteered his and Mac's "Blues Train" and carefully wrote out the music and lyrics. Trouble was that Turner couldn't read and hadn't memorized a new lyric in fifteen years. Plus, Hemmingway was legally blind. The Felliniesque trio took weeks to learn the single song, fuelled by coffee, beer and Tab; Doc would sing, Hemmingway would play, Turner would sing, then they'd all sing and play together, until slowly and painfully it cohered. After rehearsals, Doc's driver gave Turner a lift to his hotel, and Doc, Shirlee, and Turner's red-haired, freckled wife, Pat, usually joined him for the ride. Turner was tipsy on beer and smiled wide, his tiny eyes twinkling. On his best days he'd serenade Shirlee with "Still in Love," his gargantuan voice booming inside the van.

The January 1983 session took place at the small, funky Jac Studio on West Fifty-seventh Street. Miraculously, the rhythm section and horn players had learned their parts, but Turner was preoccupied with a pair of broken dentures. When it came time to record "Blues Train," Doc parked his wheelchair facing the vocal mike and held the lyrics in his shaking hand, ready to mouth or whisper them to Turner in case he forgot them. But Big Joe sailed through without a hesitation. Doc didn't realize until the tape stopped rolling that he'd sweated through his clothes.

A couple of days later, he wrote about the session in his journal. He'd begun taking down entries in cheap, spiral-bound notebooks that he kept stacked near his bed. He wrote when he was alone and feeling his worst, and it never failed to cheer him up. The bad years were behind him. For the first time he was letting himself look inside. The music he was writing with Mac was different, too. The new songs were more like the Irving Berlin standards Doc had always admired for their directness, for being simple but not simplistic. The new lyrics weren't clever or slick, nor did they conceal hidden meanings. Unlike the three-minute melodramas he'd written with Mort, they took the form of confessions or distilled personal philosophies told quietly and confidently from an adjacent bar stool.

They proved a tough sell. Mac sang the demos with such singular style that everyone who heard them thought they'd been written specifically for him. But even though they weren't placing them with Top 40 acts, Doc and Mac still had the ears of their friends and heroes. In 1980, Mac passed along a tape of their songs to B.B. King. They got the good news right away; a recording date, with Mac on piano, was already scheduled. For months Doc looked forward to being at the Hit Factory, on West Fifty-fourth Street, for the session. The date fell on a frigid January night. Ice and snow blanketed the sidewalks and roads; Doc's van had broken down. He stayed at home. To pass the time he called his bookie and watched an old boxing film while the wind rattled the windowpanes. The telephone woke him at three in the morning. B.B. King's producer Stewart Levine was calling to tell him about the session. Everyone had been sitting around the studio when B.B., who'd been looking over Doc's lyrics to a song called "There Must Be a Better World Somewhere," suddenly began to cry. He sat like that for a long time, no one around him knowing what to do. After a while he told Levine that he'd thought about the lyrics for a long time and finally understood what they meant. Later that night, B.B. recorded the song in one take.

They'd written the song late one night after Mac told Doc about a hymn Deacon Frank Lastie used to sing at his Ninth Ward "spirit church." Lastie took it slow, like a funeral dirge, and one of its lines had always stuck in Mac's mind: "This earth is no place I'm proud to call home." In 1981, "There Must Be a Better World Somewhere" won a Grammy; two years later, the Joe Turner session got nominated. The awards made for a nice coda. But Doc was most excited that B.B. King had sung his song—the story he'd written about living disabled, about feeling every morning that he was stepping into the ring with one arm tied behind his back—just the way he'd imagined:

Sometimes I wonder just what I'm fighting for
I win some battles, but I always lose the war
I keep right on stumblin' in this no man's land out here
But I know, yes I know
There must be a better world somewhere

DOC AND GEOFFREY went shopping. After stocking up on
groceries at Gristede's they headed down the block to a knick-
knack shop called Noto's, where Doc bought a stack of greeting
cards, some for holidays he'd never even heard of. It was the
summer of 1986. Geoffrey was heading off to law school at
Emory University in Atlanta, and it seemed like a pleasant way
to kill an hour. Doc came home to a strange message on the answering machine. Someone named Gary Schaffner said he
worked for Bob Dylan and left a number and an extension. Doc
called back and left a message. An hour later the phone rang:
"Doc Pomus—this is Bob Dylan," a voice said in the receiver.
Dylan told Doc that he knew all about him and wanted to get
together.

The next afternoon Doc posted Geoffrey in the lobby to make
sure no one wandered up to the apartment while Dylan and his
entourage were there. As he sat waiting, scrubbed, combed and
cologned, Doc realized he was intimidated. It was a feeling he
hadn't experienced in years. Not even John Lennon or Ray Charles
or B.B. King had given him a tremor, but he just wasn't sure
what he'd say to the enigmatic poet laureate of the twentieth
century, the boy genius who'd single-handedly demolished the
Brill Building.

Dylan showed promptly at three. He was thin and quiet and
dressed simply in a button-down shirt, slacks and low-cut white
boots. His entourage was his gangly, bashful son Sam, who got
even shier after Doc kept calling him "Steve." Dylan was serious
and modest and intensely likable. Doc cracked a few jokes but
Dylan didn't smile, which made Doc talk faster and more haltingly, afraid he was babbling. Dylan wanted to talk about writing.

He was blocked. He said that when he was young he'd felt like a transmitter at times, but now in the act of creation he was self-conscious and his thoughts wandered. It all worked for a few minutes and then fizzled. He couldn't remember anymore what it had felt like to write easily. Doc thought Dylan sounded spooked. He told him that even though he couldn't be twenty again, his songs could still be thrilling and profound. All he had to do was believe it in the deepest part of himself.

Dylan stayed until dark. He told Doc that he liked the Eastern Parkway section of Brooklyn, where the Jamaicans lived. It was one of the few places in the city where he could walk the streets unrecognized. They talked for a while about the Village. There was a Bob Dylan look-alike contest at a club there that night; Dylan thought it would be hilarious to show up. All the while they were interrupted by the telephone. Before Dylan came over, Doc had put Joel Dorn up to calling him and now the phone rang every twenty minutes. Doc apologized to Dylan, picked up the receiver, listened for a moment, and then growled, "I'm too busy to work on your film, Mr. Coppola. Try me again in six months." Dorn cackled on the other end. Doc began to regret the ruse after two or three calls but couldn't tell Dorn to cut it out without blowing his cover.

Before he left, Dylan handed Doc a tape of riffs. If he liked them maybe Doc could come up with some lyrical ideas. He'd come back in September and they'd write together. They posed for a Polaroid and said goodbye. After Dylan and his son left, Doc sat in his twilit room dazed, not sure whether he'd hallucinated the whole afternoon. Finally he popped Dylan's tape into the stereo. Imagine, he thought, a little blues street cat like Doc Pomus writing with the Great Surrealist. Doc tapped his fingers to the music and began to relax.

DOC SEARCHED FOR JIMMY SCOTT all through the early eighties. They'd lost touch after Scott left New York in the late fifties, and Doc thought he was still living in Cleveland. The local musicians' union there put him in touch with some old-timers who'd known the singer slightly, but all Doc found out was that Jimmy had been working as a shipping clerk at the Sheraton and doing occasional gigs in nearby nursing homes.

So Doc was flabbergasted when, scouring the concert listings in the paper, he saw a small ad for a gig by Little Jimmy Scott across the river in Newark. He found his old boon in a dingy club performing for an audience of five, trying valiantly to make himself heard above the braying pickup band. But it was still Jimmy—though his operatic upper range had faded, he still sang with the same exquisite phrasing and emotion. After the show, Jimmy told Doc he'd moved back to New Jersey after his wife, Earlene, persuaded him to give performing one last try.

Jimmy had lived the life of a musical Job since they'd parted. In 1962, it looked like his days of obscurity were over when Ray Charles, a devoted fan, recorded him with an orchestra for his Tangerine label. The sublime "Falling in Love Is Beautiful" was certain to finally get Jimmy noticed, but it never made it to the stores. Savoy's Herman Lubinsky claimed he had Scott under contract for years to come and threatened to sue, and Charles pulled the record. Jimmy came out of retirement in 1969 and again in 1972, when Joel Dorn coaxed him into a studio and recorded a pair of albums for Atlantic. But Lubinsky squashed them, too, and Doc's favorite singer returned to sorting mail at the Sheraton.

It was a hideous tale, but Lubinsky was dead, and Doc wasn't about to let Jimmy slip away. Doc helped him line up gigs in the city and spread the word that Jimmy Scott, the world's greatest ballad singer, was back in New York. Doc called and sent tapes to everyone he knew—label heads, managers, music writers, A&R men. Once they heard Jimmy, he was sure someone would sign him to a deal; it was just a matter of getting them to the gigs. But no matter how often Doc ranted, begged and cajoled, hardly anyone showed. He just didn't get it. Doc vented his gall in a letter published in *Billboard* under the headline "Before It's Too Late":

When we talk about Jimmy Scott we're talking about somebody who might be the best singer of contemporary or vintage ballads around. There must be some space somewhere for him. What's everyone waiting for? He's sixty-two years old, he'll die and there'll be a hot funeral. Everybody will show up in hip mourning clothes and talk about how great he was. Let's do something now. I've shed enough tears for enormously talented friends who died penniless in relative obscurity. I'm getting good and pissed at the affluent members of the music community who sit around and pontificate and let such tragedies happen again and again.

ONE NIGHT Doc's club crawl took him to The Bottom Line just a block east of Washington Square Park. He sat at his usual table and watched an empty spotlight. Cigarette smoke wafted into the shaft of light from offstage while the sax player blew Earle Hagen's "Harlem Nocturne." Finally, Willy DeVille strode out of the wings and snatched the mike. With his pedantically trimmed pencil mustache he looked like a cross between a bullfighter and a Puerto Rican pimp. The tightest black suit clung to his thin frame; he wore a purple shirt, a narrow black tie and shoes with six-inch points. A pompadour jutted out above his forehead like the lacquered hull of a submarine. The show was the most soulful Doc had seen in ages. Onstage, Willy's band, Mink DeVille, had nothing in common with the New Wave CBGB bands that the press had lumped them with. Unlike Television, the Ramones, or Blondie, at heart Mink DeVille was an R&B band, and Willy, an old-fashioned soul singer. He'd borrowed much of his phrasing from Ben E. King and couldn't believe it when someone told him that Doc Pomus wanted to meet him after the show: "You mean the guy who wrote 'Save the Last Dance for Me'?" He was even more amazed when Doc asked whether he'd write with him. "Look me up. I'm in the book," Doc hollered before rolling away.

Working with Willy was always a challenge. He was conceited and vain and laughed at all the wrong times. Sometimes he showed up at the songwriting sessions with Toots, a childhood sweetheart he'd met back when he was Billy Borsay and lived in Stamford, Connecticut. Half French and half Pima Indian, Toots favored a pair of nose rings, snow-white kabuki make-up and a Ronettes-style beehive the color of tar. She'd once put out a lit Marlboro in a woman's eye just for staring at Willy. Toots and Willy were junkies. One of them was always shooting up in the bathroom or going out to cop more smack. When they weren't shooting up, they fought like feral cats.

Doc put up with the bullshit because writing with Willy could be a blast. While Mac drew from a blues and funk palette, Willy's sensibilities were more eclectic, closer to Mort's Spanish Harlem esthetic. His melodies ran the gamut from rock to flamenco, and his arrangements strove for the inventiveness of Leiber and Stoller. His lyrics were just as capable. One night, he showed up at the Westover with a chorus to an unwritten song jangling in his head, and sang it to Doc: "There's nothing that I wouldn't do / Just to walk that little girl home." Doc searched for the rest of the lyric. He shut his eyes and gestured manically with his hands as though pulling words from the air. Finally, he looked up and spoke the opening line: "It's closing time / At some nowhere café." They thought it should be a recitation.

Willy recorded "Just to Walk That Little Girl Home," along with the two other songs he'd written with Doc, in Paris. Augmenting his band with Elvis Presley's Vegas rhythm section and the string arrangements of film composer Jean-Claude Petit, he created a record that sounded like nothing that had come before. Doc's opening line to "Just to Walk That Little Girl Home," spoken over a ticking percussion and tinkling piano, gave way to an accordion. By the time the strings came in halfway through, it was clear that Willy had realized his fantasy of a new, completely contemporary Brill Building record. To the symphonic sweetness of the Drifters he added his own Gallic romance and, in his vocal, a measure of punk rock's Bowery grit. Doc was elated when he heard it. Thinking they'd signed a New Wave band, Capitol didn't know what to do with Willy's rock and roll chanson and shelved it for a year. When it was finally released in 1980, *Le Chat Blue*, remixed by Joel Dorn, made nearly every critic's list of the year's best records.

Working with two junkies proved vexing. Before the writing dates, Doc performed his ablutions and waited in a fresh change of clothes at the poker table, his notebooks and several tins of sugar cookies stacked beside him. Sometimes he waited for hours and wondered whether Mac or Willy would show at all. One night outside Doc's front door, Willy happened across Mac, who was leaving in a hurry. When he walked in, the air in the apartment was still charged with the tension of a recent argument. Doc told Willy that he'd just lent Mac his gun. Didn't it make him sick, Doc had asked Mac, to be so worried for his life that he needed a gun—just to get a fix? "That's all I got and all I love," Mac said to him, and walked out.

Mostly, Doc managed to write with Mac without too much drama; on a good night they could hammer out three or even four songs. The process was becoming second nature. One afternoon they wrote in front of the cameras of a German documentary film crew that had pitched camp at the Westover to get footage of the two Doctors at work. The first run that Mac played on the Wurlitzer became the final melody; they finished the song, titled "Black Widow," in fifteen minutes. The German director was furious. He accused them of having staged the whole thing. Doc and Mac just grinned.

Their songs became the foundation for two of Mac's records, *City Lights* and *Tango Palace*, both loose, funky valentines to New Orleans. Doc and Mac also furnished their songs to old friends like Chuck Carbo, Jimmy Witherspoon, LaVern Baker and Irma Thomas, who'd long ago recorded Doc, Mort, and Scottie Fagan's indelible "I'm Gonna Cry Till My Tears Run Dry." But their ideal interpreter proved to be R&B veteran Johnny Adams, known around New Orleans as the "Tan Canary" for his extraordinary pipes. A teenaged Mac had produced his first record in 1959.

Adams never managed to become a chart threat but all through the eighties remained a devastating vocalist.

Adams brought a jazz singer's approach to Doc's private, ruminative lyrics. He'd been knocked around long enough to grasp exactly what they meant. Like Mabel Mercer or Sinatra, he interpreted the lyrics with an intelligence that allowed them to breathe and resonate, steadying their gospel emotiveness with a precise and steely diction. Mac's uncomplicated, blues-derived melodies provided the perfect backdrop. In Adams's hands, the best of those songs—"A World I Never Made," "Blinded by Love," "Dreams Must Be Going Out of Style"—were masterpieces of concision, whole novellas distilled into a couple of verses and a chorus. They expressed Doc's vision more completely than any before them: they had the classic simplicity of an Irving Berlin song, the inventive storytelling of the best Brill Building records, the sinuousness of a jazz ballad, and the raw emotion of the blues.

Doc had come full circle. Like his first songs, the new ones were addressed resolutely to adults. He had never written so frankly; never had his lyrics been so unencumbered with the expectations of the record-buying public. He decided it was his reward for "White Bucks and Saddle Shoes," for all the years he and Mort spent toiling for jukeboxes and sock hops. He was getting old, and in his songs he wanted to talk about the life of a grown man. The young, Doc figured, would fend for themselves.

THEY WERE BRINGING BACK the old songs, too. It seemed as if every month someone came out with another cover. Bruce Springsteen, Emmylou Harris, even Led Zeppelin tried them on, though no one as lucratively as Dolly Parton, who in 1984 had a Top 5 country hit with "Save the Last Dance for Me." The royalties on that record alone exceeded what he and Mortie had made in a year. He deposited the checks, and took Shirlee along to Nashville to accept his award from BMI.

At the hotel, Shirlee was hanging her clothes in the closet when she heard someone singing in the shower in the next room.

She thought she recognized the voice from long ago. When the water stopped, Shirlee stepped out into the hallway and knocked softly on the door. Mort Shuman opened it. Someone at BMI had decided to surprise the authors of Parton's hit by booking them into adjacent rooms. Doc and Mort embraced and spent the night in Doc's suite telling stories but mostly just looking at each other like reunited siblings. Mortie was dolled up in a pair of cowboy boots and a Stetson. He'd grown tanner and bigger and even more theatrical. He was crazy about country songs; before long he and Doc made plans to write again in New York. Doc wasn't sold on the idea of country, but he was happy to placate Mort if it meant they'd work together again.

Doc floated through the awards ceremony. He introduced Mort to Dolly and Willie Nelson, but mainly stuck close to his old partner. He felt as if a long-missing limb had been restored; just the same, it couldn't help but make him suspicious. He hadn't forgotten about Mort's Houdini-style mid-song escapes from their Hill & Range garret. Back in New York, they met again at the Westover. Doc got choked up watching Mort play his old Wurlitzer, the same one they'd written around at the Forrest all those years ago. Later, Doc took Mort to the Lone Star to meet his friends. After the second set, Mort and Joel Dorn talked about Doc on the roof beside the club's best-known landmark, an enormous plaster iguana crouching above the Fifth Avenue lights. "Don't you break his heart," Dorn told him.

When Mort showed up to write, he was surprisingly punctual. He and Doc attempted a couple of country weepers and managed to complete one song. After Mort left, Doc played it over the phone to Dorn. Doc thought it was a terrific start. He couldn't help but wonder what it would be like to pick up with Mort where they'd left off. Each of them had learned so much in the interim. He just knew it was going to work again. Then, about two weeks after they'd begun, Doc got a message on the answering machine. "Doc baby, . . ." the familiar voice began. Mortie had flown back to Europe. Suddenly, Doc knew he'd never see him again.

BY THE END OF THE EIGHTIES, Doc was getting used to goodbyes. In 1984, Millie had been an executive for the city's Department for the Aging when she collapsed one morning while getting
dressed to go to the office. Raoul's driver was waiting for her outside. Millie was eighty-three and had outlived Morris by six years.
Doc's friend Paul Case was gone, too. Down the block, a de-
ranged fan had shot John Lennon in front of the Dakota. And by
1985, Joe Turner, Doc's inspiration, was no more. After the funeral, his wife, Pat, gave Doc Joe's copy of "Piney Brown Blues,"
his photo albums and a box of his jewelry. For weeks, Doc ceremoniously handed out the rings and medallions to his friends
and family.

Shirlee had finally moved out of the Westover, and was living
nearby on Riverside Drive. In 1984 she married Howard Friedman, a graphic designer who worked with her at CBS Records.
Their son, Joshua Jeromy Friedman, who took his middle name
from Doc, was born two years later. Doc bristled at the marriage,
but knew enough to give Shirlee her space. Their relationship had
been platonic for years; still, Doc knew that they loved each other.
Shirlee wondered if this was what polygamy felt like. It took
Howard a while to get used to Doc calling every evening to tell
Shirlee good night.

Not long after Shirlee got married, Doc and Willy DeVille
wrote "Something Beautiful Is Dying." If it sounded a little like
the Righteous Brothers' "You've Lost That Loving Feeling," Doc's
tale was altogether more anguished. His ability to suggest an entire narrative in the space of a few lines, and Willy's brooding
melody, combined to create another latter-day Brill Building standard. On record, the purring synthesizers couldn't dampen Willy's
cracked, pleading vocal:

> Your eyes are still that shade of smoky gray
> They don't melt now when they look my way
> My heart is crying
> Your eyes are lying
> There's something beautiful dying

Doc's old fears of solitude proved groundless. After Shirlee moved out, he found himself less lonely than ever. Someone was always visiting or calling, and he'd never enjoyed his family more. He'd meet Raoul and Myrna at the Copper Hatch, plan a trip with Sharyn, who'd married her boyfriend Will Bratton and was working as a photographer, or take in a Mets game with Geoffrey at Shea Stadium. On weekends, Shirlee and Josh came for brunch. After forty years, Doc reconnected with his college girlfriend Barbara Silver, and found new love affairs among a growing circle of admirers and young singers.

At his apartment, Doc inaugurated a workshop for aspiring songwriters. He held forth from behind the seven-sided mahogany table he'd once used for the poker games. The students brought their weekly assignment—a love ballad or a novelty song—and passed them around. The guests were a definite bonus—Tom Waits, Marshall Crenshaw, or Mac would stop by to give a talk, and no one soon forgot when Lou Reed put in an appearance, hazy from a double tooth extraction. Reed lived two blocks away and came over in the afternoons. When they weren't watching old fights on TV, Doc played him Joe Turner or Jimmy Scott records, and they spent hours talking about songs. When Reed kept after Doc to try to write without repeating verses, Doc replied it was too late. "I'm just an old blues writer," he'd tell him. Friends that saw them together hardly recognized Reed. The notoriously arrogant, self-obsessed rock Apollinaire became protective, even meek, in Doc's presence.

It felt good to be needed again after all the years on the margins. Doc rarely said no to anything. The work kept him in a constant swirl of people. There were always at least a dozen projects to attend to: he wrote the theme for the Easter Seals, helped John Belushi put together a band for *The Blues Brothers*, contributed a rockabilly pastiche for John Waters's *Cry Baby* that Johnny Depp lip-synched onscreen. There was a wrestling LP with Cyndi Lauper, a blues benefit at the Lone Star for a charity that brought entertainers to hospital patients, and many tributes to Joe Turner.

Eunice Kennedy Shriver tapped him to host a gala for the Special
Olympics, and Doc spoke often to disabled groups about striking
out beyond the confines of the handicapped world, a message that
didn't usually go over with the organizers of the talks. And when
someone from the White House press office called to invite him
to the inauguration of President George H. W. Bush, Doc told
him to shove it.

More and more, Doc spent his time making phone calls on
behalf of the R&B performers with whom he'd gotten his start.
Many had spent decades living in poverty, unable to afford a saxophone or a stage gown or even a pair of dentures, so Doc signed
on as a founding member of the Washington, D.C.–based Rhythm
and Blues Foundation, created with a donation from Ahmet Ertegun. It was a welcome reminder that once in a while even the
music industry could be coerced into having a conscience. Doc
hated the self-congratulatory meetings and galas, but endured
them for the sake of being able to pull a performer from the brink
of destitution. Along with writer Gerri Hershey, Doc made sure
the money found its way to the neediest cases. The first check
bought two Hugo Boss tuxedos for Jimmy Scott.

Doc got his happiest phone call on December 17, 1989. Mac
had finally kicked heroin.

Doc's favorite night of the year was his birthday. For
weeks before he'd hand out invitations to his famous parties.
Usually, by the time the birthday rolled around, Doc had already
invited three or four hundred people to the two-room apartment
on West Seventy-second Street. Eventually, so many people began
to show up that Doc posted a guy with a gun at the door. But no
one got turned away. The guests sat around eating fried chicken
from Popeye's and watching the action around the Wurlitzer. All
through the night Jimmy Scott, Joe Turner, Mac, and others took
turns singing amid the bedlam. When Leiber and Stoller were in
town, Mike's wife, Corky, who used to play harp with Liberace,
manned the keyboard. All of Doc's worlds collided at the parties.

Ellie Greenwich ran into her ex-husband Jeff Barry. Doc would introduce an MTV veejay to Otis Blackwell, Dion to Tom Waits. When he woke up the following afternoon it felt like a Jewish Christmas. Doc sat in bed, sipped diet soda, and opened his presents.

In the spring of 1990, Raoul announced to Doc that he wanted to throw a joint birthday party. Something lavish. It sounded like fun. Their birthdays were roughly six weeks apart, so they split the difference and picked a day in between. On June 13, Raoul rented Katz's, the cavernous East Village pastrami joint decorated with decades-old signs that read: "Send a Salami to Your Boy in the Army." He had klieg lights set up on the sidewalk; the corner of Houston and Ludlow streets looked like an opening night at Grauman's Chinese Theater. Guests poured in to fete the rock and roll songwriter and the nation's top divorce specialist. Lou Reed, Phil Spector, Leiber and Stoller, and Mac hobnobbed with CNN anchor Lou Dobbs, Martha Stewart, and the New York police commissioner. Once Jimmy Scott finished his set, Don Byron's klezmer band kept things rolling until the early morning hours.

Afterward, Doc told Shirlee that the cigarette smoke at the party had made it hard for him to breathe. Doc couldn't understand it. It never bothered him before.

A CALL FROM DOC woke Shirlee on a hot August morning. He asked her to come right over. When she got there, he was sitting up in bed. He'd had a dream, Doc told her sheepishly: "But Shirlee, it was real and you know I don't really believe in that shit." In the dream, a war was happening somewhere, and he was high up, in front of a big window that looked out on a vast emptiness. Then, he saw sparklers or fireworks shoot across the sky. Later, he was somewhere like a theater, but not exactly. Everybody he'd ever known was there. They were getting up on a stage and talking about him. They were saying such nice things, Doc told Shirlee, that he was "getting fucking embarrassed listening. But it was as though I wasn't there. I could see everything, but I wasn't there. Then there were people performing. Then my family and you and I were leaving, going down an aisle and out the door. Then everyone stood up and applauded. Then we took a ride somewhere."

Doc couldn't shake the dream for days.

A STUBBORN COLD Doc had picked up wouldn't go away. He thought he was having trouble breathing. "There's something wrong with me," he finally told Shirlee. They spent a day at the NYU Medical Center. Still terrified of hospitals, Doc submitted to every test except the bronchoscopy—the one where a camera had to be lowered into his lungs down his windpipe. The doctors told him the tests came back negative. "There's something wrong with me, Shirl," Doc repeated after they got home. "They just didn't find it."

GERRY GOFFIN was visiting from California. One of his songs had recently been a huge chart hit, but he disparaged it, wanting to talk about the old days. Doc was more interested in the future. You're never a has-been, he said, as long as there's something you still want. His cough was wearing him out, and he looked pale and tired. After saying goodbye to Doc, Goffin took Shirlee aside. "I love that man," he told her with tears in his eyes. "Please take care of him." Shirlee was suddenly worried.

One day in January 1991, Doc couldn't catch his breath, and Sharyn called 911. The ambulance took him back to the NYU Medical Center. That afternoon, Shirlee, Raoul, Geoffrey, Sharyn and Will met there and sat waiting for the results of the bronchoscopy. Finally, a doctor came out of the examination room. He walked down the long hallway to the waiting room without looking up. "He's got lung cancer," he announced. "He'll live three months if he's lucky." Sharyn began to cry. Doc asked to see his brother. He wanted to draft a will.

HIGH UP ABOVE FIRST AVENUE, Doc's hospital room had gotten as crowded as his apartment. The phone rang so much that the nurse turned off the ringer at night. Raoul came every day with platters of chicken he'd deep-fried himself using Millie's recipe. Ray Charles sent a tape. Phil Spector flew in from California. Lou Reed brought a new song he'd written about Doc called "What's Good" and offered to replace the tiny black-and-white TV in his room with a large color set. "Lou," Doc replied, "this isn't the time for long-term investments."

The tumor in his lungs had been growing for years and had spread to his throat; surgery was out of the question. Doc thought about Carol, the terminally ill twelve-year-old he'd met during his stay at Doctor's Hospital in 1965, and especially about her parents. Now he, too, believed he was going to beat the odds, that by some miracle the tumors would shrink and vanish. On his tape, Ray Charles sang a song he'd performed every year on the Easter Seals telethon, and to cheer himself up Doc played it over and over. It was a stately mix of gospel and blues. Doc had written "There Is Always One More Time" with Kenny Hirsch, and now he wanted badly to believe the lyric:

> No matter what you've been through
> Long as there's breath in you
> There is always one more time

Mac came by the hospital room to put the finishing touches on a song they were writing for B.B. King called "I'm on a Roll." "Make it sound like an old Louie Jordan thing," Doc told Mac before they said goodbye. "And don't fuck it up."

THE MIRACLE GLIMMERED for a few weeks. The radiation treatment had shrunk his tumors slightly, and Doc was feeling optimistic. It was Valentine's Day. All night the Gulf War had been on the news, and Doc turned off the TV. Shirlee was with him. She wore the white cashmere sweater that he liked, and he rested his head on her chest, and she held him. Together, they looked out the large picture window into the darkness outside. On a balcony of an apartment building in the distance, someone was setting off fireworks.

SHIRLEE, SHARYN, AND WILL took turns sleeping on a cot in Doc's hospital room. One night Doc's voice startled Shirlee awake. He was staring at a wall covered with roughly a hundred and fifty get-well cards. "They've taken them all down!" Doc screamed. "Get me out of here. Help me." Shirlee grabbed his hand and called his name, but he didn't see or hear her.

DOC WAS HAVING TROUBLE SLEEPING. Memories and thoughts raced through his head. One night two stoned nurses woke him up to ask for an autograph. Nobody in the world knew what it was like to die. He was dying, and he didn't know either. How did you make sense of the fact that everything you knew and remembered and thought was going to stop? He was afraid. In the darkness he made out the face of Sharyn's husband, Will. "What am I going to do now?" Doc asked him. He wanted to hear the sound of his own voice.

AT THE MEDICAL CENTER, the patients called Doc's physician "Dr. Shroud." He gave bad news to terminally ill patients. On March 12, he stopped at Doc's bedside. Doc had a lung infection and an oxygen tube in his nose. The doctor said the radiation treatments hadn't worked. He told Doc to take care of his affairs; there wasn't much time. After he walked out, Doc fell into a deep sleep.

The following afternoon Shirlee was helping Joshua with a school play when she got a call from Will. Doc's blood work looked bad; she had to come to the hospital right away. When she got there, Raoul, Geoffrey, Sharyn and Will stood around the bed. All night Doc drifted in and out of consciousness. Geoffrey massaged his shoulders. Sharyn put on a Joe Turner tape, but Doc motioned her to turn it off. He asked everyone to spend a few moments alone with him, and said something to each one. At night the nurse gave him a shot of morphine to ease the pain. Around three thirty in the morning, Doc opened his eyes. He looked around him and said "thank you." A moment later he was gone.

THE RIVERSIDE FUNERAL HOME on Amsterdam Avenue was filled to capacity. Raoul had loudspeakers posted at the entrance to make sure the hundreds more who waited outside could hear the service. Doc's casket stood on a dais at the front of the hall. Seemingly everyone who'd known Doc showed up. In the chapel, record company executives sat shoulder to shoulder with every doorman from Doc's building. No one had ever played R&B in the synagogue, but as the service began a tape of Doc singing could be heard faintly over the PA. One by one, Ahmet Ertegun, Phil Spector, Mac, Lou Reed, Lone Star owner Mort Cooperman and a half-dozen others came to the podium to speak. Hunched over a tiny, wheezing organ, Mac sang "My Buddy," Gus Kahn's Tin Pan Alley standard, and "There Must Be a Better World Somewhere." Then he played while Jimmy Scott sang George and Ira Gershwin's "Someone to Watch Over Me." The vaulted ceiling echoed Jimmy's piercing tenor.

"Save the Last Dance for Me" rang out over the sound system as the service concluded. Doc's family followed the casket down the aisle. Everyone in the pews suddenly stood and applauded, and Doc's dream returned to Shirlee like a slap.

Doc had one last piece of business to take care of. During the service, Sire Records honcho Seymour Stein racked his brain about the tiny old black guy who'd sang the Gershwin ballad. Why hadn't he heard him before? As the crowd filed out of the chapel, he took hold of Jimmy Scott's arm. Shortly after the funeral, Stein signed him to a five-record deal.

Introduction to an unwritten memoir, February 21, 1984:

I was never one of those happy cripples who stumbled around smiling and shiny-eyed, trying to get the world to cluck its tongue and shake its head sadly in my direction. They'd never look at me and say, "What a wonderful, courageous fellow."

I was always too fucking mad and didn't have a chip, but a great big log on my shoulder, daring the world to get in my way or mess with me. I walked slow and straight and never swung my legs fast and awkwardly like the rest of the gimps who got around with braces and crutches. My main thing was to act and look cool—angry, and cool and sharp. I talked the hip talk of the jazzmen and dressed like Bed-Stuy and Harlem. I was gonna be the first heavy-weight boxing champion on crutches— a one punch knockout killer. Or maybe the first major league pitcher on crutches—firing endless, unhittable strikes. Or maybe I'd be the first famous bandleader waving his baton with one hand and leaning on his crutch with the other. And I was gonna make love to the most beautiful exciting women in the world, and they would all love me passionately and forever. I was going to be the most extraordinary and talented and virile man that ever lived.

And underneath I was a frightened little kid—afraid that my limited physical equipment was not enough to get me any kind of piece of the action out there. I would end up a street beggar hustling quarters, or be just another bed in a cold state institution, or live in a welfare hotel sharing a toilet with some diseased junkie or hooker. Most of the time I shut this out with the help of booze, pot, insanity or blindness; or a combination of any or all of it. But once in a while I would lay in a sleazy hotel room with the soiled bedcovers over my head—too scared to move, sometimes for days and nights—sleepless and trembling. And when it got like that I never knew when it would end, or how it would end, or if it would ever end, but it always did. Now, thirty or forty years later, it happens less and less, and I've found corners of myself and the world that I own more than once in a while. And some mornings when I wake up and look around, I even smile deep and feel like it's good to be here and to be me. But it sure took a long fucking time.

Afterword

Doc liked to joke that someday he'd be buried near a race-track. He was laid to rest near Millie and Morris in Elmont, New York, where the Belmont Stakes is run. Family and friends sat shivah at a spacious two-bedroom apartment just down the street from the Westover, on West Seventy-second Street and Broadway, where Doc had been planning to move. The mourners listened to loud R&B records and loaded up on lox and corned beef. A photo of Doc and John Lennon hung in the hallway. Doc never saw his new home.

All through 1991, nightclubs around New York staged dozens of tributes. Later that year, Doc's friend Phil Spector inducted him into the Rock and Roll Hall of Fame. The Rhythm and Blues Foundation inaugurated the Doc Pomus Financial Assistance Program, which helps pay for the living expenses of veteran R&B performers, and honored him with its Pioneer Award. Doc became the first white recipient. Bob Dylan, Lou Reed, Brian Wilson, B.B. King, Dr. John, and others recorded *Till the Night Is Gone: A Tribute to Doc Pomus*. It came out to widespread acclaim.

Following an operation on his liver, Mort Shuman died in a London hospital in November 1991, just six months after Doc. He was fifty-four.

That same year, Johnny Adams came out with a new CD. It was called *A Doc Pomus Retrospective: The Real Me* and was intended to showcase the plainspoken, personal songs Doc had been writing, some of the finest of his career.

The Tan Canary sang the title track backed only by Mac's piano:

> When I look in the mirror
> I no longer see
> The man I used to be
> Now looking back at me
> All I ever see
> Is the real me

Doc left behind more than a thousand songs. They're more popular than ever.

Discographical Note

IN AN AGE OF FILE SHARING and *iTunes*, just about any discography is bound to be at least partly pointless and grow rapidly out-of-date. This is especially true in the case of Doc, whose hits alone have been packaged in hundreds, if not thousands, of formats. What follows, then, is a list of forty favorite recordings of his songs. That number, like the performances themselves, is a purely personal choice and is intended as a starting point for an exploration of Doc's vast, and hugely rewarding, body of work.

For an overview of Doc's recordings as a singer, it's hard to go wrong with *Blues in the Red* from Rev-ola Records, a single CD spanning twenty-four tracks.

The song title is followed by the artist's name and the (in a few cases, approximate) year of the original release.

"My New Chick," Doc Pomus, 1947
"My Good Pott," Doc Pomus, 1947
"Kiss My Wrist," Doc Pomus, 1949
"Send for the Doctor," Doc Pomus, 1950
"Give It Up," Doc Pomus, 1951
"I've Got That Feelin'," Lil Green, 1951
"Don't You Cry," Joe Turner, 1952
"Still in Love," Joe Turner, 1953
"Boogie Woogie Country Girl," Joe Turner, 1956
"Lonely Avenue," Ray Charles, 1956
"I'm Going Crazy," The Tibbs Brothers, 1956
"Plain Jane," Bobby Darin, 1959
"Turn Me Loose," Fabian, 1959

"Teenager in Love," Dion and the Belmonts, 1959

"Hushabye," The Mystics, 1959

"(If You Cry) True Love, True Love," The Drifters, 1959

"This Magic Moment," The Drifters, 1960

"A Mess of Blues," Elvis Presley, 1960

"Save the Last Dance for Me," The Drifters, 1960

"I Count the Tears," The Drifters, 1960

"Havin' Fun," Dion, 1961

"(Marie's the Name) His Latest Flame," Elvis Presley, 1961

"Little Sister," Elvis Presley, 1961

"Young Boy Blues," Ben E. King, 1961

"Suspicion," Elvis Presley, 1962

"No One," Ray Charles, 1963

"Can't Get Used to Losing You," Andy Williams, 1963

"I Need Somebody to Lean On," Elvis Presley, 1964

"I'm Gonna Cry 'till My Tears Run Dry," Irma Thomas, 1964

"Hushabye," The Beach Boys, 1964

"More Than a Miracle," Garnett Mimms, 1965

"Just to Walk That Little Girl Home," Mink DeVille, 1980

"That World Outside," Mink DeVille, 1980

"There Must Be a Better World Somewhere," B.B. King, 1981

"Something Beautiful Is Dying," Mink DeVille, 1985

"A World I Never Made," Johnny Adams, 1987

"Still in Love," Johnny Adams, 1991

"There Is Always One More Time," Johnny Adams, 1991

"The Real Me," Johnny Adams, 1991

"Dreams Must Be Going Out of Style," Johnny Adams, 1995

A Note on Sources and Acknowledgments

I NEVER MET DOC. But in this attempt to tell his story, he became my biggest ally. Doc recorded his journal entries in stacks of notebooks filled with loopy, nearly impossible-to-decipher handwriting. Together with dozens of interviews, they bequeathed a vivid, real man with his loves, his frustrations, and his tremendous appetite for life intact. Doc was as frank and introspective a diarist as any chronicler could hope for. When he wanted to, he was also an effective and immensely personable writer of prose—the five passages excerpted in this book offer but a taste. In his recollections, Doc managed almost entirely to avoid exaggeration and hubris. Attempts to verify his versions of events nearly always bore out their accuracy.

In writing this book, I've tried to honor Doc's candor and gifts as a storyteller by imbuing the major characters with as much inner life as I could. Doc's interior monologue is based on his own journal entries and reminiscences. Rather than attempting an exhaustive treatment of his work and career, my intent has been to tell a story—one story—of Doc's life. Hopefully, others will follow. The emphasis throughout, then, has been on maintaining a coherent narrative. Researching events that took place fifty and sixty years ago can be uncertain work, and, inevitably, after every attempt at verification was exhausted, I was sometimes left with two or more conflicting accounts. Instead of presenting every possibility to the reader, I made a choice.

I owe a huge debt to individuals who shared their memories, insights, and mementos of Doc, and many of whom remained stoic in the face of never-ending questions and demands on their time. I'd like to thank Miriam Abramson-Bienstock, Stan Applebaum, Stephanie Chernikowski, Robert Cohen, Ed Cramer, Hank Crawford, Willy DeVille, Joel Dorn, Barbara Dorr, Tom Dowd, Ahmet Ertegun, Paul Evans, Scott Fagan, Donald Fagen, James Felder, Max Felder, Myrna Felder, Fabian Forte, Al Gafa, Brian Gari, Snuff Garrett, Leonard Gaskin, Gerry Goffin, Ellie Greenwich, Gerri Hershey, Kenny Hirsch, Gladys Kaufman, Ben E. King, Robin Lerner, Jerry Leiber, Elaine Orlando, Jerry Ragavoy, Mac Rebennack, Lou Reed, Artie Ripp, David Ritz, Neysha Sardoff, Phil Sardoff, Jimmy Scott, Neil Sedaka, Mike Stoller, Barbara Suarez, Jerry Wexler, and Sol Yaged.

David McGee generously shared his extensive and illuminating interviews with Doc. I'm indebted to Billy Vera for access to his record collection and to his staggering knowledge of American music. Spencer Leigh filled in much-needed information on Doc and Mort's visit to England; the Doc-related lore and scholarship on his Web site, www.spencerleigh.demon.co.uk, have been useful and entertaining resources. Dan Kochakian has been instrumental in preserving Doc's recorded legacy as a singer and shared printed matter, photographs, and recordings. Pia Maria Shuman's attorney Charles Negus-Fancey kindly granted access to Mort Shuman's autobiographical sketch. Ken Emerson has been a cheerleader and a friend; he graciously shared his Brill Building leads, carefully read the manuscript, offered valuable insights and advice, and kept morale high. The person who introduced me to Doc's story and encouraged me to pursue this project was Peter Guralnick. Thank you, Peter.

This book would not exist without the participation of Doc's family, who generously opened doors to Doc's journals, letters, interviews, scrapbooks, photos, home movies, personal effects, and contacts, and remained a wellspring of crucial information and guidance. Thanks to Geoffrey Felder for his support. Raoul Felder withstood years of questions with grace and candor. The courageous, thoughtful accounts of Doc's great loves—Willi Burke and

Shirlee Hauser—form the bedrock of this book. I owe the biggest debt of gratitude to Sharyn Felder and Will Bratton, who guided me through Doc's world with forbearance, the patience of Job, and endless enthusiasm. I'm happy to call them friends.

Brooke Costello, Matt Dojny, and John Wray read portions of the manuscript and provided much-appreciated comments. Thanks to Chloe Hooper, David Wondrich, Ian Frazier, Craig Seligman, Alex Kopelman, and John Jeremiah Sullivan for their sage advice and friendship. Jin Auh, Jeffrey Posternak, Margot Kaminski, and Andrew Wylie at the Wylie Agency worked hard to make this book a reality. Ben Schafer, my kind, long-suffering editor, as well as Dan Franklin at Jonathan Cape, have my heartfelt gratitude. In clearing the brush of typos and chintzy grammar, Jane McGraw was a thorough and sensitive reader. Matty Goldberg's belief in Doc's story, and in this book, made it possible. The Brooklyn Writer's Space has been a great place to work.

Finally, to my mother, Anna Halberstadt, my stepfather, Vitaly Komar, and above all to Doug Dibbern, my editor, partner, and best friend: *spasibo.*

Credits

ALLEY, ALLEY BLUES
Words and music by Doc Pomus
© 1985 Stazybo Music administered by Pomus Songs, Inc.
All Rights Reserved. Used by Permission.

CAN'T GET USED TO LOSING YOU
Words by DOC POMUS Music by MORT SHUMAN
© 1962 (Renewed) 456 MUSIC ASSOCIATES and
UNICHAPPELL MUSIC, INC.
All Rights Administered by UNICHAPPELL MUSIC, INC.
All Rights Reserved. Used by Permission.

HEARTLESSLY
Words and Music by DOC POMUS
© 1955 UNICHAPPELL MUSIC, INC.
All Rights Reserved. Used by Permission.

I COUNT THE TEARS
Words by DOC POMUS, Music by MORT SHUMAN
© 1960, 1961 (Renewed) UNICHAPPELL MUSIC, INC. and
TRIO MUSIC CO., INC.
All Rights Reserved. Used by Permission.

JUST TO WALK THAT LITTLE GIRL HOME
Words and music by Doc Pomus and Willy DeVille
© 1980 Stazybo Music and Glenwood Music Corp. & Fire
Escape Music.
Stazybo Music administered by Pomus Songs, Inc.
All Rights Reserved. Used by Permission.

Index